The Alba House Gospels

THE ALBA HOUSE
GOSPELS

So You May Believe

Translated
by
Mark A. Wauck

ALBA · HOUSE   NEW · YORK

SOCIETY OF ST. PAUL, 2187 VICTORY BLVD., STATEN ISLAND, NY 10314

ALBA stands for the four evangelists, incorporating the initials of the Latin symbols which represent the biblical authors:

Angelus (angel) = Matthew
Leo (lion) = Mark
Bos (ox) = Luke
Aquila (eagle) = John

Library of Congress Cataloging-in-Publication Data

Bible. N.T. Gospels. English. Wauck. 1992.
  The Alba House Gospels : so you may believe / translated by Mark A. Wauck.
    p.   cm.
  "Translated directly from the Greek and is based on two principal texts, the 3rd edition of the United Bible Society's The Greek New Testament and the 26th edition of Nestle-Aland's Novum Testamentum Graece" —P. ix.
    ISBN 0-8189-0625-1
    I. Wauck, Mark A.   II. Title
BS2553.W38   1992
226'.05209 — dc20   91-40303
                                                              CIP

Nihil Obstat:
    Msgr. Daniel Murray, Rector St. Charles Borromeo Seminary, Overbrook, PA
    Rev. Robert Hayden, Vice Rector Immaculate Conception Seminary, Huntington, NY
Imprimi Potest:
    Most Rev. Emil A. Wcela, Vicar Eastern Vicariate
    Diocese of Rockville Centre, NY
Imprimatur:
    Most Rev. Daniel E. Pilarczyk
    President, National Conference of Catholic Bishops
    March 22, 1991

Produced and designed in the United States of America by the
Fathers and Brothers of the Society of St. Paul,
2187 Victory Boulevard, Staten Island, New York 10314,
as part of their communications apostolate.

ISBN: 0-8189-0625-1

Printing Information:

Current Printing - first digit	1	2	3	4	5	6	7	8	9	10

Year of Current Printing - first year shown

1992	1993	1994	1995	1996	1997	1998

TABLE OF CONTENTS

Biblical Abbreviations

OLD TESTAMENT

Genesis	Gn	Nehemiah	Ne	Baruch	Ba
Exodus	Ex	Tobit	Tb	Ezekiel	Ezk
Leviticus	Lv	Judith	Jdt	Daniel	Dn
Numbers	Nb	1 Maccabees	1 M	Joel	Jl
Joshua	Jos	2 Maccabees	2 M	Amos	Am
Judges	Jg	Job	Jb	Obadiah	Ob
Ruth	Rt	Psalms	Ps	Jonah	Jon
1 Samuel	1 S	Proverbs	Pr	Micah	Mi
2 Samuel	2 S	Ecclesiastes	Ex	Nahum	Na
1 Kings	1 K	Song of Songs	Sg	Habakkuk	Hab
2 Kings	2 K	Wisdom	Ws	Zephaniah	Zp
1 Chronicles	1 Ch	Sirach	Si	Haggai	Hg
2 Chronicles	2 Ch	Isaiah	Is	Malachi	Ml
Ezra	Ezr	Jeremiah	Jr	Zechariah	Zc
		Lamentations	Lm		

NEW TESTAMENT

Matthew	Mt	Ephesians	Ep	Hebrews	Heb
Mark	Mk	Philippians	Ph	James	Jm
Luke	Lk	Colossians	Col	1 Peter	1 P
John	Jn	1 Thessalonians	1 Th	2 Peter	2 P
Acts	Ac	2 Thessalonians	2 Th	1 John	1 Jn
Romans	Rm	1 Timothy	1 Tm	2 John	2 Jn
1 Corinthians	1 Cor	2 Timothy	2 Tm	3 John	3 Jn
2 Corinthians	2 Cor	Titus	Tt	Jude	Jude
Galatians	Gal	Philemon	Phm	Revelation	Rv

PREFACE

Daniel A. Murray, STL, SSL

The Church has always encouraged the Christian faithful to learn, by the frequent reading of Scripture, that knowledge of Jesus Christ which leads to salvation. Pius X commended all who strove to promote the praiseworthy custom of reading and meditating on Scripture, seeing that it helps in no small way "to dissipate the idea that the Church is opposed to or in any way impedes the reading of Scripture in the vernacular." (*Qui piam,* Pii X Acta IV, 1123-25)

Benedict XV recommended that all the children of the Church reverence Scripture, read it piously, and meditate on it constantly. He envisioned a situation in which every Christian family would be accustomed to reading Scripture daily. *(Spiritus Paraclitus)*

Pius XII commended the immense labors undertaken by Catholic biblical scholars by which the word of God became more accessible to the faithful. He saw the reading of Scripture as the serious duty of all in the Church, and exhorted Bishops to endeavor daily to increase and promote among those committed to their care, "a greater knowledge of and love for the Sacred Books." (*Divino Afflante Spiritu,* paragraph 51)

The Second Vatican Council echoed the perennial teaching of the Magisterium on Sacred Scripture in the life of the Church in chapter six of the dogmatic constitution on Divine Revelation: "in the Sacred Books, the Father who is in heaven meets his children with great love and speaks with them; and the force and power of the word of God is so great that it remains the support and energy of the Church, the strength of faith for her children, the food of the soul, the pure and perennial source of spiritual life." (paragraph 21)

The Bishops at the Second Vatican Council were aware of the growing thirst for Scripture among the faithful. They urged everyone to put themselves in touch with the sacred text, whether through the liturgy, or through devotional reading, or through instructions suitable for the purpose. (*Divine Revelation*, paragraph 25)

Mark A. Wauck has taken this teaching to heart. He has gone back to the original Koine Greek of the New Testament and produced a most readable translation of the four Gospels.

Doctor Wauck has taken painstaking efforts to "render the sacred text as faithfully as possible and in a style which will be readily grasped by the ordinary reader." (Translator's preface) He has indeed captured, as well as one can in translation the force, color, and cadence of the original texts. Anyone who hears a public proclamation of Doctor Wauck's translation of the Gospels will sense the rhythm of each Evangelist's inspired text.

I commend Alba House for its initiative in publishing this translation. Doctor Wauck is to be congratulated for his labor of love which makes the prayerful reading and meditation of the Gospels a joy. May everyone who reads this translation experience that "new surge of spiritual vitality from intensified veneration for God's word" hoped for by the Bishops of the Second Vatican Council. (*Dogmatic Constitution on Divine Revelation*, paragraph 26)

Rev. Msgr. Daniel A. Murray, STL, SSL
Rector, St. Charles Borromeo Seminary
Overbrook, Pennsylvania

TRANSLATOR'S PREFACE

This new English version of the four Gospels has been translated directly from the Greek and is largely based on two principal texts, the 3rd edition of the United Bible Society's *The Greek New Testament* and the 26th edition of Nestle-Aland's *Novum Testamentum Graece*, although in places variant readings have been preferred.

The one overriding concern has, of course, been to render the sacred text as faithfully as possible and in a style which will be readily grasped. The English employed is basically contemporary American English. While slang has been avoided, a conscious effort has been made to model the text after the spoken language, since the Greek of the Gospels, generally speaking, reflects the spoken Koine Greek of the first century A.D. At the same time, it is recognized that, just as contemporary American English is spoken in many different forms, so, too, the Greek of the Gospels exhibits considerable stylistic variation, both among the four Gospels and, sometimes, within individual Gospels. A conscious decision was made to preserve these variations in style rather than employ a uniform "Gospel" style of English.

Since the Greek of the Gospels is so different from American English in its grammar, syntax, and idiom, it isn't possible to communicate all the stylistic peculiarities which render the Greek of the Gospels distinctive. Nevertheless, it is unquestionably desirable to communicate as much of these stylistic elements as possible and, when possible, this has been done. For the most part, syntactic (rather than grammatical) features of the Greek which find some counterpart in English have been used in order to communicate stylistic differences in a way which will be readily understandable.

In general, no attempt has been made to "improve" on the Evangelists. With the partial exception of Luke, the authors of the Gospels had no literary pretensions; their primary concern was with their message and they trusted that the Spirit would make up for what their contemporaries may have regarded as stylistic shortcomings. Countless generations can, indeed, testify that the power of the Spirit was in their work, and every effort has been made to capture the force and color of the original. To that end, the use of paraphrase and circumlocution has been held to a minimum. When resort has been made to such devices it has been done with a view to basic readability and intelligibility. In a few instances it has been felt necessary to add words to the text to make the meaning clear. Such additions are indicated by brackets when they cannot reasonably be considered to be "understood" or implied. Emphasis, indicated by italics, has also been added in some passages where this will help to convey the sense of the text.

A further feature of this translation is the use of a poetic format when the words of Jesus appear to reflect an underlying poetic structure. Scholars have long known that extensive portions of Jesus' words were composed using techniques of parallelism of thought and language as well as rhythm, similar to what is found in the Psalms and the poetic passages in the Prophets. When presented as poetry the meaning and artistry of Jesus' words are often more easily grasped, because each line or subline contains a simple unit of thought which is grasped both visually and conceptually. To accomplish this versification has not always been an easy task. There are unquestionably passages which show traces of an original poetic format which have not been so rendered in this translation, for the reason that, in the form in which they have come down to us, the poetic nature of these passages has been substantially obscured. However, in cases where the poetic format has not been preserved completely intact, but is nevertheless recognizable, it has been rendered as poetry if that would serve the purposes of readability and intelligibility.

The reader will also note that the Greek *nomos* has been rendered by the Hebrew "Torah," rather than by the English "law." This has been done for two reasons. First, "Torah" has been used to avoid the more restricted connotations of "law." "Torah" referred to the totality of

God's revelation which could serve as a guide for one's life, and it is in this sense that *nomos* is used in the Gospels. Torah was, therefore, quintessentially, the Decalogue, but it also extended far beyond the confines of the Pentateuch to areas which we would never characterize as "law," as can be seen in several New Testament passages. Secondly, the word was used to provide local color, to remind the reader that the events being read about took place at a particular time, in a particular setting.

In addition, where style and accuracy allow, inclusive language has been used. Neologisms and more abstract terms have been avoided in favor of simpler terms which are in keeping with the style of the original.

Finally, in keeping with the foregoing principles, the reader is encouraged to read the Gospels aloud, or to at least quietly enunciate them, so that the rhythms of the spoken language can help bring the Word to life.

ACKNOWLEDGMENTS

It should be apparent to all that no translation of Scripture can be done unaided, by a single person, and I am no exception. I have gratefully relied upon and availed myself of the work of generations of scholars and translators. Mention must also be made of Fr. Fred Piegl, of Northridge Prep, who selflessly devoted many hours of his time and expertise in the field of personal computers. Above all I want to express my gratitude for the patience and understanding of my wife Mary Ellen and our children, Martin, Monica, Stephen, and Joseph.

GENERAL INTRODUCTION

THE GOOD NEWS

While each of the evangelists wrote from a distinct perspective, a common purpose is evident in all four Gospels: to proclaim the "good news." What is the good news? Essentially, it is summarized by the primitive *kerygma* or preaching of the early Church: a) Jesus is the Son of God; b) he went about teaching, healing, and proclaiming the advent of the Kingdom of God; c) he was rejected by his own people, died as a sacrifice to redeem both Jews and Gentiles, and rose triumphantly; d) he passed on his authority to his successors, the apostles; e) he will come again in glory from the right hand of God where he has been exalted; f) all of this happened or will happen "in accordance with the Scriptures." This basic *kerygma* serves as the framework around which all four Gospels were written. As can be seen, at the center of the good news is a real person, Jesus of Nazareth, the Messiah, who came to transform our lives.

From this it is clear that the Gospels are not simply theological treatises or mythical constructs — they are necessarily concerned not only with ideas or theories but also with concrete facts and events. Jesus of Nazareth did, in fact, live; he did, in fact, die and later rise again; the proof of his message can be found in what he actually said and did. At the same time, it is also clear that the Gospels do not pretend to be biographies in the modern sense — those events related are not recounted for their own sake but were selected because they could help reveal the meaning of the good news. It is this concern with the concrete, factual, and historical which sets off Christianity from gnosis in every day and age, and it was this double perspective —concern for concrete events and concern for their transcendent meaning and significance — which gave rise to the Gospel as a distinct literary genre.

An important corollary to the basic fact that the purpose of the Gospels is to proclaim is that they explicitly (Jn 20:30-31) disclaim any pretension to be exhaustive, either in the biographical or theological sense. We must not expect either a complete biography or a complete account of the Christian faith. The former is not available to us, and the latter, to the extent that it's possible, is the province of the Church, for which the Gospels are no substitute.

THE SYNOPTIC PROBLEM

The Gospels of Matthew, Mark, and Luke are commonly referred to as the Synoptic Gospels because, when viewed in comparison to each other (especially in parallel columns), they show striking, often word for word, similarities. The careful reader will quickly note, however, that there are also many striking contextual differences. Many attempts have been made to explain this phenomenon. In the twentieth century the most widely accepted explanation is probably a variation of the Two Document theory. Basically, this theory holds that Mark was written first and was available to the authors of Matthew and Luke, along with collections of the sayings of the Lord, referred to as Q, in both oral and written forms. In addition, Matthew and Luke are also said to have used sources of tradition unique to themselves.

While considerable erudition has gone into this theory, its acceptance is not universal and many refinements to the basic theory have been elaborated, usually in an attempt to avoid a mechanistic, cut and paste, interpretation. In recent years several noted scholars have explored the possibility that all three synoptic evangelists had access to substantially similar sources, both written and oral, which were later developed, under the influence of differing concerns and circumstances and with varying degrees of interaction between the authors and translators, into our canonical Gospels. This approach sometimes involves a much earlier dating of the Synoptic Gospels than is the case with most versions of the Two Document theory. The reader should remember, however, that, barring truly momentous documentary discoveries, the details of any solution will probably have to be considered provisional.

DATE AND AUTHORSHIP

As is well known, the history of New Testament scholarship has witnessed repeated and heated debates over the date of composition for the four Gospels. What might be termed a middle ground of scholarship supports the following dates: Mark, prior to 70 A.D., probably the late 60's; Luke and Matthew, 75-85; John, the 90's. The dating of Matthew and Luke is largely dependent on the belief that in them Jesus' prophecies about the destruction of Jerusalem were in fact written after the event, i.e., after 70 A.D., a belief which has come under increasing fire in recent years. The dating of John relies in large part upon the highly developed nature of Johannine theology and tradition concerning John which states that he lived to an advanced old age.

The traditional datings differ in that they place Matthew first, followed by Mark and Luke, all prior to 70 A.D. Nevertheless, the accounts of this process which have come down to us are not entirely cut and dried. Tradition holds that Matthew the Evangelist is identical with Matthew the publican (Mt 9:9 ff.) and that he wrote first, in the "Hebrew" language (which may have meant Aramaic). The precise form this early version of Matthew took — whether it was similar to the hypothetical Q document or also included narrative — is not clear from our sources. Moreover, the final version of Matthew, the Greek which has come down to us, does not appear to be a simple translation of an original "Hebrew" text, but appears to be the result of at least some development. There is nothing to preclude the possibility that tradition which formed the basis of Mark was also available to, and in fact was used in the composition of, Matthew. Thus, although the process of composition which led to the canonical Gospel of Matthew may have begun first, there may also have been some chronological overlapping as well.

As to Mark, he is said to have drawn heavily from the teaching of St. Peter, having been his translator, but the Gospel may not have reached final form until after Peter's death. Luke is familiar to all as the companion of St. Paul. Under this scheme he would have completed his Gospel by the early 60's A.D., based upon the fact that Acts clearly refers to the Gospel of Luke in its prologue as already written, while Acts itself breaks off abruptly in the early 60's. His association with Mark, as recorded in Acts, explains his use of the Marcan chronology as well as other details, without necessarily requiring that Luke actually had access to canonical Mark, as postulated by the Two Document theory.

Tradition is usually considered to state that the Fourth Gospel was written by the Apostle John around 90-100 A.D., but this, too, is now questioned. In the first place, it is clear that the Johannine historical tradition is quite early and reliable. In addition, it is possible that tradition only states that St. John *lived* to an advanced age, not that he wrote as an old man. Finally, the highly developed nature of Johannine theology is no longer regarded as an indication of late composition: as Martin Hengel has stated, the basic Christological doctrines were probably largely formulated within a few years of the death of the Lord.

As can be seen, scholarship regarding the dating and authorship of the Gospels, as well as the whole issue of the Synoptic Problem, appears to be in a more fluid state than heretofore. This shift can be placed within the larger context of the growing recognition — brought about by the fact that modern archaeological, historical, and linguistic research is supportive of the general outlines of what tradition has to tell us, and also by an increasing understanding of the processes of oral and written tradition — that the skepticism of many 19th and early 20th century exegetes toward the Gospel tradition was both extreme and unwarranted. A major buttress for this line of reasoning is the fact that the Gospels reflect, in extraordinary detail, the situation in Palestine prior to the Jewish revolt of 66-70 A.D. As a result, scholars are increasingly confident that the Gospel traditions can be traced back to an origin in the ministry of Jesus himself and that these traditions are essentially reliable.

THE GOSPEL ACCORDING TO
MATTHEW

INTRODUCTION TO MATTHEW

As was noted earlier, tradition maintains that the apostle Matthew was the first to write down "reports" about the Lord, that he wrote in "Hebrew" (which many believe meant Aramaic), and that "everyone" subsequently translated it to the best of their ability. Unfortunately, not a trace remains of this early version of Matthew; the only extant Gospel of Matthew is the Greek one, and the available evidence indicates that the version of Matthew with which we are acquainted underwent at least some development before it reached its final form. The evidence also indicates that the translation from Hebrew or Aramaic to Greek probably took place at an early date in order to make it accessible to the many Christians, Jewish and Gentile, whose first language was Greek. Whether Matthew was personally involved in the entire process is not known.

Although not a great deal is known about Matthew, one thing is certain: he was quite familiar with Palestinian Judaism at the time of Jesus' ministry. He appears to have been well educated in the rabbinic traditions and in his Gospel the Pharisees appear as the typical representatives of Judaism. For this reason many scholars believe that this Gospel was written with Jewish converts in mind, although it clearly affirms the universality of Jesus' mission and early on was widely used by Gentile Christians as well. From a stylistic standpoint, Matthew (this designation also includes his translators and editors) can best be characterized as sober and competent. While his command of Greek was not comparable to Luke's, Matthew nonetheless avoids most of the less acceptable expressions which Luke tolerates. In this sense, Matthew's Gospel has perhaps the smoothest and most consistent style.

A primary theme of Matthew is that Jesus, in his coming and in his teaching, fulfills the Torah and the Prophets, and Matthew lays particular stress on the ethical effects which flow from this. In line with this concern, Matthew spends a great deal of time explaining the characteristics of Jesus' Kingdom, the new Israel, and the means of entering this Kingdom: faith in Jesus. He also stresses both the fact that the disciples have received authority in the Kingdom from Jesus, thus displacing the Jewish authorities, as well as the nature of that authority. From this we can see that Matthew had a strong sense for both the spirit of the Kingdom and the need for institutions and firm authority in the Church. A final theme which is interwoven with these others is that of the rejection of Jesus by the Jewish authorities and the extension of the Kingdom to embrace all nations.

Many different attempts have been made to analyze the structure of Matthew. The following outline is designed to help the reader relate the various passages to the main themes described above.

A. 1:1-17   The genealogy of Jesus.

B. 1:18-25   The birth of Jesus, "Emmanuel/God with us."

C. 2:1-23   The wise men and the flight into Egypt.

D. 3:1-17   The coming of the Baptist, his baptism of Jesus and the descent of the Spirit.

E. 4:1-11   The temptation of Jesus.

F. 4:12-25   Jesus returns to Galilee and begins his ministry, proclaiming the good news of the Kingdom and gaining fame for his cures.

G. 5:1-7:29   The Sermon on the Mount.

5:1-16   Characteristics of those who belong to the Kingdom.

5:17-48   True meaning of the Torah.

6:1-18   True practice of the Torah.

6:18-34   Exhortations to trust in God.

7:1-29   Further exhortations and warnings.

The people are astounded at the way Jesus teaches on his own authority.

H. 8:1-9:33   Jesus travels about, teaching and healing, revealing his divine power and authority.

I. 9:35-11:1   Jesus sends the disciples out to teach and heal, granting them his power and authority, and provides instruction and encouragement regarding discipleship.

J. 11:2-30   Jesus speaks of the significance of the Baptist and denounces those who have been too proud to follow Jesus in a spirit of simple faith.

K. 12:1-50   Controversy with the Pharisees.

    12:1-21   The Pharisees challenge Jesus regarding Sabbath observance and Jesus proclaims himself Lord of the Sabbath.

    12:22-37   The Pharisees question the source of Jesus' power and Jesus defends himself against the slander.

    12:38-50   Jesus denounces an unbelieving generation and refuses to give a "test sign."

L. 13:1-58   Parables of the Kingdom and rejection at Nazareth.

M. 14:1-36   The death of the Baptist. Jesus feeds the 5,000 and walks on the sea; the disciples' confession.

N. 15:1-20   Challenged by the Pharisees, Jesus teaches regarding true inner purification, as opposed to external observance.

O. 15:21-16:12   Jesus travels about, healing, and feeds 4,000. He again refuses to provide a sign on request and warns the disciples against the Pharisees and Sadducees.

P. 16:13-17:27   Who Jesus is: Peter's confession. The primacy of Peter, the price of discipleship, and the coming of the Son of Man foretold. Jesus is transfigured but when he returns to the people he encounters lack of faith.

Q. 18:1-35   The humble exercise of authority and the necessity of forgiveness.

R. 19:1-20:34   True discipleship and authority in the Kingdom. Jesus is questioned by the Pharisees regarding divorce and by a rich man regarding what must be done to gain eternal life. In his replies Jesus stresses simple faith and renunciation. Parable of the laborers in the vineyard. The examples of the sons of Zebedee and the blind men.

S. 21:1-22:46   Jesus enters Jerusalem in triumph, cleanses the Temple, and challenges the Jewish authorities in parables and argumentation.

T. 23:1-39   Denunciation of the Pharisees.

U. 24:1-25:46   The prophecies of the destruction of Jerusalem, coming of the Son of Man, and the end of the world. Parables of the end time.

V. 26:1-27:66   Last Supper and Passion of Jesus.

W. 28:1-20   Resurrection and appearances of Jesus. The disciples are sent to all nations. "I'll be with you."

THE GOSPEL ACCORDING TO
MATTHEW

A. THE GENEALOGY OF JESUS

1 **1** [a] A record of the lineage of Jesus Christ, son of David, son of Abraham.

2 Abraham fathered Isaac, and Isaac fathered Jacob, and Jacob fathered Judah and his brothers, **3** and Judah fathered Perez and Zerah by Tamar, and Perez fathered Hezron, and Hezron fathered Ram, **4** and Ram fathered Amminadab, and Amminadab fathered Nahshon, and Nahshon fathered Salmon, **5** and Salmon fathered Boaz by Rahab, and Boaz fathered Obed by Ruth, and Obed fathered Jesse, **6** and Jesse fathered David, the King.

And David fathered Solomon by Uriah's wife, **7** and Solomon fathered Rehoboam, and Rehoboam fathered Abijah, and Abijah fathered Asa, **8** and Asa fathered Jehoshaphat, and Jehoshaphat fathered Joram, and Joram fathered Uzziah, **9** and Uzziah fathered Jotham, and Jotham fathered Ahaz, and Ahaz fathered Hezekiah, **10** and Hezekiah fathered Manasseh, and Manasseh fathered Amos, and Amos fathered Josiah, **11** and Josiah fathered Jechoniah and his brothers at the time of the Babylonian Exile.

12 After the Babylonian Exile Jechoniah fathered Shealtiel, and Shealtiel fathered Zerubbabel, **13** and Zerubbabel fathered Abiud, and Abiud fathered Eliakim, and Eliakim fathered Azor, **14** and Azor

---

[a] Lk 3:23-28.

1:1 *Jesus* is the Greek form of the Hebrew *Joshua* and the Aramaic *Yeshua*, which mean "Yahweh is salvation." In v. 1 *Christ* appears to be used as a proper name, but elsewhere it normally translates the Hebrew *Mashiah*, "Anointed One."

fathered Zadok, and Zadok fathered Achim, and Achim fathered Eliud, **15** and Eliud fathered Eleazar, and Eleazar fathered Matthan, and Matthan fathered Jacob, **16** and Jacob fathered Joseph the husband of Mary, who gave birth to Jesus, who is called Messiah.

17 So all the generations from Abraham up to David were fourteen generations, and from David up to the Babylonian Exile were fourteen generations, and from the Babylonian Exile up to the Messiah were fourteen generations.

B. THE BIRTH OF JESUS

18 [b] Now the birth of Jesus Christ came about like this. When his mother Mary was betrothed to Joseph, but before they came together, she was found to be with child by the Holy Spirit. **19** Joseph her husband was a good and upright man so he was planning to put her away, but quietly because he didn't wish to disgrace her. **20** But while he was thinking these things over, behold, the angel of the Lord appeared to him in a dream and said, "Joseph son of David, don't be afraid to take your wife Mary into your house—the child who has been conceived in her is from the Holy Spirit. **21** She'll give birth to a son and you shall name him Jesus, because he'll save his people from their sins." **22** All this took place to fulfill what was declared by the Lord through the prophet when he said,

23   Behold, the virgin shall be with child
    and will give birth to a son,
    And they shall give him the name Emmanuel,

---

[b] Lk 2:1-7.

1:16 Up to this point the genealogy of Jesus has been traced through the male line. Here, however, there is an abrupt break at the final, crucial, link. Matthew clearly states that Jesus was generated from Mary, even though the whole genealogy led up to Joseph and Mary's lineage was nowhere mentioned. The inescapable conclusion is that Joseph was not Jesus' natural father, and beginning at 1:18 Matthew explains the origins of Jesus. It should be noted, however, that since Jesus' legal father, Joseph, was of the line of David, Jesus was entitled to claim the title "Son of David."

1:18 "Came together"; i.e., had marital relations.

1:19 The Greek word *dikaios*, usually translated "righteous," does not carry the legalistic connotations that the English word does. Rather, it conveys the notion of conformity to the will of God or the possession of a Godlike character.

1:23 Is 7:14 (Septuagint). The reference to "Emmanuel" foreshadows Jesus' promise at the conclusion of Matthew's Gospel: "I'll be with you."

which is translated, "God with us." **24** When Joseph rose from his sleep he did as the angel of the Lord had commanded him and took his wife into his house, **25** but he hadn't known her before she gave birth to her son, and he gave him the name Jesus.

C. THE WISE MEN AND THE FLIGHT INTO EGYPT

2 **1** When Jesus was born in Bethlehem of Judea in the days of King Herod, behold, Magi from the east arrived in Jerusalem **2** asking, "Where is the newborn King of the Jews? We saw his star rising and came to worship him." **3** When King Herod heard this he was troubled, and all Jerusalem with him, **4** so he gathered all the chief priests and scribes of the people and inquired of them where the Messiah was to be born. **5** And they told him, "In Bethlehem of Judea, for thus has it been written by the prophet,

> **6** **And you, Bethlehem**, land of Judah,
>> are by no means **least among the rulers of Judah;**
>> **For from you shall come the ruler**
>> **who will shepherd my people Israel."**

7 Herod secretly summoned the Magi and found out from them the time the star had appeared, **8** then he sent them to Bethlehem and said, "Go search carefully for the child and send for me as soon as you find him, so I can go worship him, too." **9** After listening to the king they departed, and, behold, the star they had seen rising went before them until it came and stopped above where the child was. **10** Now when they saw the star they rejoiced exceedingly, with great joy, **11** and when they came into the house they saw the child with his mother, Mary.

1:25 Traditionally this verse has been translated: "he did not know her until she gave birth...," which leads many not conversant with the Greek to assume that **after** Jesus' birth Joseph **did** know Mary. Unlike the English, however, the Greek carries no such implication as to the future. It states only what the situation was as of the date of Jesus' birth and is silent about what took place later.

The Vulgate reads "**firstborn** son." According to Jewish usage this title was applied to an only child, as well as to the first in a series. There is no implication whatsoever that Mary ever had another child.

2:2 The obscure expression here translated "rising" has often been translated "in the east."

2:6 Mi 5:2, 2 S 5:2.

They fell on their knees and worshipped him, and they opened their treasures and offered him gifts — gold and frankincense and myrrh. **12** Then having been warned in a dream not to go back to Herod, they departed for their country by another way.

13 When they had departed, behold, the angel of the Lord appeared in a dream to Joseph and said, "Get up, take the child and his mother and flee to Egypt and stay there until I tell you — Herod is going to search for the child to kill it." **14** So he got up and took the child and his mother and departed by night for Egypt, **15** and he stayed there until Herod's death to fulfill what was expressed by the Lord through the prophet when he said,

I called my son out of Egypt.

16 When Herod saw that he'd been tricked by the Magi he became absolutely furious, and he ordered the killing of all the children in Bethlehem and all its neighborhood from two years old and younger, according to the time he'd ascertained from the wise men. **17** Then what was declared by Jeremiah the prophet was fulfilled, when he said,

18　　　　**A voice was heard in Rama,**
　　　　　wailing and great mourning;
　　　　Rachel weeping for her children,
　　　　　and she would not be comforted,
　　　　　because they were no more.

19 After Herod died, behold, the angel of the Lord appeared in a dream to Joseph in Egypt **20** and said, "Get up, take the child and its mother and leave for the land of Israel — those who sought the child's life are dead." **21** So he got up and took the child and its mother and went into the land of Israel. **22** But when he heard that Archelaus was ruling over Judea in place of his father Herod he was afraid to go there; so, having been warned in a dream, he departed for the district of Galilee, **23** and he went and settled in a town called Nazareth to fulfill what was said by the prophets, "he shall be called a Nazorean."

2:15 Ho 11:1. This brief reference is complex in its allusions and has several levels of meaning. Most literally, Hosea has referred to the whole people of Israel as God's son. Matthew, on the other hand, uses the text to highlight the unique Sonship of Jesus. These two sonships dovetail in the doctrine of the adoptive sonship of all believers who form the Church, the Mystical Body of Jesus, the new Israel. There is also an allusion to the new Exodus which Jesus will lead, which is referred to more explicitly at Lk 9:31.

2:18 Jr 31:15.

D. JESUS AND JOHN THE BAPTIST

3 **1** ^c In those days John the Baptist appeared, preaching in the desert of Judea **2** and saying, "Repent, for the Kingdom of Heaven has come!" **3** He was the one Isaiah the prophet was referring to when he said,

A voice crying out in the desert,
Prepare the way of the Lord,
make straight his paths.

4 John had clothing made out of camel hair and wore a leather belt around his waist, and his food was locusts and wild honey. **5** At that time Jerusalem and all Judea used to go out to him and all the region around the Jordan, **6** and he baptized them in the river Jordan while they confessed their sins.

7 Now when he saw many of the Pharisees and Sadducees coming to be baptized by him he said to them, "You brood of vipers! Who warned you to flee the coming wrath? **8** Produce fruit that *shows* you've repented, **9** and don't think you can say to yourselves, 'Abraham is our father!' for I tell you, God can raise up children to Abraham from these stones. **10** The axe has already been laid at the root of the trees; any tree not producing good fruit will be cut down and thrown into the fire. **11** I baptize you with water as a token of repentance, but the one who is coming after me is more powerful than I am—I'm not worthy to carry his sandals; he'll baptize you with the Holy Spirit and fire. **12** His winnowing shovel is in his hand; he'll clean out his threshing floor and

---

Mk 1:1-8; Lk 3:1-18; Jn 1:19-28.

3:2 "Heaven" or "the Heavens" was a circumlocution for the Divine name, direct mention of which was avoided by devout Jews of that time. Alone among the Evangelists, Matthew almost invariably uses the plural, thus preserving Hebrew usage.

3:3 Is 40:3 (Septuagint).

3:7-12 Of particular interest in the Baptist's indictment of the Jewish leaders is v. 9, in which he states that descent from Abraham merits no special consideration from God and will not save them from God's wrath. In Ch. 23 Jesus presents a more detailed but basically similar indictment of the Pharisees, concluding with a lament at their refusal to repent. Following their definitive rejection of Jesus — his crucifixion — Jesus sends the disciples forth to preach the good news of the kingdom to *all* nations.

3:11 According to the Talmud, cleansing by fire is superior to cleansing by water. *Baptizo* was the common word meaning to wash or cleanse. The Talmud is a collection of Jewish oral law and commentary. It achieved written form well after the time of Jesus but includes many earlier traditions.

gather his grain into the barn, but he'll burn up the chaff with unquenchable fire."

13 [d] At that time Jesus came from Galilee to be baptized by John at the Jordan. **14** John tried to prevent him and said, *"I* need to be baptized by *you,* and *you* come to *me?"* **15** But in answer Jesus said to him, "Let it be, for now — it's fitting for us to fulfill all God's will in this way." Then he let him. **16** Now after being baptized Jesus at once came up from the water, and, behold, the heavens were opened and he saw the Spirit of God descending upon him like a dove. **17** And, behold, a voice from Heaven said, "This is My Beloved Son in whom I am well pleased!"

E. THE TEMPTATION OF JESUS

4 **1** [e] Then Jesus was led into the desert by the Spirit to be tempted by the Devil. **2** After fasting for forty days and forty nights he at last became hungry, **3** and the Tempter approached him and said, "If you're the Son of God, tell these stones to become loaves of bread." **4** But in answer he said, "It is written,

> **Not by bread alone shall man live,**
> **but by every utterance proceeding**
> **from the mouth of God."**

5 Then the Devil took him to the Holy City. He set him on the parapet of the Temple **6** and said to him, "If you're the Son of God, throw yourself down, for it's written,

> **He will give His angels orders concerning you,**
> **and on their hands they will carry you,**
> **lest you strike your foot against a stone."**

---

[d] Mk 1:9-11; Lk 3:21-22. [e] Mk 1:12-13; Lk 4:1-13.

3:15   Literally, "righteousness." This word is notoriously difficult to render into English and requires special treatment depending on the context. Cf. the note at 1:19, as well as the text at 5:6, 5:10, and 6:33.

3:17   Is 42:1.

4:4   Dt 8:3.

4:6   Ps 91:11-12.

7 Jesus said to him, "It is further written, **You shall not tempt the Lord your God!"** **8** So then the Devil took him up a very high mountain and showed him all the kingdoms of the world and their splendor, **9** and he said to him, "All these things I'll give you, if you'll fall on your knees and worship me!" **10** But Jesus said to him, "Begone, Satan! For it is written,

> **The Lord your God shall you worship,**
> **and Him** alone **shall you adore."**

11 Then the Devil left him, and, behold, angels came and served him.

F. JESUS BEGINS HIS MINISTRY IN GALILEE

12 [f] When Jesus heard that John had been arrested he returned to Galilee. **13** He left Nazareth and went and settled in Capharnaum by the sea, in the regions of Zebulon and Naphtali, **14** to fulfill what was said by Isaiah the prophet, when he said,

> **15** **Land of Zebulon and land of Naphtali,**
> **the sea road, beyond the Jordan,**
> **Galilee of the Gentiles,**
> **16** **The people living in darkness**
> **have seen a great light,**
> **And for those living in the land and shadow of death**
> **a light has dawned upon them.**

17 From that time on Jesus began to preach and to say, "Repent, for the Kingdom of Heaven has come!"

18 [g] Now as he was walking along the sea he saw two brothers —Simon, who is called Peter, and his brother Andrew — casting a throw net into the sea — they were fishermen. **19** And he said to them, "Follow me, and I'll make you fishers of men!" **20** So they left their nets at once and followed him. **21** As he continued on from there he saw two

---

[f] Mk 1:14-15; Lk 4:14-15. [g] Mk 1:16-20; Lk 5:1-11.

4:10   Dt 6:13.
4:15-16   Is 9:1-2.

more brothers, James son of Zebedee and his brother John, who were in the boat with their father Zebedee mending their nets, and he called them. **22** So they left the boat and their father at once and followed him.

23 [h] He went through all Galilee, teaching in their synagogues, proclaiming the good news of the Kingdom, and healing every disease and illness among the people. **24** News of him went out through all Syria, and they brought him all those who were sick with various diseases and were suffering torments — the demon-possessed, epileptics, paralytics — and he healed them. **25** And large crowds followed him from Galilee and the Decapolis and Jerusalem and Judea and from beyond the Jordan.

G. THE SERMON ON THE MOUNT

CHARACTERISTICS OF MEMBERS OF THE KINGDOM

5 **1** Now when he saw the crowds he went up onto the mountain. When he sat down his disciples came to him, **2** and he opened his mouth and taught them, saying,

> **3** [i] "Blessed are the poor in spirit,
> for theirs is the Kingdom of Heaven.
> **4** Blessed are those who are mourning,
> for they shall be comforted.
> **5** Blessed are the meek,
> for they shall inherit the earth.
> **6** Blessed are those who hunger and thirst
> to do God's will,
> for they shall have their fill.

---

[h] Lk 6:17-19. [i] Lk 6:20-23.

4:25 "The Decapolis" was a confederation of largely Hellenized cities. They were ten in number (Greek *deka* = ten) and all but one were located east of the Jordan. Here it was that Jesus encountered the demoniac and the herd of swine, unthinkable in a more Jewish environment.

5:1 The Greek appears to indicate a mountain that was well known.

5:4 Is 61:2-3.

7   Blessed are the merciful,
          for they shall receive mercy.

8   Blessed are the pure of heart,
          they shall see God.

9   Blessed are the peacemakers,
          for they shall be called children of God.

10   Blessed are those persecuted for
          doing God's will,
     for theirs is the Kingdom of Heaven.

11 Blessed are you when they insult you and persecute you and say every sort of evil thing against you because of me; 12 rejoice and be glad, because your reward will be great in Heaven — they persecuted the prophets before you in the same way."

13 ʲ   "You are the salt of the earth,
       But if the salt should lose its taste,
       What can it be salted with?
       It's good for nothing but to be thrown outside
       And be trampled underfoot."

14   "You are the light of the world.
       A city cannot be hid,
       which is set atop a mountain.

15   Nor do you light a lamp
       and set it beneath a bushel;
       you set it on the lampstand, instead,
       so it lights everyone in the house.

16   Let your light so shine before others
       that they'll see your good works
       and glorify your Father in Heaven."

ʲ Mk 9:50; Lk 14:34-35.

5:9   "Children." Literally, "sons."

TRUE MEANING OF THE TORAH

17 "Don't think that I came to destroy
the Torah or the Prophets;
I came not to destroy, but to fulfill.

18 For, amen, I say to you,

Until the heavens and the earth pass away,
Not one iota or one stroke will pass away
from the Torah,
Until everything has come to pass.

19 So whoever breaks one of the least of these
commandments, and teaches this to others,
shall be called least in the Kingdom
of Heaven;
But whoever obeys and teaches the commandments,
he shall be called great in the Kingdom
of Heaven.

20 For I tell you,

Unless your righteousness greatly exceeds
that of the scribes and Pharisees,
you'll never get into the Kingdom
of Heaven."

21 "You've heard that it was said to the ancients, **You shall not murder,** and that whoever does commit murder shall be liable to judgment. **22** But *I* say to you,

---

5:17 "Torah," or "law," referred to the totality of God's revelation which could serve as a guide for one's life. Torah was, therefore, quintessentially, the Decalogue, but it also extended far beyond the confines of the Pentateuch to areas which we would never characterize as "law," as can be seen in several New Testament passages.

5:18 Many writers have noted that Jesus' use of "Amen" differs significantly from the standard usage of that time. Normally it was used to invoke an authority other than oneself, but Jesus invariably uses it to invoke his *own* authority, unsupported by Scripture or tradition. Some writers consider this to be another example of Jesus claiming Divine authority for himself. In any event, the novelty of Jesus' attitude was not lost on his listeners: cf. 7:29. *Iota* is the Greek equivalent of the smallest letter of the Hebrew alphabet, *yod.*

5:19 "To bind or loose" was standard Jewish terminology meaning "to make obligatory or dispense."

5:21 Ex 20:13.

5:22 The exact meaning of *Raqa* is unclear, but in the context it is clearly abusive or insulting and is probably equivalent to "fool." *Gehenna* refers to the Hinnom Valley outside Jerusalem,

> Anyone who's angry with his brother
>> shall be liable to judgment,
> And whoever says to his brother, *'Raqa!'*
>> shall be liable to the Sanhedrin,
> And whoever says, 'You fool!'
>> shall be liable to the fire of Gehenna.

23 So if you're presenting your offering at the altar and remember there that your brother has something against you, **24** leave your offering there before the altar and go be reconciled with your brother, and then you can come and make your offering. **25** Come to terms quickly with your opponent while you're on your way with him, or your opponent may hand you over to the judge, and the judge to the guard, and you'll be thrown into prison. **26** Amen, I say to you, you won't come out of there until you pay back the last penny."

27 "You've heard that it was said, **You shall not commit adultery! 28** but *I* say to you that anyone who looks at a woman with lust for her has already committed adultery with her in his heart.

29 But if your right eye causes you to sin,
>> pull it out and throw it away from you!
> It's better for you to lose one part of your body
>> but not have your whole body thrown into
>>> Gehenna.
30 And if your right hand causes you to sin,
>> cut it off and throw it away from you!
> It's better for you to lose one part of your body
>> but not have your whole body go off to Gehenna."

31 ᵏ "And it was said, **Whoever puts his wife away, let him give her a written notice of divorce. 32** But *I* say to you,

---

ᵏ Mk 10:11-12; Lk 16:18.

where the bodies of executed criminals were burnt. In the Gospels it refers to hell. The Sanhedrin was the highest court of Judaism and had a police force, whose members were called "attendants," to enforce its decrees.

5:26　"Penny." Literally, *quadrans*. A *quadrans* was a Roman coin worth 1/4 *assarion* or 1/64 *denarius*. A *denarius* was a silver coin and was considered to be the value of a day's wages for a common laborer.

5:27　Ex 20:14.

5:31　Dt 24:1.

5:32　The traditional translation of this verse is usually "except by reason of immorality," or a

Anyone who puts his wife away —

except by reason of an unlawful union —

> makes her an adulteress,
> And whoever marries after putting her away
> commits adultery."

33 "Again, you've heard that it was said to your forefathers, **You shall not break your oaths!** and, **You shall fulfill your oaths to the Lord! 34** But *I* tell you not to swear at all, neither **by Heaven,** because **it's the throne of God, 35** nor by **the earth,** because **it's the footstool for His feet,** nor by Jerusalem, because it's **the city of the Great King, 36** nor shall you swear by your head, because you're not able to make one hair white or black. **37** Let your speech be 'yes, yes,' or 'no, no'; anything more than that is from the Evil One."

38[1] "You've heard that it was said, **an eye for an eye** and **a tooth for a tooth. 39** But *I* tell you *not* to resist the evildoer; on the contrary,

> Whoever strikes you on the right cheek,
> turn the other to him as well;
> **40** To the one who wants to go to law with you
> and take your tunic,
> give him your cloak as well,
> **41** And whoever forces you to go one mile,
> go with him two.

---

[1] Lk 6:29-30.

similar variant. That translation, however, does not adequately explain the Greek. The consensus of scholars favors the explanation of J. Bonsirven, S.J., which is based on his study of Jewish marriage law at that time and has been adopted here since it provides a clear explanation of the Greek. Most literally, the Greek reads, "except by reason of fornication," *fornication* being a term of art in Rabbinical circles indicating that, since a true marriage had not been entered into, the relationship was one of fornication. The usual reason was attempted marriage within forbidden degrees of kinship. It is clear, therefore, that Jesus is not stating an exception to the general rule forbidding divorce in valid marriages. Rather, he is distinguishing valid marriages from other relationships which do not constitute true marriages. The general rule regarding marriage naturally does not apply to such illicit or otherwise defective relationships. This has been the consistent teaching of the Church.

5:33 Nm 30:2.

5:34 Is 66:1.

5:35 Is 66:1.

5:38 Ex 21:14.

5:41 "Forces"; according to Manson this word refers to a requisition of services under compulsion, probably by the Romans. It is the same word which is used to describe the requisition of Simon of Cyrene's services to carry the cross.

42   Give to the one who asks of you,
        and don't turn away the one who wishes
           to borrow from you."

43 [m] "You've heard that it was said, **Love your neighbor!** and hate your enemy. **44** But *I* say to you,

    Love your enemies,
    And pray for those who persecute you,

45 so that you'll become sons of your Father in Heaven, because

    He causes His sun to rise on the evil and the good,
        and rains on the just and the unjust.

46   For if you love those who love you,
        what reward will you have?
           Don't the tax collectors also do the same?

47   And if you greet only your brothers,
        what great thing are you doing?
           Don't the Gentiles also do the same?

48   So *you* be perfect
        as your Heavenly Father is perfect."

TRUE PRACTICE OF THE TORAH

6 **1** "Take care not to perform your good deeds in front of others in order to be seen by them; if you do, you'll have no reward from your Father in Heaven."

2   "Whenever you give alms,
        don't sound a trumpet before you,
    Like the hypocrites do in the synagogues
        and in the streets,
        so people will praise them.

---

[m] Lk 6:27-28, 32-36.

5:43 Lv 19:18. It was a common teaching of the rabbis that "neighbor" referred only to fellow Jews. Non-Jews were in opposition to God and were therefore "enemies." Other currents of rabbinic thought, however, did manifest a more conciliatory view toward Gentiles.

5:46 Publicans or tax collectors were considered outcasts, not because of objections to the payment of taxes *per se*, but because they collected taxes for the Romans and were often extortionate and dishonest.

> Amen, I say to you,
>> they have their full reward!

3   But when you give alms,
>> don't let your left hand know what your
>>> right hand is doing,

4   So that your alms may be in secret,
>> and your Father who sees in secret
>>> will reward you."

5 [n]   "And when you pray,
>> don't be like the hypocrites —
> They love to pray standing in the synagogues
>> and on the corners of wide streets,
>>> so people will notice them.
> Amen, I say to you,
>> they have their full reward!

6   But when you pray,
>> go into your storeroom and, when you've
>>> closed the door,
> Pray to your Father who is hidden,
>> and your Father who sees what's hidden
>>> will reward you."

7   "And when you're praying,
>> don't babble on like the Gentiles —
> They think they'll be heard
>> because of their wordiness.

8   But don't be like them,
>> for your Father knows what you need
>>> before you ask Him.

9   Pray, therefore, like this:

> Our Father in Heaven,
>> hallowed be Your name,

10   Your Kingdom come, Your will be done,
> On earth, as it is in Heaven.

---

[n] Lk 11:2-4.

6:9   Several authors have suggested that "hallowed be Your name" is best understood as a prayer that God should manifest His glory, as specified in the following verses.

11   Give us this day our daily bread,

12   And forgive us our debts,
        as we forgive our debtors;

13   And lead us not into temptation,
        but deliver us from the Evil One."

14   "For if you forgive others their offenses,
        your Heavenly Father will forgive you, too;

15   But if you don't forgive others,
        neither will your Father forgive your offenses."

16   "When you fast,
        don't be gloomy like the hypocrites —
They make their faces unsightly
        to let others see they're fasting.
Amen, I say to you,
        they have their full reward!

17   But when *you* fast, anoint your head
        and wash your face,

18   so others won't see that you're fasting,
But your Father in secret *will* see,
        and your Father who sees in secret
        will reward you."

EXHORTATIONS TO TRUST IN GOD

19 °   "Don't lay up treasures for yourselves on earth,
        where moth and rust destroy,
        and where thieves break in and steal;

20   Lay up treasures for yourselves in Heaven,
        where neither moth nor rust destroy,
        and where thieves neither break in nor steal.

° Lk 12:33-34. 12:22-31.

6:13 "Evil One" is often translated, simply, "evil." The use of the masculine, however, makes the former the preferred reading. Cf. 5:37.

21   For where your treasure is,
            there, too, will your heart be."

22 P   "The eye is the lamp of the body.
        Now if your eye is generous,
        Your whole body will be full of light;
23   But if your eye is grudging,
        Your whole body will be in darkness.
        So if the light in you is darkness,
        How great is the darkness!"

24 q   "No one can serve two masters;
        Either he'll hate the one and love the other,
        Or be loyal to one and despise the other.
        You cannot serve God and Mammon!"

25   "Therefore, I tell you,

        Don't worry about your life,
            what you'll eat,
        Or about your body,
            what you'll wear;
        Isn't life more than food,
            and the body more than clothing?

26 Take a look at the birds of the sky — they neither sow nor reap nor gather into barns, yet your Heavenly Father feeds them; aren't you worth more than they are? 27 But which of you can add any time to your life by worrying? 28 And why do you worry about clothing? Look how the lilies of the field grow; they neither work nor spin. 29 But I tell you, even Solomon in all his glory wasn't arrayed like one of them. 30 But if God so clothes the grass of the fields, which is here today and thrown into the oven tomorrow, won't He clothe you much better, O you of little faith? 31 So don't go worrying, saying, 'What will we eat?' or, 'What will we drink?' or, 'What will we put on?' 32 for the Gentiles seek all those things. Your Heavenly Father knows you need them! 33 But first seek the Kingdom and the will of God and all those things will be

---

P Lk 11:34-36.   q Lk 16:13;

6:22-23   A "grudging" or "evil" eye describes the envious or acquisitive attitude toward worldly
            goods, which Jesus is counselling against in this extended passage.
6:24   *Mammon* was an Aramaic word which probably referred to worldly wealth.

given to you also. **34** So don't go worrying about tomorrow —
tomorrow will worry for itself. One day's evil is enough for a day."

FURTHER EXHORTATIONS AND WARNINGS

7 **1** [r]   "Don't judge,
            so that you won't be judged,

2   For with the judgment you judge,
            you will be judged,
        And with the measure you measure,
            it will be measured out to you.

3   But why do you see the speck in your brother's eye,
            yet don't notice the log in your own eye?

4   Or how can you say to your brother,
                'Let me take the speck out of your eye,'
            when there the log is in *your* eye!

5   You hypocrite!
        First take the log out of *your* eye,
                and then you'll see clearly to take the speck
                    out of your brother's eye."

6   "Don't give what's holy to the dogs,
            nor throw your pearls before the swine,
        Lest they trample them under their feet,
            and turn around and tear you."

7 [s]   "Ask! and it shall be given to you;
            Seek! and you shall find;
                Knock! and it shall be opened to you.

8   For everyone who asks, receives,
            and whoever seeks, will find,
                and to those who knock, it shall be opened.

---

[r] Lk 6:37-38, 41-42. [s] Lk 11:9-13.

7:6   J. Fitzmyer is one of several authors who believe that "what's holy" is a mistranslation of an
       Aramaic word meaning "rings." Such misunderstandings were possible because Aramaic,
       like Hebrew, was written without vowel signs. Depending upon what vowel sounds were
       supplied to fill out the consonant signs there could be a number of possible readings for any
       given word.

9   Or what man among you, if his son
          asked for a loaf,
            would hand him a stone?

10   Or if he asked for a fish,
            would hand him a snake?

11   So if you who are evil know how
          to give good gifts to your children,
    How much more will your Father in Heaven
          give good things to those who ask Him!

12   Therefore, whatever you want others to do for you,
          do so for them as well;
    For this is the Torah and the Prophets."

13 [t]   "Go in through the narrow gate,

    For wide is the gate and broad the way
          leading to destruction,
        and many are those who enter through it;

14   How narrow the gate and difficult the way
          leading to life,
        and few are those who find it!"

15 [u]   "Watch out for false prophets who come
          to you in sheep's clothing,
    But within are savage wolves.

16   By their fruit you will know them!
    You don't gather grapes from thorns,
    Or figs from thistles, do you?

17   Likewise, every good tree produces good fruit,
    But the worthless tree produces bad fruit;

18   A good tree can't produce bad fruit,
    Nor can a worthless tree produce good fruit.

19   Every tree not producing good fruit is cut down
    And thrown into the fire.

20   And so, from their fruit you will know them."

21 [v] "Not everyone who says to me, 'Lord, Lord!' will come into the Kingdom of Heaven; no, the one who does the will of my Father in Heaven will. 22 Many will say to me on that day, 'Lord, Lord, didn't we

---

[t] Lk 13:24. [u] Lk 6:43-44. [v] Lk 13:25-27.

prophesy in your name and drive out demons in your name and do mighty works in your name?' **23** And then I'll declare to them, 'I never knew you; get away from me, you pack of evildoers!'"

24 ᵂ "Therefore, everyone who hears these words of mine
and follows them
is like a wise man who built his house on rock.

25 And the rain fell and the floods came
and the winds blew and beat against that house,
Yet it didn't fall,
because its foundations were set firmly on rock.

26 Everyone who hears these words of mine
and *doesn't* follow them
is like a foolish man who built his house on sand.

27 And the rain fell and the floods came,
and the winds blew and beat against that house,
And it fell,
and great was its fall."

28 And it happened that when Jesus had finished these words the crowds were amazed at his teaching **29** because he was teaching them on his own authority, and not like their scribes.

H. JESUS TRAVELS, TEACHING AND HEALING

8 **1** ˣ Now large crowds followed him when he descended from the mountain **2** and, behold, a leper came up, knelt before him, and said, "Lord, if you wish to, you can make me clean." **3** Jesus reached out his hand, touched him, and said, "I *do* wish to, be made clean!" and at once his leprosy was made clean. **4** Then Jesus said to him, "See that you tell no one, but go show yourself to the priest and present the offering Moses commanded, as a witness to them."

5 ʸ Now when he came into Capharnaum a centurion came up to him, appealing to him **6** and saying, "Lord, my servant is lying paralyzed at home, terribly tormented." **7** Jesus said to him, "I'll come heal him." **8** In response the centurion said, "Lord, I'm not worthy to

---

ᵂ Lk 6:47-49. ˣ Mk 1:40-45; Lk 5:12-16. ʸ Lk 7:1-10; Jn 4:43-54.

8:7 Some scholars read this verse as a question, i.e., "Shall I come heal him?"

have you come under my roof, but just say the word and my servant will be healed. **9** For I, too, am subject to authority and have soldiers under me, and if I say to this one, 'Go!' he goes, or if I say to another, 'Come!' he comes, and if I tell my slave, 'Do this!' he does it." **10** When Jesus heard this he was amazed and said to those who were following, "Amen, I say to you, nowhere have I found such faith in Israel! **11** I tell you, many will come from east and west and will recline at table with Abraham and Isaac and Jacob in the Kingdom of Heaven, **12** but the sons of the Kingdom will be thrown out into the outer darkness;

> There there will be wailing
> and gnashing of teeth!"

13 Then Jesus said to the centurion, "Go your way! Let it be done for you as you have believed," and his servant was cured at that very moment.

14 [z] And when Jesus came into Peter's house he saw Peter's mother-in-law lying in bed, sick with a fever; **15** he touched her hand and the fever left her, and she got up and began to serve him. **16** Now when evening came they brought him many people who were demon-possessed, and he drove the spirits out with a word and cured all those who were sick **17** to fulfill what was said by Isaiah the prophet when he declared,

> **He took away our illnesses**
> **and removed our diseases.**

18 [a] Now when Jesus saw a crowd around him he gave orders to go off to the other side. **19** And a scribe came up and said to him, "Teacher, I'll follow you wherever you go." **20** Jesus said to him,

> "Foxes have holes
> And the birds of the sky have nests,
> But the Son of Man has nowhere to lay his head."

21 Then another of his disciples said to him, "Lord, let me first go bury my father." **22** But Jesus said to him, "Follow me, and let the dead bury their own dead."

---

[z] Mk 1:29-34; Lk 4:38-41. [a] Lk 9:57-62.

8:17 Is 53:4.

8:20 Manson has suggested that the "foxes," of proverbial cunning, are Herod and his hated Edomite followers who played one side off against the other to their own advantage. The "birds of the air" were the Roman overlords. Jesus would then be warning his followers about what to expect: his Kingdom would be very different.

23[b] When he got into the boat his disciples followed him. **24** And, behold, such a violent storm arose on the sea that the boat was being covered by the waves, but he kept on sleeping. **25** They came to him and got him up and said, "Lord, save us, we're going to die!" **26** And he said to them, "Why are you afraid, O you of little faith?" Then he got up and rebuked the winds and the sea, and there was a profound calm. **27** But the men were amazed and said, "What sort of man *is* this, that even the winds and sea obey him?"

28[c] When he came to the other side, to the region of the Gadarenes, two demon-possessed men who had come out from the tombs met him; they were so violent that no one could go by along that way. **29** And, behold, they cried out and said, "What do you want with us, Son of God? Have you come here to torment us before the appointed time?" **30** Now some distance away from them was a herd of many swine, feeding. **31** So the demons begged him and said, "If you drive us out, send us into the herd of swine." **32** And he said to them, "Begone!" So when they went out they went off into the swine and, behold, the whole herd rushed down the slope into the sea and died in the water. **33** Then the herdsmen fled, and when they had gone off to the town they announced everything, and what had happened to the demon-possessed men. **34** And, behold, the whole town went out to meet Jesus, and when they saw him they begged him to leave their region.

9 **1**[d] After embarking on the boat he crossed over and came to his own city. **2** And, behold, they carried a paralytic to him who was lying on a bed. When Jesus saw their faith he said to the paralytic, "Take courage, child, your sins are forgiven!" **3** And, behold, some of the scribes said to themselves, "This fellow is blaspheming!" **4** And Jesus, who knew their thoughts, said, "Why do you have evil thoughts in your hearts? **5** What's easier, to say, 'Your sins are forgiven,' or to say, 'Get up and walk'? **6** But so you'll know that the Son of Man has authority on earth to forgive sins" — then he said to the paralytic, "Get up, pick up your bed and go to your house!" **7** And he got up and went off to his house. **8** When they saw this the crowds became frightened and glorified God, Who gave such authority to men.

---

[b] Mk 4:35-41; Lk 8:22-25. [c] Mk 5:1-20; Lk 8:26-39. [d] Mk 2:1-12; Lk 5:17-26.

8:29 It was a common belief at that time that the demons had power until judgment day, hence their question of Jesus.

9 ^e As Jesus travelled on from there he saw a man named Matthew seated at a tax booth, and he said to him, "Follow me!" And he got up and followed Jesus. **10** And it happened that he sat down at table in Matthew's house, and, behold, many tax collectors and sinners had come and were at table with Jesus and his disciples. **11** When the Pharisees saw this they said to his disciples, "Why does your teacher eat with tax collectors and sinners?" **12** But when Jesus heard this he said, "The healthy aren't in need of a doctor — the sick are. **13** So go learn what *this* means, **I desire mercy and not sacrifice,** for I came not to call the righteous, but sinners."

14 ^f Then John's disciples came to him and said, "Why do we and the Pharisees fast, but your disciples don't fast?" **15** And Jesus said to them,

> "The groomsmen cannot mourn while the bridegroom
>   is with them,
> But the day will come when the bridegroom will
>   be taken from them, and then they'll fast.

16 But no one puts a patch of new cloth
>   on an old cloak,
> For its fullness takes from the cloak
>   and the tear becomes worse.

17 Nor do you put new wine into old skins;
> For then the skins burst and the wine is spilled,
>   and the skins are ruined.
> Instead, you put new wine into new skins
> And then both are preserved."

18 ^g While he was telling them these things, behold, a ruler came and knelt before him and said, "My daughter has just died, but come lay your hand on her and she'll live." **19** So Jesus and his disciples got up and followed him. **20** And, behold, a woman who had had a chronic bleeding for twelve years came up and touched the hem of his cloak from behind, **21** for she said to herself, "If I just touch his cloak I'll be saved." **22** But Jesus, turning and seeing her, said, "Take courage,

---

^e Mk 2:13-17; Lk 5:27-32. ^f Mk 2:18-22; Lk 5:33-39. ^g Mk 5:21-43; Lk 8:40-56.

9:10 "Matthew's house." Literally, "his house," but cf. Lk 5:29, where Luke specifies "Levi's house."

9:13 Ho 6:6.

daughter! Your faith has saved you!" And the woman was saved from that hour.

23 When Jesus came to the ruler's house and saw the flute players and the crowd in an uproar **24** he said, "Out with you! — the girl hasn't died, she's sleeping!" And they laughed at him. **25** But when the crowd had been driven out he went in, grasped the girl's hand, and she got up. **26** And this news went out through all that land.

27 As Jesus travelled on from there two blind men followed him, crying out and saying, "Have mercy on us, Son of David!" **28** When he had gone into the house the blind men came to him and Jesus said to them, "Do you believe that I can do this?" They said to him, "Yes, Lord!" **29** He touched their eyes and said, "Let it be done to you according to your faith!" **30** and their eyes were opened. Then he spoke sternly to them and said, "See that no one knows!" **31** But they went out and spread the news throughout that region.

32 Now when they came out, behold, the people brought him a demon-possessed dumb man, **33** and when the demon had been driven out the dumb man spoke. The crowds were amazed and said, "The like of this has never been seen in Israel!" **34** But the Pharisees said, "By the prince of demons he drives out demons."

I. THE MISSION OF THE DISCIPLES

35 Then Jesus went around all the cities and villages, teaching in their synagogues, proclaiming the good news of the Kingdom and healing every disease and illness. **36** Now when he saw the crowds he was moved with pity for them because they were worried and helpless, like sheep without a shepherd. **37** And he said to his disciples,

> "The harvest is plentiful,
> But the laborers are few;

38 so implore the Lord of the harvest to send out laborers to his harvest."

10 **1** ʰ Then he called his twelve disciples to him and gave them authority over unclean spirits, so they could drive them out

---

ʰ Mk 3:13-19; Lk 6:12-16.

and heal every disease and illness. **2** Now these are the names of the twelve apostles; first Simon who is called Peter and his brother Andrew, and James son of Zebedee and his brother John, **3** Philip and Bartholomew, Thomas and Matthew the tax collector, James son of Alpheus and Thaddeus, **4** Simon the Zealot and Judas Iscariot, who handed him over.

5 ⁱ Jesus sent these twelve out after instructing them and saying,

> "Don't go off on the road to the Gentiles,
> And don't go into the city of the Samaritans;
> **6**   Go, instead, to the lost sheep of the house of Israel.

7 But as you go, proclaim [the good news], and say, 'The Kingdom of Heaven has come!'

> **8**   Heal the sick,
>   raise the dead,
>   Cleanse lepers,
>   drive out demons;
>   Freely you have received,
>   freely give.
> **9**   Don't keep gold or silver,
>   nor brass in your belts,
> **10**   Neither a bag for the road
>   nor two tunics,
>   Nor sandals
>   nor staff,
>   For the worker is deserving of his living.

11 "Whatever town or village you enter, ask who in it is worthy and stay there until you leave.

> **12**   Now when you enter the house,
>   pay your respects,
> **13**   And if that house is worthy,
>   your peace will come upon it,

ⁱ Mk 6:7-13; Lk 9:1-6.

10:4   Literally, "Simon the Cananaean." This is generally considered to be a designation for the ultranationalist (and, therefore, anti-Roman) Zealots, but some scholars maintain that the Zealots did not become an organized movement until after the time of Jesus.

10:12   Many Greek and some Latin manuscripts add, "saying, 'Peace to this house.' "

But if it isn't worthy,
    your peace will return to you.
14 And whoever doesn't receive you
        or hear your words,
    When you've gone out of the house or that city,
        shake the dust from your feet.

15 Amen, I say to you, it will be more tolerable for the land of Sodom and Gomorrah on the day of judgment than for that city!"

16 ^j   "Behold, I'm sending you off like sheep among wolves;
        Be as wise as serpents and guileless as doves.

17 But beware of men —

    They'll hand you over to councils,
        and scourge you in their synagogues,
18 And you'll be led before governors
            and kings for my sake,
        as a witness to them and to the Gentiles.
19 But when they hand you over, don't worry
            about how to speak
        or what you should say;
    For what you should say
        will be given you in that hour,
20 For it won't be you speaking,
        but the Spirit of my Father speaking in you.
21 Brother will hand brother over to death,
        and father, child.
    And children will rebel against parents
        and put them to death.
22 And you'll be hated by all
        because of my name,
    But whoever holds out till the end,
        they will be saved.

23 And when they persecute you in one such city, flee to another; for, amen, I say to you, you will not finish with the cities of Israel before the Son of Man comes."

---

^j Mk 13:9-13; Lk 21:12-17.

24 [k] "The disciple is not above the teacher,
nor the servant above his master.

25   It's enough for the disciple to become
like his master,
and the servant like *his* master.
If they've called the householder Beelzebul,
how much more his dependents!"

26 [l] Therefore, don't be afraid of them —

Nothing is concealed
that will not be revealed,
Nor hidden
that will not be made known.

27   What I tell you in darkness,
speak in the light,
And what you hear whispered,
proclaim on the rooftops.

28   Don't fear those who can kill the body
but can't kill the soul;
Fear, instead, the One Who can kill
both soul and body in Gehenna.

29 Aren't two sparrows sold for a few cents? Yet not one of them will fall to the earth without your Father's leave. **30** But as for you, even the hairs of your head are all numbered. **31** So don't be afraid; you're worth more than many sparrows."

32 [m] "Therefore, whoever acknowledges me
before men,
I, too, will acknowledge them before my Father
in Heaven;

33   But whoever denies me before men,
I, too, will deny them before my Father
in Heaven."

34 [n] "Don't think that I came to spread peace
on the earth;
I came not to spread peace but the sword.

---

[k] Lk 6:40. [l] Lk 12:2-7. [m] Lk 12:8-9. [n] Lk 12:51-53; 14:26-27.

10:29   "A few cents." Literally, "an *assarion*." An *assarion* was a Roman copper coin worth 1/16 of a *denarius*, which was a silver coin equivalent to a common laborer's daily wage.

35   I came to turn a man **against his father,**
    And a daughter against her mother,

    And a daughter-in-law against her mother-in-law,
36   And **a man's enemies will be the members**
        of his household.

37   Whoever loves father or mother more than me
        is not worthy of me,
38   And whoever doesn't take up his cross and follow
        behind me isn't worthy of me.

39   Whoever finds his life will lose it,
    And whoever loses his life for my sake
        will find it."

40 º   "Whoever receives you
        receives me,
    And whoever receives me
        receives the One Who sent me.
41   Whoever receives a prophet
        because he's a prophet
        shall receive a prophet's reward,
    And whoever receives a good man
        because he's a good man
        shall receive a good man's reward.

42 And whoever gives even a cup of cold water to one of these little ones because he's a disciple, amen, I say to you, he will not lose his reward."

11 **1** And it happened that when Jesus had finished instructing his twelve disciples he left there to teach and preach in their cities.

J. RESPONSE IN FAITH AND REPENTANCE

2 ᴾ Now when John heard in prison about the works of the Messiah he sent by means of his disciples **3** and said to him, "Are you he who is to come, or are we to expect another?"

º Mk 9:41. ᴾ Lk 7:18-35.

10:35-36 Mi 7:6.

4 In answer Jesus said to them, "Go tell John what you hear and see:

5   **The blind can see again** and the lame walk,
        Lepers are made clean and the deaf hear,
        The dead are raised and **the poor are given
            the good news;**
6   And blessed be whoever is not scandalized by me."

7 After they had left, Jesus began to speak to the crowds about John.

        "What did you go out to the desert to see?
            A reed, shaken by the wind?
8   But what did you go out to see?
            A man wearing luxurious clothing?
        Behold, those in luxurious clothing
            are in the houses of kings!

9   But what did you go out to see?
            A prophet?
        Yes, I tell you, and one greater than a prophet.
10   He it is of whom it is written,
        **Behold, I'm sending my messenger before your face,
            who will prepare your way before you.**
11   Amen, I say to you, among those born of women
                there has not risen one greater than John
                    the Baptist,
        Yet even the least in the Kingdom of Heaven
            is greater than he is.
12   From the days of John the Baptist
                until the present
        The Kingdom of Heaven suffers violence,
            and the violent take it by force.

11:5   Is 35:5-6; 61:1.

11:10   Ml 3:1. This prophecy continues by stating that Yahweh Himself will come in judgment. If John the Baptist is the messenger, as Jesus says, then Jesus is equating himself with Yahweh, a point likely not missed by his listeners.

11:12   This obscure verse probably refers to attempts by those hostile to Jesus to prevent the acceptance of the Kingdom.

13 For all the Prophets and the Torah up to John prophesied, **14** and if you can accept it, he's Elijah — he who is destined to come.

15   Whoever has ears,
          let them hear!"

16 "But to what shall I compare this generation? It's like children sitting in the marketplace who call to each other **17** and say,

'We piped for you and you didn't dance,
          we wailed and you didn't mourn.'

18   For John came neither eating nor drinking,
                    and they said,
          'He has a demon';
19   The Son of Man came eating and drinking,
                    and they said,
          'Look at him, a glutton and a drunkard, a friend
                    of tax collectors and sinners!'
          Yet wisdom is justified by her works!"

20 ᑫ Then he began to denounce the cities in which most of his mighty works had taken place, because they hadn't repented. **21** "Woe to you, Chorazin! Woe to you, Bethsaida! Because if the mighty works that happened in *you* had taken place in Tyre or Sidon, they would have repented in sackcloth and ashes long ago. **22** But I say to you, Tyre and Sidon, it will be more tolerable for you on the day of judgment. **23** And you, Capharnaum!

You'll be exalted to Heaven, will you?
You'll be brought down to Hell!

because if the mighty works that happened in you had taken place in Sodom it would have remained to this day. **24** But I say to you, it will be more tolerable for the land of Sodom on the day of judgment than for you!"

25 ʳ At that time Jesus raised his voice and said,

ᑫ Lk 10:13-15. ʳ Lk 10:21-22.

11:13   Jesus here characterizes the Torah as a prophetic witness, perhaps in opposition to the understanding of it as a code of law which will remain entirely unchanged for all time.

11:19   This accusation against Jesus meant that his accusers considered him to be deserving of stoning. Cf. Dt 21:20.

11:23   Is 14:13, 15.

> "I praise you, Father,
>> Lord of Heaven and earth,
> Because You hid these things from the wise
>> and intelligent,
>> and revealed them to babes;

26 Yes, Father,
>> for such was Your desire.

27 All things have been given to me by my Father,
>> and no one knows the Son except the Father,
> Nor does anyone know the Father except the Son,
>> and to whomever the Son wishes to reveal Him.

28 Come to me, all you grown weary and burdened,
>> and I will refresh you.

29 Take my yoke upon you
>> and learn from me,
> For I am gentle and humble hearted,
>> and you will find rest for your souls;

30 For my yoke is easy,
>> and my burden light."

K. CONTROVERSY WITH THE PHARISEES

THE LORD OF THE SABBATH

12 **1** ˢ At that time Jesus was going through the grain fields on the Sabbath; now, his disciples became hungry and began to pluck the heads of grain and eat them. **2** When the Pharisees saw this they said to him, "Look, your disciples are doing what it's unlawful to do on the Sabbath!" **3** But he said to them, "Haven't you read what David did when *he* was hungry, as well as those with him? **4** How he went into the house of God and ate the loaves of offering, which it wasn't lawful for

---

ˢ Mk 2:23-28; Lk 6:1-5.

11:28-30 "Yoke." This was a common way of referring to the Torah, and every pious Jew was to accept this "yoke" joyfully. Here Jesus contrasts his own authoritative teaching with the Pharisees' interpretation of the Torah.

him to eat nor for those with him but was for the priests alone? **5** Or haven't you read in the Torah that on the Sabbath the priests serving in the Temple violate the Sabbath yet are not considered guilty? **6** But I say to you, something greater than the Temple is here. **7** If you had known what this means, **I desire mercy and not sacrifice,** you wouldn't have condemned the innocent. **8** For the Son of Man is Lord of the Sabbath."

9 [t] He left there and went to their synagogue, **10** and, behold, a man with a withered hand was there. And they demanded to know of him, "Is it lawful to heal on the Sabbath?" in an effort to find an accusation they could bring against him. **11** But he said to them, "Is there a man among you who, if he had one sheep and it fell into a ditch on the Sabbath, wouldn't take hold of it and pull it out? **12** How much more is a man worth than a sheep! And so it's lawful to do good on the Sabbath." **13** Then he said to the man, "Hold out your hand." He held it out and it was restored, as sound as the other. **14** But the Pharisees went out and plotted to do away with Jesus.

15 Now Jesus realized this and departed from there. Many people followed him and he healed them all **16** and commanded them not to make him known, **17** so he would fulfill what was said by Isaiah the prophet, when he proclaimed,

18	Behold my Servant whom I have chosen,
	my Beloved in whom my soul is well pleased;
	I will put my Spirit upon him,
	and he will proclaim judgment to the Gentiles.
19	He will not quarrel or shout out angrily,
	nor will anyone hear his voice in the streets.
20	He will not snap off a broken reed,
	and he will not snuff out a smoldering wick,
	Until he leads justice to victory,
21	and the Gentiles will hope in him.

---

[t] Mk 3:1-6; Lk 6:6-11.

12:7   Ho 6:6.
12:18-21   Is 42:1-4 (Septuagint).

JESUS AND BEELZEBUL

22 [u] Then they brought him a demon-possessed blind and dumb man, and he healed him so that the dumb man could speak and see. **23** And all the crowds went wild and said, "Could this be the Son of David?" **24** But the Pharisees heard and said, "If Beelzebul, prince of demons, weren't helping him, this fellow wouldn't be able to drive out demons!" **25** Now he knew their inmost thoughts and so he said to them,

> "Every kingdom divided against itself
> is laid waste,
> And every city or house divided against itself
> will not stand.

26 And if Satan drives out Satan,
> he's divided against himself;
> How, then, will his kingdom stand?

27 And if I drive out demons by Beelzebul,
> by whom do *your* followers drive them out?
> Therefore, *they'll* be your judges!

28 But if I drive out demons by the Spirit of God,
> then the Kingdom of God has come upon you!

29 How can someone enter the strong man's house and carry off his possessions if he doesn't first tie the strong man up? *Then* he can plunder the house.

30 Whoever isn't with me is against me,
> And whoever doesn't gather with me scatters.

31 Therefore I say to you,

---

[u] Mk 3:20-30; Lk 11:14-23; 12:10.

12:27   "*Your* followers"; literally, "*your* sons."

12:28   This is one of the few instances where Matthew uses "Kingdom of God" rather than "Kingdom of Heaven." The two expressions are equivalent, but the latter phrase reflects the Jewish desire to avoid using the Divine name. For other examples of the use of "Kingdom of God" in Matthew cf. 19:24 and 21:43.

12:29   Here Jesus compares Satan to a "strong man" and the present age to Satan's house. It is Jesus who has entered Satan's house, bound him, and freed those in Satan's power. Jesus' power over demons is a sign of this mastery and of the coming of the Messianic age.

Every sin and blasphemy will be forgiven you,
But blasphemy against the Spirit
    will not be forgiven.
32   And whoever says a word against the Son of Man
    will be forgiven,
But whoever speaks against the Holy Spirit
    will not be forgiven in this age
        or the coming one.
33 ᵛ Either make the tree good and its fruit good,
Or make the tree bad and its fruit bad,
For from the fruit the tree is known.
34   You brood of vipers!
How can you speak good things
    when *you're* evil?
For the mouth speaks from the abundance
    of the heart.
35   The good man brings forth good things
    from his good treasure,
And the evil man brings forth evil things
    from his evil treasure.
36   But I tell you that for every slighting
    utterance you make,
You'll give an accounting on the day
    of judgment,
37   For by your words you'll be justified,
And by your words you'll be condemned."

THE SIGN OF JONAH

38 ᵂ Then some of the scribes and Pharisees spoke up and said to him, "Teacher, we want to see a sign from you." **39** But in answer he said to them,

---

ᵛ Lk 6:43-45. ᵂ Mk 8:11-12; Lk 11:29-32.

12:36   Often translated "every idle word." The context makes it abundantly clear, however, that Jesus is addressing those attempting to simply dismiss him.

12:39   "The sign of Jonah," also referred to at 16:4, probably referred primarily to the extension of God's mercy to the Gentiles and their preference over those Jews who rejected Jesus. It is so understood by Luke, cf. Lk 11:29-32.

"A wicked and adulterous generation seeks a sign,
Yet no sign will be given it but the sign of Jonah
the prophet.

40   For just as **Jonah was in the belly of the whale
for three days and three nights,**
So will the Son of Man be in the heart of the earth
for three days and three nights.

41   The men of Nineveh will stand in judgment
against this generation and will condemn it,
Because they repented as a result of Jonah's
preaching,
And, behold, one greater than Jonah is here.

42   The queen of the South will rise up at the judgment
against this generation and condemn it,
Because she came from the ends of the earth
to hear the wisdom of Solomon,
And, behold, one greater than Solomon is here."

43[x] "Now when an unclean spirit comes out of a man it goes about through waterless places seeking relief, and finds none. **44** Then it says, 'I'll return to the house I came out of,' and when it comes it finds it empty, swept out, and decorated. **45** Then it goes and brings with it seven other spirits worse than itself, and it goes in and settles there, and the last state of that man becomes worse than the first. That's how it will be with this evil generation, too."

46[y] While he was still speaking to the crowds, behold, his mother and brothers came and stood outside, seeking to speak with him. **47** Now someone said to him, "Look, your mother and your brothers are standing outside — they want to speak with you!" **48** But in answer he said to the one who had spoken to him, "Who is my mother, and who are my brothers?" **49** And stretching out his hand to his disciples he said, "Here are my mother and my brothers, **50** for whoever does the will of my Father in Heaven, he's my brother and sister and mother."

[x] Lk 11:24-26. [y] Mk 3:31-35; Lk 8:19-21.

12:40   Jon 1:17.

12:46   In Semitic usage, close relatives such as cousins could be referred to as brothers or sisters. That these "brothers" were not additional sons of Mary, the mother of Jesus, can be seen from other passages such as Mt 27:60. Cf. below at 13:55 for a further discussion.

L. PARABLES OF THE KINGDOM
AND REJECTION AT NAZARETH

13 1 ᶻ That day when Jesus left the house he sat down by the sea, **2** and such large crowds gathered around him that he got into a boat and seated himself, while the whole crowd stood on the shore. **3** Then he told them many things in parables and said,

"Behold, the sower went out to sow!
4 And as he sowed, some seed fell along the path,
and the birds came and ate it up.
5 Now other seed fell on rocky ground, where it
didn't have much soil
and it sprouted at once, since the soil
had no depth.
6 But when the sun rose it got scorched,
and since it had no roots it withered away.
7 But other seed fell among the thorns,
and the thorns came up and choked it.
8 Still other seed fell on the good earth
and gave fruit,
the one a hundredfold, the other sixtyfold,
yet another thirtyfold.
9 Whoever has ears,
let them hear!"

10 ᵃ And the disciples came forward and said to him, "Why are you speaking to them in parables?" **11** In answer he said, "To you it's given to know the secrets of the Kingdom of Heaven, but to them it isn't given.

12 For whoever has, it will be given to him
and it will be more than enough,
But whoever does not have, even what he has
will be taken from him.

13 Therefore, I speak to them in parables, because

ᶻ Mk 4:1-9; Lk 8:4-8. ᵃ Mk 4:10-12; Lk 8:9-10.

Although they look,
they don't see,
And though they listen,
they neither hear nor understand,

14 and in them is being fulfilled the prophecy of Isaiah, who said,

**For all you listen,
you will hear yet not understand,
And though you look,
you will see yet not perceive.**

15 **For the heart of this people has been hardened,
and it has been difficult for them to hear
with their ears,
And they closed their eyes lest they see
with their eyes
and hear with their ears
And understand with their heart and return,
and I will heal them.**

16 But blessed are your eyes because they see,
and your ears because they hear.

17 Amen, I say to you,
Many of the prophets and the righteous longed
to see what you're seeing,
yet didn't see,
And to hear what you're hearing,
yet didn't hear."

18 [b] "Listen, then, to the parable of the sower. **19** When anyone hears the word of the Kingdom yet doesn't understand, the Evil One comes and carries away what was sown in his heart; this is what was sown along the footpath. **20** What was sown on the rocky ground, this is the one who hears the word and at once receives it joyfully, **21** but he's not well rooted but is only for the moment and when trouble or persecution arises because of the word he at once falls away. **22** Now what was sown among the thorns, this is the one who hears the word, yet worldly cares and the deception of wealth choke the word and it's

---

[b] Mk 4:13-20; Lk 8:11-15.

13:14-15 Is 6:9-10.

unfruitful. **23** But what was sown on good earth, this is the one who hears the word and understands, who, indeed, bears fruit, and produces a hundredfold, or sixtyfold, or thirtyfold."

24   He presented another parable to them and said, "The Kingdom of Heaven has been compared to a man who sowed good seed in his field.   **25** While everyone was sleeping his enemy came and sowed weeds among the wheat and went off, **26** so when the shoots sprouted and bore fruit the weeds appeared then, too. **27** The householder's servants came to him and said, 'Master, didn't you sow good seed in your field? Then where did the weeds come from?' **28** But he said to them, 'An enemy did this.' So the slaves said to him, 'Do you want us to gather them up, then?'   **29** But he said, 'No, you might uproot the wheat at the same time you're gathering the weeds. **30** Let them both grow together until the harvest, and at the harvest time I'll tell the harvesters, "First gather the weeds and tie them in bundles to be burned, but gather the wheat into my barn."'"

31 ᶜ   He presented another parable to them and said, "The Kingdom of Heaven is like a grain of mustard seed, which a man took and sowed in his field. **32** Although it's the smallest of seeds, when it's fully grown it's the biggest of garden plants and becomes a tree, so that the birds of the air come and nest in its branches."

33 He told them another parable. "The Kingdom of Heaven is like yeast that a woman took and mixed into a bushel of wheat flour until all of it was leavened."

34 ᵈ Jesus spoke all these things to the crowds in parables and he said nothing to them except in a parable, **35** so that what was said by the prophet would be fulfilled, when he said,

> **I will open my mouth in parables,**
> **I will proclaim what has been hidden since**
> **the beginning of the world.**

ᶜ Mk 4:30-32; Lk 13:18-21. ᵈ Mk 4:33-34.

13:25   "Weeds." Lit., "darnel." Darnel is a weed which is very similar in appearance to wheat.

13:33   "A bushel." Lit., "a *saton*." A *saton* was a dry measure equaling 21.6 pints; three *satons* would be just about one bushel — a hyperbolically large amount.

13:35   Ps 78:2.

36 After he left the crowds he went into the house, and his disciples came to him and said, "Explain the parable of the weeds in the field to us." **37** In answer he said, "The one who sowed good seed is the Son of Man, **38** while the field is the age; now the good seed, these are the children of the Kingdom, while the weeds are those who belong to the Evil One, **39** and the enemy who sowed them is the Devil; now the harvest is the end of the age, and the harvesters are the angels. **40** Just as the weeds are gathered and burned with fire, so also will it be at the end of the age; **41** the Son of Man will send his angels, and they'll gather all who cause others to sin from his Kingdom and all those who do evil, **42** and they'll thrust them into the furnace of fire;

> There there will be wailing
> and gnashing of teeth!

43 Then the righteous will shine like the sun in the Kingdom of their Father.

> Whoever has ears,
> let them hear!"

44 "The Kingdom of Heaven is like a treasure hidden in a field which a man found and hid, and in his joy he went off and sold all he had and bought that field."

45 "Again, the Kingdom of Heaven is like a merchant seeking fine pearls; **46** when he found one very precious pearl he went and sold off all he had and bought it."

47 "Again, the Kingdom of Heaven is like a dragnet cast into the sea which gathered every sort of fish; **48** when it was filled they dragged it ashore and gathered the good ones into containers, but they threw the bad ones out. **49** It will be like that at the end of the age; the angels will go out and sort the evil out from among the righteous **50** and throw them into the furnace of fire;

> There there will be wailing
> and gnashing of teeth."

51 "Have you understood all these things?" "Yes," they said to him. **52** Then he said to them,

---

13:38   "Children." Lit., "sons." "Those who belong to." Lit., "the sons of."
13:43   Dn 12:3.

"Every scribe who is a disciple
    of the Kingdom of Heaven
Is like a man who is master of a house,
Who brings out from his treasure
    new things and old."

53 [e] And it happened that when Jesus finished these parables he left there. **54** When he came to his home town he taught them in their synagogue, with the result that they were amazed and said, "Where does this fellow get this wisdom and these mighty works? **55** Isn't this the carpenter's son? Isn't his mother called Mary, and his brothers James and Joseph and Simon and Judas? **56** And his sisters — aren't they all here among us?" **57** And they rejected him. But Jesus said to them, "A prophet is without honor only in his hometown and in his own house." **58** And because of their unbelief he didn't do many mighty works there.

M. THE DEATH OF THE BAPTIST AND TWO SIGNS

14 **1** [f] At that time Herod the Tetrarch heard reports about Jesus, **2** and he said to his servants, "This is John the Baptist; he's been raised from the dead and that's why these powers are at work in him." **3** For Herod had seized John, bound him, and thrown him into prison because of Herodias, the wife of his brother Philip, **4** because John had been telling Herod, "It isn't lawful for you to have her." **5** Herod wished to kill him, but he feared the [reaction of the] people, because they regarded John as a prophet. **6** Now when Herod's birthday celebration was held Herodias' daughter danced before the guests, and she pleased Herod so much **7** that he promised with an oath to give her whatever she asked for. **8** So, prompted by her mother, she said, "Give me, right here on a platter, the head of John the Baptist." **9** And the king,

---

[e] Mk 6:1-6; Lk 4:16-30. [f] Mk 6:14-29; Lk 9:7-9.

13:55   Church tradition has consistently maintained that the "brothers" of Jesus referred to here were merely close relatives, not sons of the same mother. It is instructive to compare this passage to 27:60 (and parallel passages in the other Gospels, esp. Mk 15:40 - 16:1 and Lk 23:49 - 24:10) where these brothers are again referred to as sons of "Mary," but this time it is unambiguously clear that *this* Mary was not Mary the mother of Jesus. Such usage was typically Semitic.

grieved because of his oath and those reclining at table with him, ordered that it be given to her. **10** He sent and had John beheaded in prison **11** and his head was brought on a platter and given to the girl, and she brought it to her mother. **12** His disciples came and took the corpse and buried it. Then they came and informed Jesus.

13 ᵍ Now when Jesus heard about it he left there privately by boat for a desert place, and when the crowds heard this they followed him on foot from the cities. **14** When he got out [of the boat] he saw a large crowd, and he was moved with pity for them and healed their sick. **15** Now when evening had come his disciples came to him and said, "This is a desert place and the day has already come to a close; send the crowds away so they can go off to the villages and buy themselves some food." **16** But Jesus said to them, "There's no need for them to go away; *you* give them something to eat." **17** They said to him, "We have nothing here except five loaves and two fish." **18** But he said, "Bring them here to me." **19** After ordering the crowds to recline on the grass he took the five loaves and the two fish and, looking up to heaven, he gave a blessing, and after breaking them he gave the loaves to his disciples and his disciples gave them to the crowds. **20** They all ate and were filled, and they picked up what was left of the fragments — twelve baskets full. **21** Now there were about five thousand men who ate, apart from women and children.

22 ʰ At once he made his disciples get into the boat and go on ahead of him to the other side while he sent the crowds away, **23** and after sending the crowds away he went up the mountain to pray in private. When evening came on he was there alone, **24** while the boat was already several miles away from land, tossed about by the waves, for the wind was against it. **25** Now shortly before dawn he came toward them, walking on the sea. **26** When the disciples saw him walking on the sea they were terrified and said, "It's a ghost!" and they cried out in fear. **27** But he spoke to them at once and said, "Take courage! It's me! Don't be afraid!" **28** In answer to him Peter said, "Lord, if it's you, command me to come to you on the water." **29** So he

---

g Mk 6:30-44; Lk 9:10-17; Jn 6:1-14. h Mk 6:45-52; Jn 6:15-21.

14:24 "Several miles." Lit., "many *stadious*." A *stadioi* (the Greek word is plural) was about 607 ft.
14:25 "Shortly before dawn." Lit., "at the fourth watch of the night." The fourth watch would have been just before dawn. The Romans considered night to extend from six p.m. to six a.m. and divided it into four equal parts. Thus, the fourth watch was between three a.m. and six a.m.

said, "Come!" Peter got out of the boat and began to walk on the water and drew near to Jesus, **30** but when he saw the wind he became frightened and, as he began to sink, he cried out and said, "Save me, Lord!" **31** At once Jesus reached out his hand and caught him and said to him, "O you of little faith, why did you doubt?" **32** And when they got into the boat the wind ceased. **33** Then those in the boat worshipped him and said, "Truly you're the Son of God!"

34 [i] After crossing over they came to land at Gennesaret. **35** The men of that place recognized him and sent to all that neighborhood, and they brought all those who were sick to him **36** and begged him to just let them touch the hem of his cloak, and those who touched it were cured.

N. TRUE PURIFICATION

15 **1** [j] Then Pharisees and scribes from Jerusalem came up to Jesus and said, **2** "Why do your disciples disobey what was handed down by the elders? They don't wash their hands when they eat bread!" **3** In answer he said to them, "And why do *you* disobey the commandment of God through what you hand down? **4** God said, 'Honor your father and your mother,' and, 'Let whoever curses his father or mother be put to death,' **5** but you say, 'Whoever says to his father or mother, "Whatever benefit you might have of me is an offering to God," **6** need not honor his father,' and you set aside the word of God for what *you* hand down. **7** You hypocrites! Surely Isaiah prophesied about you when he said,

8   **This people honors me with their lips,**
            but their heart is far distant from me;
9   **In vain do they worship me,**
                teaching as doctrines the commandments
                    of men."

---

[i] Mk 6:53-56. [j] Mk 7:1-23.

15:8-9   Is 29:13 (Septuagint).

10 Then he called the crowd to himself and said to them, "Hear and understand!

11   What goes into the mouth
            is not what makes a man unclean;
        On the contrary, what comes out of his mouth,
            that makes a man unclean."

12 The disciples came and said to him, "Do you know that, when they heard, the Pharisees took offense at what you said?" **13** But in answer he said, "Every plant not planted by my Heavenly Father will be pulled out by the roots. **14** Let them be. They're blind guides. Now,

            If a blind man leads a blind man,
            Both will fall into a ditch."

15 In response Peter said to him, "Explain the parable to us." **16** Jesus said, "Can you still be that dense? **17** Don't you see that everything that enters the mouth goes into the stomach and is expelled into the latrine? **18** But the things that leave the mouth come from the heart, and those are the things that make you unclean. **19** For from the heart come wicked thoughts, murder, adultery, fornication, theft, false witness, and blasphemy. **20** These things are what make a person unclean, but eating with unwashed hands doesn't make you unclean."

O. HEALINGS AND SIGNS

21 [k] When he left there Jesus withdrew to the district of Tyre and Sidon. **22** And, behold, a Canaanite woman from that region came and cried out, "Have mercy on me, Lord, Son of David! My daughter is severely possessed by a demon!" **23** But not a word did he answer her. His disciples came forward and begged him and said, "Send it away—

---

[k] Mk 7:24-30.

15:14   Ex 20:12; Dt 5:16.

15:16   "You." The Greek word is plural, so that Jesus is not singling Peter out.

15:23   "Send it away." Literally, "send *her* away." The substitution of "it" presupposes an Aramaic original. Since Aramaic has no neuter gender, it was possible to mistakenly translate an Aramaic feminine pronoun literally rather than changing it to the neuter, if that would be required in Greek. The context appears to support this interpretation. If it is read "her," then Jesus' reply to the disciples is a nonsequitur, since he would be granting neither the woman's request that her daughter be healed, nor the disciples', that she be sent away.

she keeps crying out behind us!" **24** But in answer he said, "I was sent only to the lost sheep of the house of Israel." **25** So she came and knelt before him and said, "Lord, help me!" **26** But in answer he replied, "It isn't right to take the children's bread and throw it to the dogs." **27** But she said, "O yes, Lord — even the dogs eat the crumbs that fall from their masters' table!" **28** In answer, then, Jesus said to her, "O woman, great is your faith! Let it be done for you as you wish!" And her daughter was healed from that very hour.

29 After leaving there Jesus went along the sea of Galilee, and he ascended the mountain and sat down there. **30** Large crowds came to him who had with them lame, blind, crippled, dumb people, and many others, and they put them down at his feet and he cured them, **31** so that the crowd marvelled when they saw the dumb speaking, cripples sound, the lame walking, and the blind seeing, and they glorified the God of Israel.

32 [1] Then Jesus called his disciples together and said, "I'm overcome with pity for the crowd — they've stayed with me for three days now and don't have anything to eat, yet I don't want to send them away hungry — they might faint on the way." **33** And the disciples said to him, "Where can we get enough loaves in the desert to feed such a large crowd?" **34** Jesus said to them, "How many loaves do you have?" "Seven, and a few fish," they replied. **35** After ordering the crowd to sit down on the ground **36** he took the loaves and the fish and gave thanks, and he broke them and kept giving them to his disciples, and the disciples gave them to the crowds. **37** They all ate and were filled, and they picked up the leftover fragments — seven large baskets full. **38** Now there were four thousand men who ate, apart from the women and children. **39** Then after sending the crowds away he got into the boat and came to the regions of Magadan.

16 **1** [m] The Pharisees and Sadducees came to test him, and they asked him to show them a sign from Heaven. **2** But in answer he said to them, "In the evening you say, 'Fair weather — the sky is red,'

---

[1] Mk 8:1-10. [m] Mk 8:11-13; Lk 12:54-56.

On the other hand, if "it" is substituted, it makes excellent sense: the disciples beg Jesus to grant the woman's request and send *it* (the demon) away just to quiet the woman, but he at first declines to grant the woman this favor because she is a non-Israelite. This is clearly seen in the parallel passage at Mk 7:24 ff.

3 and in the morning, 'Today will be stormy — the sky is red and darkened.' You know how to read the face of the sky, yet you can't tell the signs of the times!

    4 [n]   A wicked and adulterous generation seeks a sign,
        Yet no sign will be given it but the sign of Jonah."

Then he left them and went away.

    5 And when the disciples went to the other side they forgot to bring bread. 6 Now Jesus said to them, "Take care, and guard against the leaven of the Pharisees and Sadducees!" 7 But they kept arguing among themselves and said, "Why didn't we bring bread?" 8 So Jesus, realizing this, said, "O you of little faith, why are you arguing among yourselves because you don't have bread? 9 Do you still not understand? Don't you remember the five loaves for the five thousand and how many baskets you picked up? 10 Or the seven loaves for the four thousand and how many large baskets you picked up? 11 How can you not understand that I wasn't talking to you about bread? Be on guard, then, against the leaven of the Pharisees and Sadducees." 12 Then they realized that he wasn't saying to be on guard against the leavening but against the teaching of the Pharisees and Sadducees.

P. JESUS, PETER, TRANSFIGURATION

    13 [o] Now when Jesus came to the district of Caesarea Philippi he began to question his disciples, "Who do they say the Son of Man is?" 14 So they said, "Some say John the Baptist, others, Elijah, still others, Jeremiah or one of the prophets." 15 Then he asked them, "But *you* — who do *you* say I am?" 16 Peter replied, "You're the Messiah, the Son of the Living God!" 17 And in response Jesus said to him,

        "Blessed are you, Simon son of Jonah,
        For it wasn't flesh and blood that
            revealed this to you,
        But my Father in Heaven.

---

[n] Mk 8:14-21. [o] Mk 8:27-30; Lk 9:18-21.

18   And now *I* tell *you,* that you are Peter,
And on this rock I will build my church,
And the gates of Hell will not prevail
    against it.

19   I will give you the keys of the Kingdom
    of Heaven,
And whatever you bind on earth will have been
    bound in Heaven,
And whatever you loose on earth will have been
    loosed in Heaven."

20 Then he ordered the disciples not to tell anyone that he was the Messiah.

21 P From then on Jesus began to explain to his disciples that he had to go on to Jerusalem and suffer terrible things at the hands of the elders and chief priests and scribes and be put to death and rise on the third day. **22** Peter took him aside and began to remonstrate with him and said, "God have mercy on you, Lord! This will never happen to you!" **23** But he turned to Peter and said, "Get behind me, Satan! You're an occasion of sin for me—you're not thinking the thoughts of God but of men." **24** Then Jesus said to his disciples,

    "If anyone would come after me,
      let him deny himself,
    And let him take up his cross
      and follow me.

25   For whoever would save his life
      will lose it,
While whoever loses his life for my sake
      will find it.

26   For what good will it do a man if he gains
      the whole world,
      but forfeits his life?

P Mk 8:31 - 9:1; Lk 9:22-27.

16:18   "Peter...rock"; a play on words is involved here. In Greek, "Peter" = *Petros* and "rock" = *petra*. This play on words undoubtedly was derived from the original Aramaic; Peter was known in the early Church as "Kephas," derived from *kepha,* the Aramaic word for "rock." Verse 19 with its symbolism of the keys and reference to binding and loosing makes it clear that Peter will receive both Divine authority and Divine guidance in matters relating to the Kingdom, which the Church has taught as pertaining to faith and morals.

27 For the Son of Man will come in the glory
of his Father
with his angels,
And then he'll pay each
according to his work.

28 Amen, I say to you, some of those standing here will not taste death until they see the Son of Man coming to his Kingdom."

17 **1** ᑫ Six days later Jesus took Peter and James and his brother John along and led them up a high mountain by themselves. **2** And he was transformed in front of them and his face shone like the sun, while his clothing became as white as light. **3** And, behold, Moses appeared to them as well as Elijah, and they were speaking with him. **4** So in response Peter said to Jesus, "Lord, it's good for us to be here; if you wish, I'll put up three dwellings here, one for you, one for Moses, and one for Elijah." **5** While he was still speaking, behold, a bright cloud overshadowed them and, behold, a voice from the cloud said, "This is My Beloved Son, in whom I am well pleased; hear him!" **6** When the disciples heard it they fell on their faces and were overwhelmed with fear, **7** but Jesus came and touched them and said, "Get up; don't be afraid any more!" **8** And when they raised their eyes they saw no one but Jesus alone.

9 As they were descending the mountain Jesus commanded them, "Tell no one the vision until the Son of Man has risen from the dead." **10** And the disciples questioned him and said, "Why, then, do the scribes say that Elijah must come first?" **11** In answer he said, "Elijah *is* coming and he'll restore all things; **12** but I say to you that Elijah has *already* come, yet they didn't acknowledge him; instead, they did to him whatever they wanted. So, too, the Son of Man will suffer at their hands." **13** Then the disciples realized that he was talking to them about John the Baptist.

14 ʳ And as they were coming toward the crowd a man came up to him, knelt before him, **15** and said, "Lord, have mercy on my son.

ᑫ Mk 9:2-13; Lk 9:28-36. ʳ Mk 9:14-29; Lk 9:37-43.

17:4   "Dwellings." This Greek word also means "tents," but was applied to the booths which the Jews constructed during the Feast of Tabernacles; they were meant to recall the way the Israelites lived during the Exodus.

17:15   "Epileptic." Lit., "moonstruck." Epileptics were thought at that time to be influenced by the moon.

He's epileptic and suffers terribly — many times he falls into the fire and many times into the water. **16** I brought him to your disciples, but they couldn't cure him." **17** But in answer Jesus said,

> "O unbelieving and perverse generation!
> How long will I be with you?
> How long will I put up with you?

Bring him here to me!" **18** And Jesus rebuked it and the demon went out of him, and the child was cured from that very hour. **19** Then the disciples came to Jesus privately and said, "Why couldn't *we* drive it out?" **20** But he said to them, "Because of your weak faith, for, amen, I say to you, if you have faith like a grain of mustard seed you'll say to this mountain, 'Move from here to there!' and it *will* move, and nothing will be impossible for you." **[21]**

22 ˢ Now while they were together in Galilee Jesus said to them, "The Son of Man is going to be handed over into the hands of men **23** and they'll put him to death, but on the third day he'll rise." And they were terribly distressed.

24 When they came to Capharnaum those who were collecting the Temple tax came up to Peter and said, "Doesn't your Teacher pay the Temple tax?" **25** "Certainly he does!" he said. And when he came into the house Jesus anticipated him by saying, "What do you think, Simon? The kings of the earth — from whom do they collect tax or toll? From their followers or from others?" **26** And when he said, "From others," Jesus said to him, "So then their followers are exempt! **27** But so we don't offend them, go to the sea, cast a hook in, and take the first fish that comes up, and when you open its mouth you'll find a silver coin, worth twice the Temple tax; take it and give it to them for me and you."

ˢ Mk 9:30-32; Lk 9:43-45.

17:21   The best manuscript tradition omits this verse: "But this type doesn't come out except through prayer and fasting."

17:24   This was the annual temple tax which every Jew was required to pay. The coin used, the *didrachma,* was a Greek one equivalent to two *denarii.* It was collected just before the Passover.

17:25-26 "Followers." Literally, "sons."

17:27   "A silver coin, worth twice the temple tax." Lit., "a *stater.*" A *stater* was worth two *didrachmas,* cf. 17:24 above.

Q. TRUE AUTHORITY AND FORGIVENESS

18 1 [t] At that time the disciples came to Jesus and said, "Who's the greatest in the Kingdom of Heaven?" **2** He called a child forward, stood it before them, **3** and said, "Amen, I say to you,

> Unless you turn about and become like children,
> you won't *enter* the Kingdom of Heaven!
> **4** Therefore, whoever humbles himself like this child,
> he's the greatest in the Kingdom of Heaven.
> **5** And whoever receives one child such as this one
> in my name,
> receives me."

6 [u] "But whoever causes one of these little ones who believe in me to sin, it'd be better for him to have a donkey's millstone hung around his neck and be sunk in the depths of the sea. **7** Woe to the world because of occasions of sin! It's inevitable that occasions of sin will come, yet woe to the man through whom the occasion of sin comes!

> **8** So if your hand or your foot causes you to sin,
> cut it off and throw it away from you!
> It's better for you to enter that life
> crippled or lame,
> than to have two hands or two feet and be thrown
> into eternal fire.
> **9** And if your eye causes you to sin,
> pluck it out and throw it away from you!
> It's better for you to enter that life one-eyed,
> than to have two eyes and be thrown
> into the hell of fire."

10 [v] "See that you don't look down on one of these little ones, for I tell you, their angels in Heaven continually look upon the face of my

---

[t] Mk 9:33-37; Lk 9:46-48. [u] Mk 9:33-37; Lk 9:46-48. [v] Lk 15:3-7.

18:6   For everyday household use in Palestine a stone hand mill or quern was used. The millstone referred to here was a much larger and heavier one, requiring the use of a donkey for its operation.

18:8-9   "That life"; i.e., the life of the Kingdom, as opposed to "the hell of fire." This last expression is a typically Semitic turn of phrase which means "fiery hell."

Father in Heaven. [11] **12** What do you think? If a man has a hundred sheep and one of them strays away, won't he leave the ninety-nine on the mountain and go look for the one that went astray? **13** And if he happens to find it, amen, I say to you, he rejoices more over it than over the ninety-nine that *didn't* go astray. **14** Likewise, it isn't the will of your Father in Heaven to lose one of these little ones."

15 ᵂ "Now if your brother should sin against you, go show him his error between you and him alone. If he listens to you, you've won back your brother; **16** but if he doesn't listen, take one or two more with you, so that **every statement may stand upon the testimony of two or three witnesses. 17** If he refuses to listen to *them,* tell the church, but if he refuses to listen even to the church, let him be like a Gentile or a tax collector to you."

18 "Amen, I say to you,

> Whatever you bind on earth
> > will have been bound in Heaven,
> And whatever you loose on earth
> > will have been loosed in Heaven.

19 Again I say to you, if two of you agree on earth about any matter they ask for, it will come to be for them through my Father in Heaven. **20** For where two or three are gathered in my name, I am there among them."

21 Then Peter came up and said to him, "Lord, how many times can my brother sin against me and I'll have to forgive him? Up to seven times?" **22** Jesus said to him, "I don't say to you up to seven times, but instead up to seventy-seven times. **23** Therefore, the Kingdom of Heaven may be compared to a king who wanted to settle accounts with his servants. **24** Now when he began settling up a debtor was brought to him who owed ten thousand *talents,* **25** and when he was unable to pay it back the lord ordered him to be sold, as well as his wife and children and everything he had, and payment to be made. The servant fell down, therefore, knelt before him, and said, **26** 'Be patient with me and I'll pay you back everything!' **27** So, deeply moved, the lord of that

---

ᵂ Lk 17:3.

18:11   The best manuscript tradition omits this verse: "For the Son of Man came to save the lost."
18:16   Dt 19:15.
18:24   An astronomically large sum, impossible to repay, since each *talent* was worth
         5,000 - 6,000 *denarii.*

servant released him and forgave him the debt. **28** But when that servant went out he found one of his fellow servants who owed him a hundred *denarii*, and he grabbed him and started choking him and said, 'Pay back what you owe!' **29** So the fellow servant fell down and begged him and said, 'Be patient with me and I'll pay you back!' **30** But he wouldn't; instead, he went off and threw him into prison until he could pay back what was owed. **31** Now when his fellow servants saw what had happened they were terribly distressed, and they went and told their lord everything that had happened. **32** Then when his lord had summoned him he said to him, 'You wicked servant! I forgave you all that debt when you begged me; **33** shouldn't you have had mercy on your fellow servant, too, as I had mercy on you?' **34** And in his anger the lord handed him over to the jailors until he could pay back all that was owed. **35** That's what my Heavenly Father will do to you, too, unless each of you forgives your brother from your heart.''

R. DISCIPLESHIP AND AUTHORITY, FAITH AND RENUNCIATION

19 **1** [x] And it happened that when Jesus finished these words he left Galilee and went to the regions of Judea beyond the Jordan. **2** Large crowds followed him and he cured them there.

3 And Pharisees came up to him and tested him by asking, "Is it lawful for a man to put his wife away for any reason?" **4** But in answer he said, "Haven't you read that He Who created them from the beginning **made them male and female? 5** And He said, **For this reason a man shall leave father and mother and be united with his wife, and the two shall become one flesh. 6** So, then, they're no longer two but one flesh. Therefore,

> What God has joined together
> let man not separate.''

---

[x] Mk 10:1-12.

19:4   Gn 1:27.
19:5   Gn 2:24.

7 They said to him, "Then why did Moses command us **to give a notice of divorce and put her away?"** **8** He said to them, "Moses allowed you to put your wives away because of the hardness of your hearts, but it wasn't that way from the beginning. **9** So *I* say to you, whoever puts his wife away — not in [the case of] an unlawful union — and marries another commits adultery." **10** His disciples said to him, "If *that's* the relationship between a man and his wife, it's better not to marry!" **11** But he said to them, "Not everyone can accept this teaching — only those to whom it's been given. **12** For there are some who are eunuchs from their birth, and some who are eunuchs were made eunuchs by men, and some who are eunuchs make themselves eunuchs for the sake of the Kingdom of Heaven. Let whoever can accept this accept it!"

13 [y] Then children were brought to him so he could lay his hands on them and bless them, but the disciples rebuked them. **14** But Jesus said,

> "Let the children be,
> And don't stop them from coming to me,
> For of such as these
> Is the Kingdom of Heaven!"

15 And after laying his hands on them he went away from there.

16 [z] And, behold, a certain man came up to Jesus and said, "Teacher, what good should I do so that I'll have eternal life?" **17** But he said to him, "Why do you ask *me* about what's good? One there is Who is good. If you want to go into life, keep the commandments." **18** He said to him, "Which ones?" So Jesus said, "These — **you shall not murder, you shall not commit adultery, you shall not steal, you shall not bear false witness, 19 honor your father and mother,** and **love your neighbor as yourself."** **20** The young man said to him, "I've obeyed all of these; what else do I need to do?" **21** Jesus said to him, "If you want to be perfect, go sell your possessions and give to the poor and you'll

---

[y] Mk 10:13-16; Lk 18:15-17. [z] Mk 10:17-31; Lk 18:18-30.

19:7   Dt 24:1.

19:9   For a detailed discussion of Jesus' teaching on divorce cf. above at 5:32. Jesus is not stating an exception to the general rule forbidding divorce in valid marriages. Rather, he is distinguishing valid marriages from other relationships which do not constitute true marriages. The general rule regarding marriage naturally does not apply to such illicit or otherwise defective relationships. This has been the consistent teaching of the Church.

19:18-19 Ex 20:12-16.

have treasure in Heaven, and come follow me." **22** Now when the young man heard this he went away sadly, because he had many properties.

23 Then Jesus said to his disciples, "Amen, I say to you, with difficulty will the rich man enter the Kingdom of Heaven! **24** Yet again I say to you, it's easier for a camel to go through a needle's eye than for a rich man to go into the Kingdom of God." **25** Now when the disciples heard this they were very much amazed and said, "Then who can be saved?" **26** But Jesus gazed at them and said,

> "For men this is impossible,
> But for God all things are possible."

27 Then in response Peter said to him, "You see we've left everything and followed you; what will there be for us, then?" **28** And Jesus said to them, "Amen, I say to you, you who have followed me—in the new age, when the Son of Man takes his seat on his throne of glory — you, too, will sit on twelve thrones judging the twelve tribes of Israel. **29** And everyone who has left houses or brothers or sisters or father or mother or children or fields for the sake of my name will receive a hundredfold and will gain eternal life.

> **30** But many who are first will be last,
> and the last, first."

20 **1** "For the Kingdom of Heaven is like a landowner who went out early in the morning to hire workers for his vineyard **2** and, after agreeing with the workers on a *denarius* for the day, he sent them into his vineyard. **3** And when he went out at about the third hour he saw others standing idle in the market place, **4** and he said to those, 'You go into the vineyard, too, and I'll give you whatever's just.' **5** So they went off. When he went out again at about the sixth and ninth hours he did the same. **6** Now at about the eleventh hour when he went out he found others standing there, and he said to them, 'Why have you stood here idle the whole day?' **7** They said to him, 'Because nobody hired us.' He said to them, 'You go into the vineyard, too.' **8** Now when evening came the lord of the vineyard said to his foreman, 'Call the workers and pay them their wages, beginning from the last up to the first.' **9** When those of the eleventh hour came they each got a *denarius*. **10** And when

---

19:28   Dn 7:9, 22.

the first ones came they thought they'd receive more, yet they, too, each received a *denarius*. **11** Now when they received it they began to grumble against the landowner **12** and say, 'These last ones worked one hour, yet you made them equal to us, who endured the whole day and the scorching heat!' **13** But in answer to one of them he said, 'My friend, I do you no injustice; didn't you agree on a *denarius* with me? **14** Take what's yours and go! I wish to give this last one the same as I gave to you. **15** Isn't it lawful for me to do what I want with what's mine? Or are you jealous because I'm good?' **16** Thus,

> The last shall be first,
> and the first, last."

17 ᵃ And as Jesus was going up to Jerusalem he took the Twelve aside privately, and as they walked he said to them, **18** "Behold, we're going up to Jerusalem, and the Son of Man will be handed over to the chief priests and the scribes; they'll condemn him to death **19** and hand him over to the Gentiles to be mocked and scourged and crucified, and on the third day he'll rise."

20 ᵇ Then the mother of the sons of Zebedee came up to him with her sons and knelt down to make a request of him. **21** So he said to her, "What do you want?" She said to him, "Say that these two sons of mine can sit, one at your right hand and one at your left hand, in your Kingdom." **22** But in answer Jesus said, "You don't know what you're asking for! Can you drink the cup *I'm* going to drink?" They said to him, "We can." **23** He said to them, "You will, indeed, drink my cup, but as for sitting at my right hand or left, that isn't mine to give — it's for those for whom it's been prepared by my Father." **24** And when the other ten heard they became indignant at the two brothers. **25** So Jesus called them together and said, "You know that

> The rulers of the Gentiles lord it over them,
> And their leaders exercise authority over them,

26 but it won't be like that among you; instead,

> Whoever would be great among you,
> let him be your servant,

---

a Mk 10:32-34; Lk 18:31-34. b Mk 10:35-45.

20:15 "Are you jealous." Literally, "is your eye evil."

27 And whoever would be first among you,
> let him be your slave;

28 Just as the Son of Man came, not to be served,
>> but to serve,
> and to give his life as a ransom for many."

29 [c] When they left Jericho a large crowd followed him. **30** And, behold, there were two blind men sitting by the road, and when they heard that Jesus was passing by they cried out and said, "Have mercy on us, Son of David!" **31** The crowd ordered them to be quiet, but they cried out all the more, "Lord, have mercy on us, Son of David!" **32** Jesus stopped, called them over, and said, "What do you want me to do for you?" **33** They said to him, "Lord, let our eyes be opened!" **34** So Jesus, deeply moved, touched their eyes, and at once they could see again and they followed him.

S. JESUS' MINISTRY IN JERUSALEM

21 **1** [d] When they drew near to Jerusalem and had come to Bethphage, on the Mount of Olives, Jesus sent two disciples **2** and said to them, "Go into the village opposite you, and at once you'll find a donkey tied up and a colt with it; untie them and lead them to me. **3** And if anyone says anything to you, say, 'The Lord needs them,' and he'll send them at once." **4** Now this took place to fulfill what was said by the prophet when he said,

5 Tell the daughter of Zion,
> 'Behold your king is coming to you,
>> humble, and mounted on a donkey,
> and on a colt, the offspring of an ass.'

---

[c] Mk 10:46-52; Lk 18:35-43. [d] Mk 11:1-11; Lk 19:28-38; Jn 12:12-19.

21:1ff   Beginning with Jesus' entry into Jerusalem the fulfillment of Jesus' mission moves inexorably to its climax. As seen through the eyes of faith, all these events are "in accordance with the scriptures," and the account is punctuated with frequent references to scripture in order to underline this. All Jesus' words and actions are now seen in their full eschatological significance: the Kingdom has come and, following the Lord's atoning death, it will be proclaimed to all nations.

21:5   Is 62:11.

6 When the disciples had gone and done as Jesus had instructed them **7** they led the donkey and the colt to him and put their cloaks on them, and he sat upon them. **8** Most of the crowd spread their cloaks on the road, while others cut branches from the trees and spread them on the road. **9** And the crowds that were going ahead, as well as those following him, kept shouting, saying,

> "**Hosanna** to the Son of David!
> **Blessed is he who comes in the name of the Lord!**
> **Hosanna** in the highest!"

10 When he came into Jerusalem the whole city was caught up in the excitement and asked, "Who is this?" **11** So the crowds said, "This is the prophet Jesus, from Nazareth in Galilee!"

12[e] Then Jesus went into the Temple and drove out all those who were selling and buying in the Temple, and he overturned the tables of the moneychangers and the seats of those who sold the doves, **13** and he said to them, "It is written,

> **My house shall be called a house of prayer,**
> but you're making it **a robbers' den!**"

14 And the blind and lame came up to him in the Temple, and he healed them. **15** Now when the chief priests and scribes saw the wonders he was performing and the children who were shouting in the Temple and saying, "Hosanna to the Son of David!" they were indignant **16** and said to him, "Do you hear what they're saying?" But Jesus replied, "Certainly. Haven't you ever read that

> **Out of the mouths of babes and sucklings**
> **You have brought perfect praise?**"

17 Then he left them and went out of the city to Bethany and spent the night there.

18[f] Now early in the morning, as he was returning to the city, he was hungry. **19** He noticed a fig tree by the road and so he went over to it, but he found nothing on it but leaves, and he said to it, "May no fruit

---

[e] Mk 11:15-19. [f] Mk 11:12-14, 20-24.

21:9   Ps 118:26. *Hosanna* probably signified "royal power."
21:13   Is 56:7
21:16   Ps 8:2 (Ps. 8:3 in the Septuagint).

ever come from you again, forever!" And the fig tree shrivelled up immediately. **20** When the disciples saw it they were amazed and said, "How did the fig tree shrivel up immediately?" **21** In answer Jesus said to them, "Amen, I say to you, if you have faith and never doubt, you'll not only do what was done to the fig tree but also, if you say to this mountain, 'Be taken away and thrown into the sea,' it will happen. **22** Whatever you ask for in prayer and believe in, you'll receive."

23 [g] And when he went into the Temple the chief priests and elders of the people came up to him as he was preaching and said, "By what authority do you do these things? Who gave you this authority?" **24** But in answer Jesus said to them, "I'll ask you one question, too; if you answer it for me I'll tell you by what authority I do these things. **25** Where was John's baptism from? From Heaven or from men?" They began to argue among themselves, saying, "If we say, 'From Heaven,' he'll say, 'Then why didn't you believe him?' **26** But if we say, 'From men,' we're afraid of the people — they all consider John a prophet." **27** So in answer to Jesus they said, "We don't know." And Jesus said to them, "Nor will I tell you by what authority I do these things."

28 "What do you think, now? A man had two sons. He came up to the first one and said, 'Son, go work in the vineyard today.' **29** And in answer he said, 'I don't want to!' but later he changed his mind and went. **30** So he went up to the other one and said the same thing, and the second son answered, 'I'm going, lord!' but he didn't go. **31** Which of the two did the will of the father?" They said, "The first." Jesus said to them, "Amen, I say to you, tax collectors and prostitutes are entering the Kingdom of God ahead of you. **32** For John came to you preaching the way of repentance and fulfillment of God's will and you didn't believe him, whereas the tax collectors and prostitutes *did* believe him, but though you saw it you didn't change your minds and believe him."

33 [h] "Listen to another parable! There was a man, a landowner, who **planted a vineyard and put a hedge around it and dug a winepress in it and built a tower** and let it out to vinedressers and left on a journey. **34** Now when harvest time drew near he sent his servants to the vinedressers to get his fruits. **35** And the vinedressers took hold

---

[g] Mk 11:27-33; Lk 20:1-8. [h] Mk 12:1-12; Lk 20:9-19.

21:32 Literally, "in the way of righteousness."
21:33 Is 5:1-2.

of his servants and beat one, killed another, and stoned yet another. **36** Once more he sent other servants, more than the first group, and they did the same to them. **37** So, finally, he sent his son to them, saying, 'They'll feel shame before my son.' **38** But when the vinedressers saw the son they said to themselves, 'This is the heir; come on, let's kill him and have his inheritance!' **39** And they took hold of him, threw him out of the vineyard, and killed him. **40** So, then, when the lord of the vineyard comes, what will he do to those vinedressers?" **41** They said to him, "He'll put those evil men to a miserable death and let out the vineyard to other vinedressers who'll give him the fruits in their seasons." **42** Jesus said to them, "Haven't you ever read in the scriptures,

> **The stone rejected by the builders**
> **has become the cornerstone;**
> **By the Lord has this been done,**
> **and it is wonderful in our eyes.**

43 Therefore, I say to you, the Kingdom of God will be taken from you and given to a people who produce its fruits." **[44]**

45 When the chief priests and Pharisees heard his parables they knew that he was speaking about them, **46** and while they considered seizing him they feared the crowds, for they regarded him as a prophet.

22 **1**[i] And in response Jesus spoke to them again in parables and said, **2** "The Kingdom of Heaven may be compared to a king who held a wedding feast for his son. **3** And he sent his servants to call those invited to the feast, but they didn't want to come. **4** Once more he sent other servants and said, 'Tell those who were invited, "Behold, I've prepared my dinner; my oxen and fatted calves have been killed and everything's ready; come to the feast!"' **5** But they ignored the invitation and went off, one to his farm and another to his business, **6** and the rest seized his servants, treated them shamefully, and killed them. **7** The king became furious, then, and he sent his soldiers and killed those murderers and burnt their city down. **8** Then he said to his servants, 'The wedding feast is ready, but those invited weren't worthy. **9** So go

---

[i] Lk 14:15-24.

21:42 Ps 118:22-23.

21:44 The best manuscript tradition omits this verse: "And whoever falls on this stone will be broken to pieces, while it will crush whoever it falls upon."

to the highways and invite whoever you find to the wedding feast.' **10** The servants went out on the roads and gathered everyone they found, evil as well as good, and the feast was full of guests. **11** But when the king went in to see the guests he saw there a man who wasn't dressed in a wedding garment, **12** and he asked him, 'My friend, how did you come in here without a wedding garment?' But he remained silent. **13** Then the king said to his servants, 'Tie his hands and feet and throw him out into the outer darkness;

> There there will be wailing
>> and gnashing of teeth,'
> **14** For many are called,
>> but few are chosen."

15 [j] Then the Pharisees went and planned how they could entrap him in his speech. **16** And they sent their disciples to him with the Herodians who said, "Teacher, we know you're truthful and truly teach the way of God and are influenced by no one, for you don't consider the person. **17** So tell us what you think; is it lawful to pay the tax to Caesar or not?" **18** But Jesus, aware of their evil intent, said, "You hypocrites! Why are you testing me? **19** Show me the coin for the tax!" So they brought him a *denarius*. **20** And he said to them, "Whose image is this, and whose inscription?" **21** They said to him, "Caesar's." Then he said to them,

> "Render, therefore, to Caesar
>> the things that are Caesar's,
> And to God
>> the things that are God's."

22 When they heard this they were amazed, and they left him and went away.

23 [k] That same day the Sadducees came to him claiming that there's no resurrection, and they put this question to him: **24** "Teacher, Moses said, **If anyone should die without children, his brother shall marry his wife and raise up offspring for his brother.** **25** Now there used to be seven brothers among us, and the first married and died, and

---

[j] Mk 12:13-17; Lk 20:20-26. [k] Mk 12:18-27; Lk 20:27-40.

22:24 Dt 25:5; Gn 38:8.

since he had no offspring he left his wife to his brother. **26** Likewise also the second and the third, up to the seventh. **27** And last of all the woman died. **28** At the resurrection, then, whose wife will she be of the seven, since they all had her?" **29** But in answer Jesus said to them, "You go astray because you neither understand scripture nor realize the power of God — **30** at the resurrection they'll neither marry nor be given in marriage but will be like angels in Heaven. **31** But as for the resurrection of the dead, haven't you read what was said to you by God when He declared, **32 I am the God of Abraham and the God of Isaac and the God of Jacob.** He's not God of the dead but of the living." **33** And when the crowds heard this they were astounded at his teaching.

34 ¹ Now when the Pharisees heard that he'd silenced the Sadducees they came in a group, **35** and one of them, a lawyer, asked him as a test, **36** "Teacher, which is the greatest commandment in the Torah?" **37** So he said to him, **"You shall love the Lord with all your heart and with all your soul and with all your understanding; 38** this is the first and greatest commandment. **39** And the second is like it, **You shall love your neighbor as yourself.** 40** All the Torah and the Prophets rests on these two commandments."

41 ᵐ Now while the Pharisees were gathered there Jesus began to question them, **42** "What do you think about the Messiah? Whose son is he?" "David's," they replied. **43** "Then how," he asked, "can David, in the Spirit, call him 'Lord' when he says,

44   **The Lord said to my Lord,**
          'Sit at My right hand
                till I put your enemies under your feet.'

45 If David calls him 'Lord,' how can he be his son?" **46** And no one could answer him a word, nor from that time on did anyone dare question him further.

ˡ Mk 12:28-34; Lk 10:25-28. ᵐ Mk 12:35-37; Lk 20:41-44.

22:32 Ex 3:6.
22:37 Dt 6:5.
22:39 Lv 19:18.
22:44 Ps 110:1.

T. DENUNCIATION OF THE PHARISEES

23 1 [n] Then Jesus spoke to the crowds and to his disciples **2** and said,

"The scribes and the Pharisees sit
on the chair of Moses.

3 So do and observe whatever they tell you,
But don't do their works,
because they talk but don't act.

4 Instead, they tie up heavy burdens and put them
on men's shoulders,
but they won't lift a finger to move them.

5 They do all their works
in order to be seen by others,
They broaden their phylacteries
and enlarge their tassels,

6 They love the first place at banquets
and the first seats in the synagogues,

7 And greetings in the markets
and being called 'Rabbi,'

8 But don't *you* be called 'Rabbi,'
for One is your teacher, and all of you
are brothers.

9 And call no one on earth your father,
for One is your Father — in Heaven.

10 Nor shall you be called teachers,
for one is your teacher, the Messiah.

11 Instead, the greatest among you
shall be your servant.

---

[n] Mk 12:38-40; Lk 11:37-52, 20:45-57.

23:1 ff.   Cf. the note on 3:7-12. At the time of Jesus the rabbis were adopting ever more restrictive and burdensome interpretations of the Torah. A primary purpose for this was to maintain the separateness of Israel from the Gentiles. However, as Bonsirven notes, the tendency to put ritual obligations on the same level as moral obligations was recognized to be a danger in rigoristic interpretations of the Torah — hypocrisy and formalism were known even then as "the plague of the Pharisees."

23:8-10   Jesus here warns against excessive respect for merely human authority, using the hyperbolic style favored in these types of orations.

12 For whoever exalts himself shall be humbled,
And whoever humbles himself shall be exalted."

13 "But woe to you, scribes and Pharisees,
you hypocrites!
You shut the Kingdom of Heaven
in men's faces —
you aren't going in, nor will you allow
those who *are* to go in."**[14]**

15 "Woe to you, scribes and Pharisees,
you hypocrites!
You travel over land and sea to win
one proselyte,
and when he becomes one you make him twice
the son of Gehenna that *you* are."

16 "Woe to you,
blind guides! who say,
'Whoever swears by the sanctuary,
that's nothing,
but whoever swears by the gold
of the sanctuary is bound.'

17 You're foolish and blind!
For what's greater, the gold
or the sanctuary that sanctifies
the gold?

18 And, 'Whoever swears by the altar,
that's nothing,
but whoever swears by the offering
upon it is bound.'

19 You're blind! For what's greater, the offering
or the altar that sanctifies the offering?

23:13   In the "seven woes" Jesus condemns, not outward expressions of piety *per se*, but their self-serving use to enhance personal prestige.

23:14   The best manuscript tradition omits this verse: "Woe to you, scribes and Pharisees, you hypocrites! because you eat up widows' homes and as a pretense say long prayers; therefore, you will receive the greater condemnation."

23:15   This verse reflects the extensive missionary efforts of the Pharisees prior to the destruction of the Temple. A proselyte was a Gentile who accepted all the requirements of the Torah, including circumcision. For obvious reasons, Gentile sympathizers were more numerous than actual proselytes.

20   Therefore, whoever swears by the altar
              swears by it
              and also by everything on it,
21   And whoever swears by the sanctuary
              swears by it
              and also by what's housed within it,
22   And whoever swears by Heaven swears
              by the throne of God
              and also by the One seated upon it."

23   "Woe to you, scribes and Pharisees,
              you hypocrites!
    You tithe mint and dill and cumin,
              yet you've neglected the weightier things
                      of the Torah, justice and mercy
                      and faith.
    You should have acted upon these things
              and neglected the others!
24   Blind guides!
    You strain out the gnat
              and swallow the camel."

25   "Woe to you, scribes and Pharisees,
              you hypocrites!
    You purify the outside of the cup
              and the plate,
              but inside they're full of greed
              and self indulgence.
26   Blind Pharisees!
    First purify the inside of the cup
              so that the outside will also be pure."

27   "Woe to you, scribes and Pharisees,
              you hypocrites!
    You're like whitewashed tombs, which outside
              appear beautiful,
              but inside are full of dead men's bones
              and all kinds of impurity.

28   You too appear to be righteous on the outside,
                 but inside you're filled with hypocrisy and
                 lawlessness."

29   "Woe to you, scribes and Pharisees,
                 you hypocrites!
           You restore the tombs of the prophets
                 and adorn the monuments of the righteous,

30 and you say, 'If *we* had been there in the days of our fathers, *we* wouldn't have taken part in shedding the blood of the prophets!' **31** And thus you bear witness against yourselves, because you're the sons of the prophets' murderers. **32** Go ahead, then; complete the work of your fathers! **33** You snakes! You brood of vipers! How will you escape being condemned to Gehenna? **34** Therefore, behold, I'm sending you prophets and wise men and scribes, some of whom you'll kill and crucify, and some of whom you'll scourge in your synagogues and pursue from city to city, **35** so that all the guilt will come upon you for every righteous man who died on earth, from Abel the Righteous to Zechariah the Righteous, son of Barachiah, whom you murdered between the sanctuary and the altar. **36** Amen, I say to you, all these things will befall this generation!"

37 ° "Jerusalem, Jerusalem!
           Who killed the prophets
                 and stoned those sent to her!
           How often I wished
                 ＼ to gather your children,
           Like a hen gathers her brood
                 under her wings,
           But you would not!
38   Behold, **there remains to you
                 your desolate house.**
39   For I say to you, you shall not see me
                 until you say,
                 **Blessed is he who comes in the name
                 of the Lord!"**

° Lk 13:34-35.

23:38   Jr 22:5.
23:39   Ps 118:26.

U. PROPHECIES AND PARABLES OF THE END TIME

24 1 P When Jesus came out of the Temple he left, and his disciples came up to him to show him the Temple buildings, **2** but in answer he said to them, "Do you see all these things? Amen, I say to you, not a stone here will be left upon a stone which will not be torn down."

3 q Now while he was sitting on the Mount of Olives his disciples came up to him privately and said, "Tell us when these things will happen, and what will be the sign of your coming and of the end of the age." **4** In answer Jesus said to them, "See that no one leads you astray, **5** for many will come in my name, saying, 'I'm the Messiah,' and they'll lead many astray. **6** You're going to hear of wars and rumors of wars; take care not to be alarmed, for all this must happen, but it will not yet be the end.

7　　For nation shall rise against nation,
　　　　　and Kingdom against Kingdom,

and there will be famines and earthquakes in various places; **8** but all this is the beginning of the birth pains. **9** Then they'll hand you over to suffering and kill you, and you'll be hated by all nations because of my name. **10** And then many will lose faith and they'll hand each other over and hate each other, **11** and many false prophets will rise up and they'll lead many astray, **12** and because of the spread of lawlessness the love of many will grow cold. **13** But whoever holds out till the end, they will be saved. **14** And this good news of the Kingdom will be proclaimed in all the inhabited world as a witness to all the nations, and then the end will come."

15 r "So when you see **the Abomination of Desolation** spoken of by Daniel the prophet set **in the holy place** — let the reader understand — **16** then let those in Judea flee to the mountains, **17** let the man on his housetop not descend to take things from his house, **18** and let the man in his field not turn back to get his cloak. **19** But woe to women who are with child and to those who are nursing in those days! **20** Pray that your flight will not take place in winter or on the Sabbath, **21** for then

---

P Mk 13:1-2; Lk 21:5-6. q Mk 13:3-13; Lk 21:7-19. r Mk 13:14-23; Lk 21:7-19.

24:7-31　　This passage retains signs of parallelism and poetic structure which, however, are more clearly preserved in Mark and, especially, in Luke.

there will be great **suffering such as has not been from the beginning of the world until now**, nor will be. **22** And if those days weren't shortened no fleshly creature would be saved, but for the sake of those who were chosen those days will be shortened. **23** Then, if anyone says to you, 'Look, here's the Messiah!' or, 'Over here!' don't believe it, **24** for false Messiahs and false prophets will rise up and they'll produce great signs and wonders so as to lead astray, if possible, even those who were chosen; **25** behold, I've told you ahead of time! **26** Therefore, if they say to you, 'There, he's in the desert!' don't go out; 'Here, in the inner room!' don't believe it. **27** For as lightning comes from the east and can be seen clear to the west, so it will be with the coming of the Son of Man. **28** Where the corpse is, there will the vultures gather!"

29 [s] "But immediately after the suffering of those days,

> **The sun will be darkened,**
> > **and the moon will not give its light,**
> **And the stars will fall** from the heavens,
> > **and the powers of the heavens** will be shaken.

30 And then the sign of the Son of Man will appear in the heavens, and then **all the tribes of the earth will mourn** and they'll see **the Son of Man coming on the clouds of Heaven** with power and great glory. **31** And he'll send his angels forth with a great trumpet blast, and they'll gather his chosen ones together from the four winds, from one end of the heavens to their other end."

32 [t] "So learn the parable from the fig tree. As soon as its branch becomes tender and is putting out leaves, you know that summer is near. **33** So also you, when you see all these things, you'll know that he's near, at the very gates. **34** Amen, I say to you, this generation will not pass away until all these things come to pass.

---

[s] Mk 13:24-27; Lk 21:25-28. [t] Mk 13:28-31; Lk 21:29-33.

24:15   Dn 9:27, 11:31, 12:11. "The Abomination of Desolation" refers to the desecration of the Temple by the Seleucids in 167 B.C. The Feast of Hanukkah celebrates the rededication of the Temple in 164 B.C.

24:21   Dn 12:1; Jl 2:2.

24:26   This may refer to the Essene belief that in the last days the faithful would withdraw to the desert.

24:29   Is 13:10.

24:30   Dn 7:13-14.

35   The heavens and the earth will pass away,
        But my words will not pass away."

36 ^u   "But as for that day and hour,
        no one knows —
    not the angels in Heaven, nor the Son,
        but only the Father.

37   But just as the days of Noah were,
        so will the coming of the Son of Man be.

38   For just as they kept on eating and drinking,

marrying and giving in marriage in the days before the flood right up to the day Noah went into the ark, **39** and didn't find out until the flood came and swept them all away,

        that's how the coming of the Son of Man will be.

40   Then if two men are in the field —
        one will be taken and one will be left;

41   If two women are grinding at the mill —
        one will be taken and one will be left.

42 So stay awake! because you don't know what day your Lord is coming. **43** But know this, that if the householder had known at what watch the thief was coming he would have stayed awake and wouldn't have let his house be broken into. **44** Therefore, you be ready too! because the Son of Man is coming at an hour you don't expect."

45 ^v   "Who, then, is the wise and faithful servant
        whom the Lord set over his household servants
    To give them their share of food
        at the proper time?

46   Blessed that servant who, when he comes,
        his lord finds doing so!

47   Amen, I say to you,
        he'll set him over all his possessions.

48   But if that wicked servant says in his heart,
        'My master is delayed,'

49   And begins to beat his fellow servants
        and to eat and drink with drunkards,

---

^u Mk 13:32-37; Lk 17:26-30, 34-36.   ^v Lk 12:41-48.

50 The master of that servant will come on a day
      he doesn't expect,
      and at an hour he doesn't know.
51 He'll cut him in pieces
      and assign him the lot of the hypocrites.
    There there will be wailing
      and gnashing of teeth.'"

25

1 "At that time the Kingdom of Heaven will be compared to ten virgins who took their lamps and went out to meet the bridegroom. 2 Now five of them were foolish and the other five were wise, 3 for when the foolish ones took their lamps they didn't take oil with them, 4 while the wise ones *did* take oil in vessels along with their lamps. 5 Now when the bridegroom was delayed they all grew drowsy and fell asleep. 6 At midnight the cry arose, 'Here he is, the bridegroom! Come out to meet him!' 7 Then all those virgins got up and trimmed their lamps. 8 But the foolish ones said to the wise ones, 'Give us some of your oil — our lamps are going out!' 9 The wise ones answered by saying, 'But then there might not be enough for us as well as for you! Go instead to the dealers and buy some for yourselves.' 10 But when they went off to buy some the bridegroom came, and the ones who were ready went in with him to the wedding feast and the door was shut. 11 Then, finally, the other virgins came, too, and said, 'Lord, lord, open up for us!' 12 But in answer he said, 'Amen, I say to you, I don't know you!' 13 Stay awake, therefore, because you don't know the day or the hour."

14 [w] "For it's like a man who was leaving on a journey who called his servants and turned over his possessions to them, 15 and to one he gave five *talents,* and to one, two, and to one, one; to each according to his ability. Then he left on a journey. At once 16 the one who got the five *talents* went and invested them and earned another five. 17 Likewise, the one with the two earned another two. 18 But the one who got the one went off and dug a hole in the ground and hid his lord's silver. 19 Now after a long time the lord of those servants came and settled accounts with them. 20 And when the one who got the five *talents* came forward he brought the other five *talents* and said, 'Lord, you turned five *talents* over to me; look! I've earned another five *talents.*' 21 His lord said to him,

[w] Lk 19:11-27.

'Well done, good and faithful servant!
You were faithful over a few things,
So now I'll set you over many.
Come into your lord's joy!'

22 Now when the one who got the two *talents* came forward he said, 'Lord, you turned two *talents* over to me; look! I've earned another two *talents.*' **23** His master said to him,

'Well done, good and faithful servant!
You were faithful over a few things,
So now I'll set you over many.
Come into your lord's joy!

24 But when the one who got the one *talent* came forward he said, 'Lord, I knew you were a hard man, reaping where you didn't sow and gathering where you didn't scatter, **25** and since I was afraid I went off and hid your *talent* in the ground; look! you have what's yours.' **26** In answer his lord said to him, 'You evil and lazy servant! You knew that I reap where I didn't sow and gather where I didn't scatter? **27** You would have done better to give my silver to the bankers, and when I came I would have received what was mine with interest. **28** Therefore, take the *talent* from him and give it to the one with ten *talents*,

29 For to all who have it will be given,
   and it will be more than enough,
 But from the one who doesn't have,
   even what he has will be taken from him.

30 And throw the worthless servant out into the outer darkness;

 There there will be weeping
   and gnashing of teeth.'"

31 "But when the Son of Man comes in his glory,
   and all his angels with him,
 He'll sit on the throne of his glory,
32   and all the nations will be gathered
    together before him,
 And he'll separate them from each other,

25:32 Jl 4:2.

74

like a shepherd separates the sheep
    from the goats,

33 And he'll set the sheep at his right hand
    and the goats at his left hand.

34 "Then the King will say to those
        at his right hand,
    'Come, you blessed of my Father,
    Receive the Kingdom prepared for you
        from the foundation of the world,

35 For I was hungry and you gave me to eat,
        I was thirsty and you gave me to drink,
    I was a stranger and you took me in,

36   naked and you clothed me,
    I was sick and you cared for me,
        I was in prison and you came to me.'

37 "Then the righteous will answer him by saying,
    'Lord, when did we see you hungry and feed you,
        or thirsty and give you to drink?

38 And when did we see you a stranger
        and take you in,
    or naked and clothe you?

39 And when did we see you sick,
    or in prison and come to you?'

40 "And in answer the King will say to them,
        'Amen, I say to you,
    Insofar as you did it for one of these least
        of my brothers,
        you did it for me.'"

41 "Then he'll say to those at his left hand,
    'Get away from me, you cursed,
        into the eternal fire prepared for the Devil
            and his angels,

42 For I was hungry and you *didn't* give me to eat,
        I was thirsty and you *didn't* give me to drink,

25:35-36 Is 58:7.
25:46   Dn 12:2.

43   I was a stranger and you *didn't* take me in,
          naked and you *didn't* clothe me,
    Sick,
          and in prison and you *didn't* care for me.'

44 Then they'll answer by saying, 'Lord, when did we see you hungry or thirsty or a stranger or naked or sick or in prison and not care for you?'

45   Then he'll answer them by saying,
          'Amen, I say to you,
    Insofar as you did not do it for one
              of the least of these,
          you didn't do it for me, either.'
46   And these will go off to eternal punishment,
          but the righteous to eternal life."

V. LAST SUPPER AND PASSION OF JESUS

26 **1** ˣ And it happened that when Jesus had finished all these words he said to his disciples, **2** "You know that the Passover will be in two days, and the Son of Man will be handed over to be crucified." **3** Then the chief priests and elders of the people gathered in the palace of the high priest, who was named Caiaphas, **4** and they plotted to seize Jesus on a pretext and kill him, **5** but they said, "Not at the festival, or there might be an outcry among the people."

6 ʸ Now while Jesus was at Bethany in Simon the leper's house **7** a woman came up to him with an alabaster jar of a precious oil and poured it over his head as he reclined at table. **8** When the disciples saw this they were indignant and said, "To what purpose was this waste? **9** It could have been sold for a great deal and given to the poor!" **10** Now Jesus knew this and said to them, "Why are you bothering the woman? She's done a beautiful thing for me.

11   For the poor you always have with you,
          But me you will not always have.

ˣ Mk 14:1-2; Lk 22:1-2; Jn 11:45-53. ʸ Mk 14:3-9; Jn 12:1-8.

---

12 When she put this oil on my body she did it to prepare me for burial. **13** Amen, I say to you, wherever this good news is proclaimed in the whole world, what she did will also be told in memory of her."

14 ᶻ Then one of the Twelve, the one called Judas Iscariot, went to the chief priests **15** and said, "What are you willing to give me if I hand him over to you?" **So they paid** him **thirty pieces of silver 16** and from then on he sought the right time to hand him over.

17 ᵃ Now on the first day of the Unleavened Bread the disciples came to Jesus and asked, "Where do you want us to prepare for you to eat the Passover?" **18** So he said, "Go into the city to a certain man and say to him, 'The Teacher says, "My time is at hand; I'll celebrate the Passover at your house with my disciples." ' " **19** The disciples did as Jesus had instructed them, and they prepared the Passover.

20 Now when evening had come he reclined at table with the Twelve, **21** and while they were eating he said, "Amen, I say to you, one of you will hand me over." **22** They were greatly distressed and one after the other they said to him, "Surely not me, Lord?" **23** But in answer he said, "One who dipped his hand into the bowl with me, he'll hand me over. **24** The Son of Man is going as it's written about him, but woe to that man by whom the Son of Man is handed over; it would have been better for him if that man had not been born!" **25** In response Judas, the one who handed him over, said, "Surely it isn't me, Rabbi?" And Jesus said to him, *"You* said it."

26 ᵇ Now while they were eating Jesus took bread, blessed it, broke it, gave it to his disciples and said, "Take and eat it; this is my body." **27** Then he took the cup and blessed it, gave it to them and said, "Drink from it, all of you, **28** for this is my blood of the covenant which will be poured out for many for the forgiveness of sins. **29** I say to you, I will not drink again of the fruit of the vine until that day when I drink it new with you in my Father's Kingdom." **30** And after singing a hymn they went out to the Mount of Olives.

ᶻ Mk 14:10-11; Lk 22:3-6. ᵃ Mk 14:12-21; Lk 22:7-14, 21-23; Jn 13:21-30. ᵇ Mk 14:22-26; Lk 22:15-20.

26:15   Zc 11:12.

26:17   The eight day period during which unleavened bread was eaten was closely linked to the Passover, but had its origins in a festival marking the beginning of the barley harvest.

26:28   Is 53:12.

31 [c] Then Jesus said to them, "This night you'll all lose your faith in me, for it is written,

> **I will strike the shepherd,**
> **and the sheep of the flock will be scattered,**

32 but after I rise I'll go ahead of you into Galilee." **33** In response Peter said to him, "Even if all the others lose faith in you, I will never lose faith!" **34** Jesus said to him, "Amen, I say to you, this night, before the cock crows, you'll deny me three times." **35** Peter said to him, "Even if it comes to dying with you, I won't deny you!" And all the other disciples said so, too.

36 [d] Then Jesus came with them to a place called Gethsemane, and he said to the disciples, "Sit here while I go over there and pray." **37** He took Peter and the two sons of Zebedee along and he began to be upset and troubled. **38** Then he said to them, "My soul is greatly distressed, to the point of death; stay here and stay awake with me." **39** And he went ahead a little and fell face down in prayer, and he said, "My Father, if it's possible, let this cup pass away from me, yet not as I wish but as you do." **40** When he came to the disciples he found them sleeping, and he said to Peter, "So, you couldn't stay awake with me for one hour? **41** Stay awake and pray that you won't come to the test,

> For the spirit is willing,
> But the flesh is weak."

42 He went off a second time and prayed again, saying, "My Father, if it isn't possible for this cup to pass by without me drinking it, let your will be done." **43** And when he came he again found them sleeping, for their eyes were heavy. **44** And he left them and went off again and prayed for the third time, saying the same thing once more. **45** Then he came to the disciples and said to them, "Are you still sleeping and resting? Behold, the hour has arrived and the Son of Man will be handed over into the hands of sinners. **46** Get up! Let's be going! Behold, the one who will hand me over has arrived!"

47 [e] While he was still speaking, behold, Judas, one of the Twelve, came, and with him a large crowd with swords and clubs from the chief priests and elders of the people. **48** Now the one handing him over had

---

[c] Mk 14:27-31; Lk 22:31-34; Jn 13:36-38. [d] Mk 14:32-42; Lk 22:39-46.

26:31 Zc 13:7.

given them a sign and said, "Whoever I kiss is him; seize him!" **49** And he came up to Jesus at once and said, "Hail, Rabbi!" and kissed him. **50** But Jesus said to him, "What are you here for, my friend?" Then they came forward and laid hands on Jesus and seized him. **51** And, behold, one of those with Jesus reached out his hand, drew his sword, and struck the high priest's slave and cut off his ear. **52** But Jesus said to him, "Put your sword back in its place — all those who take up the sword will die by the sword! **53** Or do you think that I couldn't call on my Father and have him at once send me more than twelve legions of angels? **54** But then how could the scriptures be fulfilled, that this is the way it must be?" **55** Then Jesus said to the crowds, "You came out with swords and clubs to seize me, as if you were after a robber? Every day I sat in the Temple teaching, yet you didn't seize me! **56** But all this has happened so that the writings of the prophets would be fulfilled." Then all the disciples forsook him and fled.

57 [f] Now after seizing Jesus they led him off to Caiaphas, the high priest, where the scribes and elders had gathered. **58** But Peter followed him at a distance up to the courtyard of the high priest, and he went inside and sat down with the Temple attendants to see the outcome. **59** Now the chief priests and the whole Sanhedrin were seeking false testimony against Jesus so they could put him to death, **60** but they found none, although many false witnesses came forward. But finally two men came forward **61** and said, "This fellow said, 'I can tear down the sanctuary of God and in three days build it up.'" **62** The high priest stood up and said to him, "Do you make no answer? Why are these men testifying against you?" **63** But Jesus remained silent. Then the high priest said to him, "I put you under oath by the Living God to tell us if you're the Messiah, the Son of God." **64** Jesus said to him, *"You* said it. Moreover, I say to you, from now on you will see

> **the Son of Man, seated at the right hand of**
> **Power, and coming on the clouds of Heaven!"**

---

[e] Mk 14:43-50; Lk 22:47-53; Jn 18:3-12. [f] Mk 14:53-65; Lk 22:54-55, 63-71; Jn 18:13-14, 19-24.

26:50 This is a short, rather cryptic, verse: literally, "My friend, concerning that which you are here?" Some would translate it as an imperative: "[Do that] concerning which you are here."
26:64 Ps 110:1; Dn 7:13.

65 Then the high priest tore his robes and said, "He has blasphemed! What further need do we have for witnesses? Look! Now *you* heard him blaspheme! 66 What's your opinion?" So in answer they said, "He deserves to die!" 67 Then they spit in his face and struck him, and while they were hitting him 68 they said, "Prophesy to us, O Messiah! Who was it that struck you?"

69 ᵍ Now as Peter was sitting outside in the courtyard a certain maidservant came up to him and said, "You were with Jesus of Galilee, too!" 70 But he denied it in front of everyone and said, "I don't know what you're saying." 71 And as he was going out to the gate another maidservant saw him and said to those who were there, "This fellow was with Jesus of Nazareth!" 72 And he denied it again with an oath: "I don't know the man!" 73 But a little later those standing there came up to Peter and said, "Surely *you* were one of them, too — even your speech gives you away!" 74 Then he put himself under a curse and swore, "I don't know the man!" At once a cock crowed, 75 and Peter remembered what Jesus told him when he said, "Before the cock crows you'll deny me three times," and he went outside and wept bitterly.

27 1 ʰ When morning had come all the chief priests and elders of the people came up with a plan against Jesus in order to put him to death, 2 and they bound him and led him off and handed him over to Pilate, the governor.

3 Then when Judas, the one who handed him over, saw that he'd been condemned, out of remorse he returned the thirty pieces of silver to the chief priests and elders 4 and said, "I sinned when I handed over innocent blood." But they said, "What's that to us? *You* take care of it!" 5 And after flinging the silver pieces into the sanctuary he left, and he went off and hung himself. 6 Now when the chief priests had picked up the silver pieces they said, "It isn't lawful to put these into the Temple treasury, since it was the price of blood." 7 So after conferring they bought the Potter's Field with them for the burial of strangers. 8 Therefore, to this day that field has been called the Field of Blood. 9 Then what was said by Jeremiah the prophet was fulfilled, when he stated, **and they took the thirty pieces of silver, the price of a man with a price**

g Mk 14:66-72; Lk 22:56-62; Jn 18:15-18, 25-27. h Mk 15:1; Lk 23:1-2; Jn 18:28-32.

26:67 Is 50:6.
27:9 Zc 11:12-13; Jr 32:6-9.

set on him, the price set on him by some of the Sons of Israel, **10** and they gave them for the potter's field, as the Lord instructed me.

11 [i] Now Jesus stood before the governor, and the governor questioned him and said, "Are *you* the King of the Jews?" But Jesus said, *"You* say so." **12** And he made no answer while the chief priests and elders were making accusations against him. **13** Then Pilate asked him, "Don't you hear how many things they're alleging against you?" **14** And not one word did he answer him to anything, to the great amazement of the governor.

15 [j] Now at the festival it was the governor's custom to release to the crowd any one prisoner they wanted. **16** At that time they had a notorious prisoner named Barabbas, **17** so when they had gathered, Pilate said to them, "Who do you want me to release to you, Barabbas or Jesus, who's called the Messiah?" — **18** he knew they'd handed him over out of envy. **19** And while he was sitting on the judgment seat his wife sent to him and said, "Have nothing to do with that innocent man — I suffered greatly in a dream today because of him!" **20** Now the chief priests and elders persuaded the crowds to ask for Barabbas but to have Jesus killed. **21** So in response the governor said to them, "Which of the two do you want me to release to you?" But they said, "Barabbas!" **22** Pilate said to them, "Then what should I do with Jesus, who's called the Messiah?" They all said, "Let him be crucified!" **23** "But what wrong has he done?" he asked. But they shouted all the more and said, "Let him be crucified!" **24** Now when Pilate saw that he was doing no good, but instead a riot was beginning, he took water and washed his hands in full view of the crowd and said, "I'm innocent of this man's blood! See to it yourselves!" **25** And in answer the whole people said, "His blood be upon us, and upon our children!" **26** Then he released Barabbas to them, but he had Jesus scourged and handed him over to be crucified.

27 [k] Then the governor's soldiers took Jesus along to the praetorium and gathered the whole cohort around him. **28** They stripped him and put a scarlet robe on him, **29** and after weaving a crown of thorns they put it on his head and a reed in his right hand, and they knelt before him and mocked him, saying, "Hail, King of the Jews!" **30** and after spitting

---

[i] Mk 15:2-5; Lk 23:3-5; Jn 18:33-38. [j] Mk 15:6-15; Lk 23:13-25; Jn 18:39 - 19:16. [k] Mk 15:16-20; Jn 19:2-3.

on him they'd take the reed and beat him over the head. **31** And when they had mocked him they stripped the robe off him and dressed him in his own clothes and led him off to be crucified.

32 [1] Now as they were going out they found a man named Simon of Cyrene; they forced this man to carry his cross. **33** And when they came to the place called *Golgotha*, which is to say "the Place of the Skull," **34** they gave him wine mixed with gall to drink, but when he tasted it he didn't want to drink it. **35** Now after crucifying him "they divided his clothes among them by casting lots," **36** and they sat down and kept watch over him there. **37** And they placed the written charge against him over his head, "This is Jesus the King of the Jews." **38** Then two robbers were crucified with him, one on his right hand and one on his left hand. **39** The passersby kept blaspheming him, **shaking their heads 40** and saying, "You who would tear down the sanctuary and build it up in three days, save yourself! If you *are* the Son of God, come down from the cross!" **41** The chief priests along with the scribes and elders also mocked him and said, **42** "He saved others but can't save himself! If he's the King of Israel, let him come down now from the cross and we'll believe in him. **43 He trusted in God, let God deliver him** now **if He wants him,** since he said, 'I'm the Son of God.'" **44** And the robbers who were crucified with him derided him in the same way.

45 [m] Now from the sixth hour darkness came upon the land until the ninth hour. **46** Then about the ninth hour Jesus cried out with a loud voice and said, *"Eli, Eli, lema sabachthani?"* that is, **"My God, my God, why have You forsaken me?"** **47** When some of those standing there heard this they said, "The fellow's calling Elijah!" **48** And at once one of them ran and took a sponge and filled it with wine, and he placed it on a reed and tried to give him a drink. **49** But the rest said, "Hold on, let's see if Elijah comes to save him!" **50** But Jesus cried out again with a loud voice and gave up the spirit. **51** And, behold, the curtain of the sanctuary was torn in two from top to bottom, and the earth was shaken

---

[l] Mk 15:21-32; Lk 23:26-43; Jn 19:28-30. [m] Mk 15:33-41; Lk 23:44-49; Jn 19:28-30.

27:35 The best manuscript tradition omits: "to fulfill what was spoken through the prophets when they said,
They divided my garments among them,
and for my clothing they cast lots." (Ps 22:19)
27:39 Ps 22:7.
27:43 Ps 22:8.
27:46 Ps 22:2.

and the rocks torn apart, **52** and the tombs were opened and many bodies of the saints who had fallen asleep arose, **53** and they came out of the tombs after his resurrection and went into the holy city and appeared to many people. **54** When the centurion and those watching Jesus with him saw the earthquake and what had happened they were terrified and said, "Truly this man *was* the Son of God!" **55** Now there were many women there, watching from a distance, who had followed Jesus from Galilee to serve him; **56** among them were Mary Magdalen and Mary the mother of James and Joseph and the mother of the sons of Zebedee.

57 [n] When evening had come a rich man from Arimathea named Joseph, who had also been a disciple of Jesus, came; **58** he went to Pilate and requested the body of Jesus. Then Pilate ordered it to be given to him. **59** Joseph took the body and wrapped it in a clean linen shroud **60** and placed it in his new tomb, which he had hewn in the rock, and after rolling a large stone up to the door of the tomb he went away. **61** Now Mary Magdalen and the other Mary were there, sitting across from the sepulchre.

62 The next day, that is, the day after the Day of Preparation, the chief priests and Pharisees gathered before Pilate **63** and said, "Lord, we remember that that imposter said, while still alive, 'After three days I'll rise.' **64** Therefore, order the sepulchre to be made secure until the third day, lest his disciples come steal him and say to the people, 'He's risen from the dead!' and the last imposture will be worse than the first." **65** Pilate said to them, "You have a guard; go secure it as well as you know how." **66** So they went and set a watch on the tomb and sealed the stone with the guard.

W. RESURRECTION AND APPEARANCES OF JESUS

28 **1** [o] Now after the Sabbath, as it began to dawn on the first day of the week, Mary Magdalen and the other Mary came to see the sepulchre. **2** And, behold, there was a great earthquake; an angel of the Lord came down from Heaven, came up to the stone, and rolled it

---

[n] Mk 15:42-47; Lk 23:50-56; Jn 19:38-42.　[o] Mk 16:1-8; Lk 24:1-12; Jn 20:1-10.

away and sat upon it. **3** Now his appearance was like lightning and his clothing as white as snow, **4** and for fear of him those who were on guard trembled and became like dead men. **5** But in response the angel said to the women, "Don't be afraid — I know you're looking for Jesus, who was crucified. **6** He isn't here — he's risen, just like he said; come see the place where he lay. **7** And go quickly to tell his disciples, 'He's risen from the dead and, behold, he's going ahead of you into Galilee; you'll see him there.' Behold, I've told you!" **8** They quickly left the tomb with fear and great joy and ran to tell the disciples. **9** And, behold, Jesus met them and said, "Hail!" But they came forward, took hold of his feet, and worshipped him. **10** Then Jesus said to them, "Don't be afraid! Go tell my brothers to go to Galilee, and they'll see me there."

11 Now as they were going, behold, some of the guard came into the city and told the chief priests all that had happened. **12** And after getting together with the elders and coming up with a plan they gave the soldiers a considerable amount of silver **13** and said, "Say, 'His disciples came at night and stole him away while we were sleeping.' **14** And if word of this gets to the governor, we'll satisfy him and keep you out of trouble." **15** So they took the silver and did as they'd been instructed. And this story has been spread among the Jews to this day.

16 P But the eleven disciples went into Galilee to the mountain Jesus had directed them to. **17** And when they saw him they worshipped him, but some were doubtful. **18** And Jesus came to them and spoke to them and said, "All authority in Heaven and on earth has been given to me. **19** Go, therefore, and make disciples of all nations, baptizing them in the name of the Father and of the Son and of the Holy Spirit, **20** and teach them to observe all that I've commanded you and, behold, I'll be with you all the days until the end of the age."

P Mk 16:14-18; Lk 24:36-49; Jn 20:19-23.

THE GOSPEL ACCORDING TO
M A R K

INTRODUCTION TO MARK

Both tradition and modern scholarship are in general agreement that the author of the second Gospel was John Mark, well known to Christians from the Acts of the Apostles and also mentioned in several epistles. He apparently cooperated in the ministries of both Peter and Paul, and there is strong testimony in tradition to the effect that Mark's Gospel reflects Peter's teaching, that Mark, in fact, committed some of Peter's preaching to writing and incorporated it in his Gospel. Some scholars find support for this in the vivid eyewitness tone of those passages in which Peter is involved. At the same time, it is also clear that Mark used more than one source, and such a well travelled Christian, acquainted with important leaders of the Church, would have had access to many eyewitnesses to the ministry of Jesus.

It is usually supposed that Mark's Gospel was written primarily for Gentile Christians since he shows none of Matthew's interest in specifically Jewish concerns and seems to assume his readers will need an explanation when such matters are mentioned. This accords well with the persistent tradition that Mark wrote this Gospel at the request of the church at Rome, a mixed community.

Mark's Greek style has been much criticized by some and it's true that his style is rough in comparison to Matthew. He makes grammatical mistakes at times; he sometimes shifts his whole train of thought in mid-sentence; his use of tenses appears inconsistent; in particular, his typically Hebrew use of "and" as an all-purpose introductory particle sometimes grates on modern ears (as it probably did on native Greek ears, as well). Nevertheless, Mark had sound literary instincts and the Gospel as a whole is skillfully organized from a thematic standpoint.

When combined with his vivid, highly human, portrait of Jesus, these factors overcome Mark's linguistic shortcomings and help to account for the strong impression his Gospel makes.

The literary technique Mark uses to great advantage is to juxtapose several of his basic themes within the framework of a short narrative passage. For example, Israel's lack of faith may be juxtaposed with the faith of a Gentile, or the disciples' spiritual blindness may be contrasted with the simple faith of a, literally, blind man. Mark's general themes are relatively few in number and can be summarized as follows. Jesus was the Son of God and clearly revealed his divinity in his miracles. Nevertheless, his own people were blind to these clear proofs and even his disciples failed to understand him at the time. Jesus manifested constant concern for the "little ones," those who respond to the good news with simple faith, and regularly admonished his disciples to exercise the authority he gave them with humility. Finally, Mark stresses, more strongly, perhaps, than any of the other evangelists, that Israel rejected Jesus and that Jesus' good news is for all who respond to him with faith — including the Gentiles.

A. 1:1-13   John the Baptist and the beginning of Jesus' ministry; his baptism and the descent of the Spirit; his temptation.

B. 1:14-3:35   Jesus begins his Galilean ministry by proclaiming the imminence of the Kingdom and the need for repentance and faith. Jesus manifests his divine authority both in deed, through his miracles, and in word, by arrogating to himself the divine power to forgive sins and legislate. This leads to conflict with the Pharisees, who cling stubbornly to their traditions even in the face of the divine power which is being manifested.

C. 4:1-41   Parables of the Kingdom. Jesus calls upon each individual to be fruitful, singlemindedly pursuing the Kingdom. He then manifests his divine power and authority.

D. 5:1-6:6   Jesus continues to manifest his divine power and authority, yet is rejected in his hometown. While

Jesus is accepted as a miracle worker, the people are blind to what this says about who he is.

E. 6:7-29   The disciples are sent out to teach and heal; the death of the Baptist.

F. 6:30-56   Jesus feeds 5,000 and walks on the sea, yet the disciples fail to understand.

G. 7:1-37   Jesus' indictment of the Pharisees: they care only for their traditions and fail to understand the true meaning of God's law, over which he asserts his authority. Jesus travels outside Israel and cures the Gentile woman's daughter because of her persistent faith. When he returns to Israel the people are astounded by his miracles and begin to suspect that Jesus may be the Messiah.

H. 8:1-26   Jesus feeds 4,000 but the Pharisees are blind and demand a sign. Jesus heals a blind man.

I. 8:27-9:29 Jesus travels outside Israel again and is transfigured, but when he returns he encounters a continuing lack of understanding.

J. 9:30-50   Jesus teaches the disciples privately regarding the exercise of authority, especially the need to respect God's "little ones."

K. 10:1-31   Jesus leaves Galilee for Transjordan, where he teaches regarding divorce and discipleship. Moses gave Israel permission to divorce because of their hardened hearts, but the disciples are to accept the Kingdom like little children. The danger of wealth in preventing this childlike acceptance.

L. 10:32-52 Jesus heads for Jerusalem. Jesus again must teach the disciples regarding humility in the exercise of authority, because of their continuing blindness. At Jericho blind Bartimaeus receives his sight because he believes.

M. 11:1-25   Jesus enters Jerusalem in triumph, seated on the humble mount of the King of Peace for all nations. He cleanses the Temple to prepare a house of prayer for all nations and teaches the disciples regarding faith and forgiveness.

N. 11:27-12:12   The leaders of Israel challenge Jesus' authority. Jesus foretells that they will be rejected by God and the vineyard (Israel) will be given to others — their authority will be given to others.

O. 12:13-44   The leaders of Israel again challenge Jesus but are vanquished. Jesus sets forth the true essence of the law — love of God and neighbor — and again contrasts the arrogant exercise of authority with the worth of the humble believer.

P. 13:1-37   The coming of the Son of Man foretold and the need to be watchful.

Q. 14:1-15:47   The Passion. The Gentile centurion correctly sees who Jesus really is.

R. 16:1-20   The Resurrection and appearances of Jesus. The disciples are sent to all nations.

THE GOSPEL ACCORDING TO

M A R K

A. THE BEGINNINGS OF JESUS' MINISTRY

1 **1**[a] The beginning of the good news of Jesus Christ, the Son of God. **2** As it is written in the prophet Isaiah —

> **Behold, I'm sending my messenger**
> **before your face,**
> **who will prepare your way,**
> **3** **The voice of one crying out in the desert,**
> **'Prepare the way of the Lord,**
> **make straight his paths'** —

4 so it was that John appeared, baptizing in the desert and proclaiming a baptism of repentance for the forgiveness of sins. **5** All the Judean countryside went out to him as well as those in Jerusalem, and they were baptized by him in the river Jordan while they confessed their sins. **6** John was clothed in camel hair with a leather belt around his waist, and he ate locusts and wild honey. **7** He preached and said, "One more powerful than I am is coming after me, the strap of whose sandal I'm not worthy to stoop down and untie. **8** I've baptized you with water, but he'll baptize you with the Holy Spirit."

9[b] And it happened in those days that Jesus came from Nazareth

---

[a] Mt 3:1-12; Lk 3:1-9, 15-17; Jn 1:19-28. [b] Mt 3:13-17; Lk 3:21-22.

1:2-4 Mark opens his Gospel by likening John the Baptist to the herald announcing the coming of Yahweh, thus clearly equating Jesus with God.

1:2 Ml 3:1.

1:3 Is 40:3 (Septuagint).

in Galilee and was baptized in the Jordan by John. **10** As he was coming out of the water he saw the heavens torn apart and the Spirit descending upon him like a dove, **11** and a voice came from Heaven, "You are My Beloved Son; in you I am well pleased!"

12 ᶜ Then the Spirit drove him out into the desert. **13** He stayed in the desert for forty days being tempted by Satan. He was with the wild animals, and angels served him.

B. AUTHORITY OF JESUS
AND CONFLICT WITH THE PHARISEES

14 ᵈ Now after John was arrested, Jesus came into Galilee proclaiming the good news of God **15** and saying, "The proper time has been fulfilled and the Kingdom of God has come; repent and believe in the good news!"

16 ᵉ As he was walking along the Sea of Galilee he saw Simon and Simon's brother Andrew casting a throw net into the sea — they were fishermen. **17** He said to them, "Follow me, and I'll make you fishers of men!" **18** And they left their nets at once and followed him. **19** He continued on a little way and saw James son of Zebedee and his brother, John — they were in the boat mending the nets. **20** He called them at once, and they left their father Zebedee in the boat with the hired men and followed him.

21 ᶠ They entered Capharnaum, and so he went into the synagogue and taught on the Sabbath. **22** The people were amazed at the way he taught — he was teaching them on his own authority, unlike the scribes. **23** And there was a man with an unclean spirit in the synagogue who cried out, **24** "What do you want with us, Jesus of Nazareth? Have you come to destroy us? I know who you are — the Holy One of God!" **25** Jesus rebuked him and said, "Be silenced and come out of him!" **26** And after throwing him into convulsions and crying out with a loud voice, the unclean spirit came out of him. **27**

ᶜ Mt 4:1-11; Lk 4:1-13. ᵈ Mt 4:12-17; Lk 4:14-15. ᵉ Mt 4:18-22; Lk 5:1-11. ᶠ Lk 4:31-37.

1:11 Is 42:1.
1:27 Literally: "a new teaching with authority." The import is that Jesus didn't invoke God but cast out demons and taught as the ultimate authority himself. The implicit claim of divine authority was not lost on his listeners.

Those gathered there were so astounded that they began to argue with one another and say, "What's going on? A new teaching given on his authority; he even gives orders to the unclean spirits, and they obey him!" **28** So word of him went out everywhere in the whole district of Galilee.

29 [g] Then after coming out of the synagogue he went to Simon and Andrew's house with James and John. **30** Now Peter's mother-in-law was consumed by a fever, and so they told Jesus about her. **31** He approached her, grasped her hand and raised her up, and the fever left her and she began to serve them. **32** Now when evening had come, when the sun had set, they brought him all those who were sick and were demon-possessed, **33** and the whole city was gathered at the door. **34** He cured many who were sick with all kinds of diseases and drove out many demons, and he didn't allow the demons to speak, because they knew him.

35 [h] Early in the morning, long before daylight, he got up, went out, and went off to a desert place, and there he prayed. **36** Simon and those with him searched for him **37** and found him, and they said to him, "Everyone's looking for you!" **38** He said to them, "Let's go elsewhere, to the neighboring country towns, so I can preach there as well — this is what I came for!" **39** And he went through all Galilee, preaching in their synagogues and driving out demons.

40 [i] And a leper came up to him, begging him and kneeling down and saying to him, "If you wish to, you can make me clean!" **41** Greatly moved, he reached out his hand, touched him, and said to him, "I *do* wish it; be made clean!" **42** and at once the leprosy left him and he was made clean. **43** After admonishing him Jesus at once sent him away **44** and said to him, "See that you tell no one, but go show yourself to the priest and offer for your cleansing what Moses commanded, as a witness to them." **45** But the man went out and began to proclaim and spread the word so energetically that Jesus wasn't even able to come

---

g Mt 8:14-17; Lk 4:38-41. h Lk 4:42-44. i Mt 8:1-4; Lk 5:12-16.

1:40-44   The Greek indicates that Jesus was moved by a strong emotion, but his brusqueness toward the leper throughout the passage seems to indicate his indignation, perhaps at the implicit assumption in the leper's words (v. 40) that Jesus' mercy is applied arbitrarily. This shows a lack of faith. For a similar response by Jesus to a plea for a cure, cf. 9:17-27. In other instances where this Greek word is used, however, the emotion which moves Jesus is pity.

into a city openly; instead, he stayed out in desert places, and the people came to him from all directions.

2 1 ʲ He came into Capharnaum again a few days later, and it became known that he was at home. **2** So many people gathered around that there was no longer room even in front of the door, and he spoke the word to them. **3** Then some people came to him carrying a paralytic, borne by four men. **4** And since they couldn't bring him through the crowd they took off the roof where Jesus was, and after opening it up they lowered the cot on which the paralytic was laid. **5** When Jesus saw their faith he said to the paralytic, "Child, your sins are forgiven!" **6** Now, some of the scribes were seated there and they questioned in their hearts, **7** "How can the fellow talk like that? He's blaspheming! Who but God alone is able to forgive sins?" **8** Jesus realized at once in his spirit that they were questioning within themselves in this way, and so he said to them, "Why are you questioning these things in your hearts? **9** What's easier, to say to the paralytic, 'Your sins are forgiven,' or to say, 'Get up, pick up your cot, and walk'? **10** But so you'll know that the Son of Man has authority to forgive sins on earth" — he said to the paralytic, **11** "I say to you, get up, pick up your cot, and go to your house!" **12** And he got up, picked up his cot at once and went out in full sight of everyone, so that everyone was amazed and glorified God, saying, "We've never seen the like!"

13 ᵏ Once again he went out along the sea, and the whole crowd came to him and he taught them. **14** As he walked along he saw Levi son of Alpheus seated at his tax booth, and he said to him, "Follow me!" And he got up and followed him. **15** Now he reclined at table in Levi's house, and many tax collectors and sinners were at table with Jesus and his disciples; many, indeed, were there. Also following him **16** were scribes of the Pharisees, and when they saw that he was eating with sinners and publicans they said to his disciples, "Why is he eating with tax collectors and sinners?" **17** When he heard this Jesus said to them, "The healthy aren't in need of a doctor — the sick are! I came to call sinners, not the righteous. "

18 ˡ John's disciples and the Pharisees were fasting, and people came and said to Jesus, "Why are John's disciples and the disciples of

---

ʲ Mt 9:1-8; Lk 5:17-26. ᵏ Mt 9:9-13; Lk 5:27-32. ˡ Mt 9:14-17; Lk 5:33-39.

2:15 "Levi's house." Literally, "his house," but Lk 5:29 specifies "Levi's house."

the Pharisees fasting, but your disciples aren't fasting?" **19** Jesus said to them,

> "Can the groomsmen fast
>   while the bridegroom is with them?
> As long as the bridegroom is with them
>   they cannot fast,

20 But the days will come when the bridegroom
>   will be taken from them,
>   and then, on that day, they'll fast.

21 No one sews a patch of unshrunken cloth
>   onto an old cloak,
>   Otherwise, the patch tears away from it,
>   the new from the old,
>   and the tear becomes worse.

22 And no one puts new wine
>   into old skins,
>   Otherwise, the wine will burst the skins,
>   and both wine and skins are ruined;

on the contrary,

> 'new wine in new skins.'"

23 [m] It happened that as he was going through the grain fields on the Sabbath his disciples began plucking the heads of the grain as they made their way through. **24** And the Pharisees said to him, "Look! Why are they doing what's unlawful on the Sabbath?" **25** He said to them, "Haven't you ever read what David did when *he* was in need and was hungry, as well as those with him? **26** How he went into the house of God when Abiathar was high priest and ate the loaves of offering" — which it's only lawful for the priests to eat — "and he gave some to those with him as well?" **27** And he said to them,

> "The Sabbath was made for Man,
>   not Man for the Sabbath;

28 thus the Son of Man is Lord even of the Sabbath."

---

[m] Mt 12:1-8; Lk 6:1-5.

2:26   1 S 21:1-6.

3 1 [n] Once again he went into the synagogue. Now a man was there who had a withered hand 2 and they were watching closely to see whether Jesus would cure him on the Sabbath, so they could make some accusation against him. 3 So he said to the man with the withered hand, "Stand out in the middle." 4 Then he said to them,

> "Is it lawful on the Sabbath to do good
> or to do evil,
> to save a life or to put to death?"

But they remained silent. 5 And after looking around at them in anger, greatly upset at the hardness of their hearts, he said to the man, "Hold out your hand." The man held his hand out and it was restored. 6 Then the Pharisees went out with the Herodians and began to plot to do away with Jesus.

7 Then Jesus departed with his disciples for the sea. A large crowd from Galilee followed and, having heard all he was doing, a large crowd as well from Judea 8 and from Jerusalem and from Idumea and beyond the Jordan and around Tyre and Sidon came to him. 9 He told his disciples to ready a small boat for him because of the crowd, so they wouldn't crush him — 10 he was curing so many that those who had diseases pressed close upon him so they could touch him. 11 As soon as the unclean spirits saw him they'd fall down before him and cry out, "You're the Son of God!" 12 And he'd sternly command them not to make him known.

13 [o] Then he went up on the mountain and called those he wanted, and they came to him. 14 He chose twelve, whom he also called apostles. They were to stay with him so he could send them out to preach 15 and to have power to drive out demons. 16 He chose the Twelve and he gave the name Peter to Simon, and James son of Zebedee 17 and James' brother John, and he gave them the name Boanerges, that is, Sons of Thunder, 18 and Andrew and Philip and Bartholomew and Matthew and Thomas and James son of Alpheus and Thaddeus and Simon the Zealot 19 and Judas Iscariot, who handed him over.

20 [p] He went into a house, and once again such a crowd gathered that they weren't even able to eat. 21 When his relatives heard this they went out to seize him, because people were saying, "He's lost his

---

[n] Mt 12:9-14; Lk 6:6-11. [o] Mt 10:1-4; Lk 6:12-16. [p] Mt 12:22-32; Lk 11:14-23, 12:10.

mind!" **22** And scribes from Jerusalem came down and said, "He's possessed by Beelzebul! By the prince of demons he drives out demons!" **23** So he called them to himself and said to them in parables, "How can Satan drive out Satan?

> **24** If a kingdom is divided against itself,
> that kingdom is unable to stand,
> **25** If a house is divided,
> that house will be unable to stand.
> **26** And if Satan rebels against himself
> and is divided,
> he cannot last, but comes to an end.

27 On the contrary, no one can enter the strong man's house to plunder his possessions unless he first ties the strong man up; *then* he can plunder his house. **28** Amen, I say to you,

> Everything will be forgiven the sons of men,
> their sins and the blasphemies they
> may blaspheme,
> **29** But whoever blasphemes the Holy Spirit
> never has forgiveness,
> but is liable for an eternal sin —"

30 because they were saying, "He has an unclean spirit!"

31 q His mother came as well as his brothers; they stood outside and sent someone in for him, to call him. **32** A crowd was seated around him, and they said to him, "Look, your mother and brothers are outside asking for you." **33** In answer he said to them, "Who is my mother and my brothers?" **34** Then he looked around at those seated in a circle

---

q Mt 12:46-50; Lk 8:19-21.

3:27 Here Jesus compares Satan to a "strong man" and the present age to Satan's house. It is Jesus who has entered Satan's house, bound him, and freed those in Satan's power. Jesus' power over demons is a sign of this mastery and the coming of the Messianic age.

3:29 The blasphemy against the Spirit consists in imputing to Satan what is in fact the lifegiving activity of the Spirit.

3:31 Church tradition has consistently maintained that the "brothers" of Jesus referred to here were merely close relatives, not sons of the same mother. It is instructive to compare this passage to 15:40-16:1 and parallel passages in the other Gospels (especially Mt 27:60 and Lk 23:49-24:10) where these brothers are again referred to as sons of "Mary," but this time it is unambiguously clear that *this* Mary was not Mary the mother of Jesus. Such usage was typically Semitic.

around him and said, "Here are my mother and my brothers. **35** For whoever does the will of God, he's my brother and sister and mother."

C. PARABLES OF THE KINGDOM

4 **1** [r] Once again he began to teach by the sea. And such a large crowd gathered around him that he sat in a boat on the sea, while the whole crowd gathered along the sea on the land. **2** Then he taught them many things in parables and in his teaching he said to them, **3** "Listen now!

> Behold, the sower went out to sow!
> **4** And it happened as he sowed that some fell
> > along the footpath,
> > and the birds came and ate it up.
> **5** And some fell on the rocky ground where it
> > didn't have much soil,
> > and it sprouted at once, since the soil
> > had no depth,
> **6** And when the sun rose it got scorched,
> > and since it had no roots it withered away.
> **7** And some fell among the thorns and the thorns
> > grew up,
> > and they choked it and it gave no fruit.
> **8** And some fell on the good earth, and it grew up
> > and increased and gave fruit,
> > and one bore thirtyfold, and one sixtyfold,
> > and one a hundredfold."

9 Then he said,

> "Whoever has ears to hear,
> let them hear!"

10 [s] When he happened to be alone, those about him with the Twelve asked him about the parables. **11** And he said to them, "To you

---

[r] Mt 13:1-9; Lk 8:4-8. [s] Mt 13:1-17; Lk 8:9-10.

is given the secret of the Kingdom of God, but to those outside everything is given in parables, **12** so that

> **Although they look,**
> **they may see yet not perceive,**
> **And though they listen,**
> **they may hear yet not understand,**
> **Lest they turn back**
> **and receive forgiveness."**

13 [t] Then he said to them, "You don't understand this parable? Then how will you understand *any* of the parables? **14** The sower sows the word. **15** Now, these are the ones where the word is sown on the footpath, and when they hear, Satan comes at once and takes away the word sown among them. **16** And these are the ones sown on the rocky ground — when they hear the word they at once receive it joyfully, **17** but they aren't well rooted and last only for the moment, and then when trouble or persecution arises because of the word they give up their faith at once. **18** Others are those sown among the thorns, which are those who hear the word, **19** but worldly cares and the deception of wealth and desires for all the other things come in and choke the word, and it's unfruitful. **20** Then there are those sown on the good earth, which hear the word and welcome it and bear fruit, one thirtyfold, one sixtyfold, and one a hundredfold."

21 [u] And he said to them, "The lamp isn't brought in to be put under the grain basket or under the bed, is it? Isn't it so it can be placed on the lampstand?

> **22** For nothing is hidden unless it is
> to be revealed,
> Nothing is covered up unless to be brought
> into the open.

> **23** If anyone has ears to hear,
> let them hear!"

24 And he said to them, "Consider what you hear.

---

[t] Mt 13:18-23; Lk 8:11-15. [u] Lk 8:16-18.

4:12 Is 6:9-10 (Septuagint).

With the measure you measure, it will be measured
out to you,
and more will be added as well.

25 For whoever has,
to him it shall be given,
And whoever does *not* have,
even what he has will be taken from him."

26 And he said,

"The Kingdom of God is like this,
as if a man should throw seed upon the earth

27 And sleep and rise by night and day,
and the seed should sprout and grow
while he's unaware.

28 The earth bears fruit on its own,
first the shoot, then the head of grain,
then the full grain in the head.

29 When it puts forth fruit he at once sends
for the sickle,
because the harvest has come."

30 ^v And he said,

"How may we compare the Kingdom of God,
or in what parable can we present it?

31 It's like a grain of mustard seed
which, when it's sown upon the earth, is the
smallest of all the seeds on the earth,

32 Yet when it's sown it grows and becomes
the biggest of all the garden plants
and puts out big branches, so that the birds
of the sky are able to nest
in its shade."

33 ^w He spoke the word to them in many such parables, in so far as they were able to understand, **34** but he spoke to the people only in parables and explained everything to his own disciples in private.

---

v Mt 13:31-32; Lk 13:18-19. w Mt 13:34-35.

4:29 Jl 4:13.

35 [x] That day when evening had come he said to them, "Let's cross over to the other side." **36** After dismissing the crowd they took him as he was, in the boat, and other boats were with it. **37** A violent wind squall came up and the waves were breaking over the boat so that by this time the boat was filling up, **38** yet he was in the stern, sleeping on the cushion. So they woke him and said to him, "Teacher, doesn't it matter to you that we're going to die?" **39** Then he woke up and rebuked the wind and said to the sea, "Silence! Be calm!" The wind ceased and there was a profound calm, **40** and he said to them, "Why are you afraid? Do you still not have faith?" **41** Then they were seized with fear and said to each other, "Who *is* he, then, that both the wind and sea obey him?"

D. JESUS MANIFESTS HIS AUTHORITY BUT IS REJECTED

5 **1** [y] He went to the other side of the sea to the region of the Gerasenes, **2** and when he got out of the boat a man with an unclean spirit came up to him from among the tombs. **3** This man made his dwelling among the tombs and no one was able to put him in chains or even bind him — **4** he'd been put in chains and restrained many times, yet he'd broken the chains and restraints to bits and scattered them, and no one was able to control him. **5** He spent all night and day among the tombs and on the mountains, and kept crying aloud in his madness and cutting himself with stones. **6** He saw Jesus from a distance and rushed up and knelt before him, **7** crying out in a loud voice, "What do you want with me, Jesus, Son of the Most High God? I beg you in the name of God not to torment me!" **8** because Jesus had been saying to him, "Come out of the man, unclean spirit!" **9** Jesus asked him, "What's your name?" and he said to him, "My name is Legion, because there are many of us." **10** And he begged Jesus not to send them out of the region.

11 Now there was a large herd of swine on the hillside there, feeding, **12** and they begged him and said, "Send us into the swine; let

---

[x] Mt 8:23-27; Lk 8:22-25. [y] Mt 8:28-34; Lk 8:26-39.

5:1 This area was in the Decapolis and was, therefore, heavily Gentile.

us enter into them!" **13** So he gave them permission and when the unclean spirits had gone out they went into the swine, and the herd, numbering about two thousand, rushed down the slope into the sea and was drowned. **14** The men who had been feeding them fled and spread the news in the town and the fields, and the people came to see what had happened. **15** When they came up to Jesus and saw the demon-possessed man seated, clothed and in his right mind — the one who had been possessed by Legion — they became frightened. **16** Then they — those who had seen [it all] — told how this had come about for the demon-possessed man, and also about the swine. **17** And the people began to beg him to leave their district. **18** When he had gotten into the boat the man who had been demon-possessed begged him to let him go with him, **19** but he wouldn't allow him to; instead he told him, "Go off to your home, to your own people, and proclaim to them what your Lord has done for you and how He had mercy on you." **20** So he went off and began to proclaim in the Decapolis what Jesus had done for him, and they were all astounded.

21 ᶻ When Jesus had again crossed over to the other side a large crowd gathered around him, as he stood by the sea. **22** One of the rulers of the synagogue, Jairus by name, came and, when he saw him, fell at his feet **23** and begged him, saying, "My little daughter is dying; come lay your hands on her and save her life!" **24** So he went off with him.

A large crowd was following him and kept crowding in on him. **25** Now a woman was there who had had a heavy flow of blood for twelve years **26** and had suffered greatly at the hands of many doctors. She'd spent all she had but had gained nothing; on the contrary, it kept getting worse. **27** Having heard about Jesus, she came with the crowd and touched his cloak from behind, **28** because she said, "If I can just touch even part of his cloak I'll be saved." **29** At once her flow of blood dried up, and she knew in her body that she was cured from the illness. **30** Jesus himself realized at once that power had gone out from him and he turned around in the crowd saying, "Who touched my cloak?" **31** His disciples said to him, "You see the crowd pressing in on you! How can you say, 'Who touched me?'" **32** But he kept looking around to see

---

ᶻ Mt 9:18-26; Lk 8:40-56.

5:20 "The Decapolis" was a confederation of largely Hellenized cities. They were ten in number (Greek *deka* = ten) and all but one were located east of the Jordan. To have encountered the herd of swine in a more Jewish environment would have been unthinkable.

who had done it. **33** Then the woman, trembling and afraid because she knew what had happened to her, came and fell down before him and told him the whole truth. **34** But he said to her, "Daughter, your faith has saved you; go in peace and be cured of your illness."

35 While he was still speaking some people came from the ruler of the synagogue's household and said, "Your daughter has died; why trouble the teacher further?" **36** But Jesus paid no attention to what was being said and said to the ruler of the synagogue, "Don't be afraid; just believe!" **37** And he didn't allow anyone to accompany him except Peter and James and James' brother John. **38** When they came to the leader of the synagogue's house Jesus saw the confusion and the people weeping and wailing loudly, **39** and when he entered he said to them, "Why are you upset and weeping? The child hasn't died, she's sleeping!" **40** And they just laughed at him. But after driving them all out he took the father of the child and the mother and those who were with him, and he went in to where the child was; **41** and after taking hold of the child's hand he said to her, *"Talitha koum,"* which, translated, is, "Little girl, I say to you, arise!" **42** At once the little girl got up and began to walk around — she was twelve years old. And at once they were completely overcome with amazement. **43** Then he gave strict orders that no one should know of this and said to give her something to eat.

6 **1** [a] Jesus left there and came to his hometown, and his disciples followed him. **2** When the Sabbath came he began to teach in the synagogue, and many of those who were listening were amazed and said, "Where did this fellow get all this? What's the wisdom given this man that such mighty works should come about at his hands? **3** Isn't this the carpenter, the son of Mary and the brother of James and Joses and Judas and Simon? Aren't his sisters right here among us?" And they rejected him. **4** Jesus said to them, "A prophet is without honor only in his hometown and among his kinsmen and in his own house." **5** He was unable to do any mighty works there, except that he cured a few sick people by laying his hands on them, **6** and he was astounded at their unbelief.

---

[a] Mt 13:53-58; Lk 4:16-18.

6:3   Cf. 3:31 above for more detailed discussion. In Semitic usage any close male relative could be referred to as a brother.

E. MISSION OF
THE DISCIPLES AND DEATH OF THE BAPTIST

[b] Then he went around the surrounding villages teaching. 7 He called the Twelve to him and began to send them out two by two, and he gave them authority over the unclean spirits 8 and ordered them to take nothing on the road but one staff — not bread, not a bag, nor coppers in their belts — 9 but instead to put sandals on their feet and not to wear two tunics. 10 And he said to them, "Whenever you go into a house, stay there until you leave the place. 11 But if any place doesn't receive you or give you a hearing, when you're leaving there shake the dust off from the soles of your feet in witness against them." 12 So they went out and proclaimed that the people should repent, 13 and they drove out many demons and anointed many sick people with oil and cured them.

14 [c] King Herod heard [about Jesus], for his name had become known, and he said, "John the Baptizer has been raised from the dead, and that's why these powers are at work in him." 15 But others said, "He's Elijah," while others said, "He's a prophet like one of the Prophets." 16 But when Herod heard he said, "John whom I beheaded, he's been raised!" 17 For Herod himself had sent and had John seized and kept him in prison because of Herodias, the wife of his brother Philip, because he'd married her. 18 For John had been telling Herod, "It isn't lawful for you to have your brother's wife." 19 Now Herodias held it against him and wanted to kill him, but she was unable to 20 because Herod feared John, knowing him to be an upright and holy man. So he kept an eye on him and when he listened to him he was greatly disturbed, and yet he liked to listen to him. 21 Now when the proper day had come Herod held a feast for his top men and the tribunes and the most important men from Galilee, 22 and when Herodias' own daughter came in and danced she pleased Herod and the guests. The king said to the girl, "Ask me whatever you want and I'll give you it," 23 and he swore to her, "Whatever you ask me for I'll give you, up to half my kingdom." 24 She went out and said to her

---

[b] Mt 10:1, 5-15; Lk 9:1-6. [c] Mt 14:1-12; Lk 9:7-9.

6:8 "Coppers" were the smaller coins used in Palestine and were often carried wrapped in a belt. More valuable coins, such as the *denarius*, were made of silver.

mother, "What should I ask for?" And her mother said, "The head of John the Baptizer." **25** So she hurried in at once to the king and made her request — "I want you to give me, right now, the head of John the Baptist on a platter." **26** The king was greatly distressed; because of the oaths and the guests he didn't want to refuse her, **27** and so he sent an executioner at once and ordered the head to be brought. He went off and beheaded John in the prison, **28** and he brought the head on a platter and gave it to the girl, and she gave it to her mother. **29** And when his disciples heard they came and carried the corpse away and laid it in a tomb.

F. TWO SIGNS AND LACK OF FAITH

30 [d] Then the apostles gathered around Jesus and told him all they had done and had taught. **31** And he said to them, "Come away privately, just yourselves, to a desert place and rest for a bit." For there were so many people coming and going that they didn't even have time to eat. **32** So they went off alone in the boat to a desert place, **33** but people saw them leaving and many of them found out where he was going, and they ran ahead on foot from all the towns and got there before them. **34** When he disembarked he saw a large crowd, and he was moved with pity for them because they were like sheep without a shepherd, and he began to teach them many things. **35** Now when the hour was already late his disciples came to him and said, "This is a desert place and the hour is already late; **36** send them away so they can go off to the farms and villages and buy themselves something to eat." **37** But in answer he said to them, "*You* give them something to eat." And they said to him, "Should we go buy two hundred *denarii* worth of bread and give it to them to eat?" **38** But he said, "How many loaves do you have? Go see." And when they found out they said, "Five, and two fish." **39** Then he ordered them all to recline in groups on the green grass, **40** and they sat down in groups of a hundred and of fifty. **41** Taking the five loaves and the two fish, he looked up to Heaven, blessed and broke the loaves, and kept giving them to the disciples so they

---

[d] Mt 14:13-21; Lk 9:10-17.

6:39 "Green grass"; John (6:10) also mentions that "there was a lot of grass" at this spot. These details indicate that it was probably early spring, quite possibly Passover time. John specifically states (6:5) that "the Passover ... was near."

could distribute them to the people, and he divided the two fish among them all. **42** They all ate and were filled, **43** and they picked up twelve baskets of fragments of bread as well as some of the fish. **44** Now there were five thousand men who ate.

45 [e] Then he made his disciples get into the boat and go on ahead to the other side, near Bethsaida, while he sent the crowd away. **46** And after he took leave of them he went up the mountain to pray. **47** When evening came on, the boat was in the middle of the sea, while he was alone on land. **48** He saw them hard pressed as they rowed — the wind was against them — and at about the fourth watch of the night he came toward them, walking on the sea, and he was going to go past them. **49** Now when they saw him walking on the sea they thought he was a ghost, and they cried out because **50** they all saw him and were terrified. But he at once spoke with them and said to them, "Take courage! It's me! Don't be afraid!" **51** Then he got into the boat with them and the wind ceased. And they were utterly amazed, **52** for they hadn't understood about the loaves; instead, their hearts were hardened.

53 [f] After crossing over they came to land at Gennesaret and moored the boat. **54** As they were getting out of the boat the people recognized him at once — **55** they ran around the whole district there and began to carry those who were sick on cots to where they heard he was. **56** Wherever he entered the villages or cities or farms they put the sick in the market places and begged him to let them just touch the hem of his cloak, and all those who touched it were saved.

G. ISRAEL'S HARDNESS OF HEART

7 **1** [g] The Pharisees and some of the scribes from Jerusalem were gathered around him, **2** and when they saw that some of his disciples ate bread with unclean, that is, unwashed, hands — **3** for the

---

[e] Mt 14:22-33. [f] Mt 14:34-36. [g] Mt 15:1-20.

6:48   "Shortly before dawn." Literally, "at the fourth watch of the night." The fourth watch would have been just before dawn. The Romans considered night to extend from six p.m. to six a.m. and divided it into four equal parts. Thus, the fourth watch was between three a.m. and six a.m.

7:3   This is a very obscure passage. The idea appears to be that the Pharisees wash their hands carefully, but the literal meaning is that they wash "with the fist," or perhaps, "by rubbing their hands."

Pharisees and all the Jews don't eat unless they wash their hands, holding fast to what was handed down by the elders, **4** and they don't eat after coming from the marketplace unless they wash and they hold fast to many other things that were handed down, washing of cups and pitchers and bronze vessels — **5** the Pharisees and scribes asked him, "Why don't your disciples walk according to what was handed down by the elders, but instead eat bread with unclean hands?" **6** But he said to them, "Surely Isaiah prophesied about you hypocrites, as it is written,

> **This people honors me with their lips,**
> > **but their heart is far from me;**
> **7** **In vain do they worship me,**
> > **teaching as doctrines the commandments of men.**
> **8** You forsake the commandment of God,
> > yet hold fast to what was handed down by men."

9 And he said to them, "Surely you *do* set aside the commandment of God so you can set up what *you* handed down. **10** For Moses said, **Honor your father and your mother,** and, **Let whoever curses his father or mother be put to death; 11** but you say, 'If a man should say to his father or mother, "Whatever help you might have from me is *Qorban*"'" that is, an offering to God — **12** "you no longer allow him to do anything for his father or mother; **13** thus you set aside the word of God for the tradition you've handed down among yourselves, and you do many other similar things."

14 Then he called the crowd to himself again and said to them, "Listen to me, all of you, and understand!

> **15** Nothing that enters a man from outside of him
> > can make him unclean;
> It's what goes forth from a man
> > that makes the man unclean."

[16] 17 When he came into the house from the crowd his disciples questioned him about the parable. **18** And he said to them, "Are you

---

7:6-7 Is 29:13 (Septuagint).

7:10 Ex 20:12; Ex 21:17.

7:11 *"Qorban."* This "gift to God" allowed the giver to continue using what was "given," leaving open the possibility for serious abuses.

7:16 The best manuscript tradition omits this verse: "If anyone has ears to hear, let him hear!"

that dense, too? Don't you see that nothing that enters a man from outside can make him unclean **19** because it enters his stomach, not his heart, and goes out into the latrine?" — thus he declared all foods to be clean. **20** Then he said, "What goes forth from a man is what makes a man unclean, **21** for from within, from the hearts of men, come evil thoughts, fornication, theft, murder, **22** adultery, greed, evil intentions, deceit, indecency, jealousy, blasphemy, arrogance, and foolishness. **23** All such evil comes forth from within and makes a man unclean."

24 ʰ Now after departing from there he went off to the regions of Tyre. He went into a house and didn't want anyone to find out, but he couldn't hide; **25** instead, a woman whose daughter had an unclean spirit heard about him at once and came and fell at his feet. **26** Now the woman was a Greek, a Syrophoenician by birth, and she kept begging him to drive the demon out of her daughter. **27** And he said to her, "Let the children be fed first — it isn't right to take the children's bread and throw it to the dogs." **28** But she answered and said to him, "Lord, even the dogs beneath the table eat the children's crumbs." **29** Then he said to her, "Because of what you've said, go your way; the demon has come out of your daughter." **30** And when she went off to her house she found the child lying on the bed, and the demon gone.

31 When he left the region of Tyre again he went through Sidon to the Sea of Galilee, through the region of the Decapolis. **32** The people there brought him a deaf and tongue-tied man and begged him to lay his hands on him. **33** He took him off alone away from the crowd and put his fingers into his ears, and after spitting he touched his tongue. **34** Then he looked up to Heaven, sighed, and said to him, *"Ephphatha,"* that is, "Be opened!" **35** At once his ears were opened and the knot in his tongue was loosed and he spoke properly. **36** Jesus ordered them to tell no one, but the more he ordered them all the more did they proclaim it. **37** The people were utterly astonished and said, "Surely he's done everything! He makes the deaf hear and the dumb speak!"

ʰ Mt 15:21-28.

7:37 "He's done everything," i.e., everything the Messiah was supposed to do.

H. A SIGN AND CONTINUED BLINDNESS

8 **1** [i] In those days there was once again a large crowd which had nothing to eat. So he called his disciples together and said to them, **2** "I'm overcome with pity for the crowd because they've stayed with me for three days now and don't have anything to eat, **3** yet if I send them off to their homes hungry they'll faint on the way, and some of them have come from far off." **4** His disciples answered him, "How could anyone give them their fill of bread here in a desert place?" **5** And he asked them, "How many loaves do you have?" "Seven," they said, **6** Then he ordered the crowd to recline on the ground and, after taking the seven loaves, he gave thanks and broke them and gave them to his disciples to distribute, and they distributed them to the crowd. **7** They had a few small fish, and after blessing them he said to distribute them as well. **8** The people ate and were filled, and they picked up the leftover fragments — seven large baskets. **9** Now there were about four thousand men there. And he sent them away. **10** Then he got into the boat with his disciples and went to the district of Dalmanutha.

11 [j] The Pharisees came out and began to argue with him, demanding of him a sign from Heaven and putting him to the test. **12** And after groaning deeply in his spirit he said,

> "Why does this generation seek a sign?
> Amen I say to you, *no* sign will be given
> to this generation."

13 Then he left them, embarked once again, and went off to the other side.

14 [k] Now they had forgotten to bring bread, and except for one loaf they had none with them in the boat. **15** He was instructing them and saying, "Take care! Watch out for the leaven of the Pharisees and the leaven of Herod!" **16** but they kept arguing among themselves as to why they didn't have bread. **17** Realizing this, he said to them, "Why are you arguing because you don't have bread?

> Do you still neither see nor understand?
> Do *you* have hardened hearts?

---

[i] Mt 15:32-39. [j] Mt 16:1-4. [k] Mt 16:5-12.

18   Can't you see with your eyes?
        Can't you hear with your ears?

Don't you remember **19** when I broke the five loaves for the five thousand, how many baskets full of pieces you picked up?" "Twelve," they said. **20** "And the seven for the four thousand, how many large baskets full of fragments did you pick up?" "Seven," they said. **21** Then he said to them, "Do you still not understand?"

22 They came to Bethsaida. Some people there brought a blind man to him and begged him to touch him. **23** So he took the blind man by the hand and led him out of the village. After spitting on his eyes and laying his hands on him Jesus asked him, "Do you see anything?" **24** And when the man looked up he said, "I see men, as if I'm looking at trees walking around." **25** Once again he laid his hands on the man's eyes; then his vision was restored and he was able to see everything clearly. **26** Then Jesus sent him to his house, saying, "Don't even go into the village."

I. TRANSFIGURATION AND LACK OF FAITH

27 [l] Then Jesus and his disciples went out to the villages of Caesarea Philippi, and on the way he asked his disciples, "Who do people say I am?" **28** So they told him, "[Some say,] 'John the Baptist,' and others, 'Elijah,' while others say, 'One of the prophets.'" **29** He asked them, "But *you* — who do *you* say I am?" In answer Peter said to him, "You're the Messiah!" **30** Then Jesus commanded them not to tell anyone about him.

31 [m] Then he began to teach them that the Son of Man had to suffer greatly and be rejected by the elders and the chief priests and the scribes and be put to death and rise after three days, **32** and he said this openly. Peter took him aside and began to remonstrate with him, **33** but when Jesus turned and saw his disciples he rebuked Peter and said, "Get behind me, Satan — you're not thinking the thoughts of God but of men!" **34** Then he called the crowd to him, along with his disciples, and said to them,

---

[l] Mt 16:13-20; Lk 9:18-21. [m] Mt 16:13-20; Lk 9:22-27.

8:18   Jr 5:21.

"If anyone would come after me,
    let him deny himself
And take up his cross
    and follow me.
35 For whoever would save his life
    will lose it,
And whoever loses his life for the sake
        of the good news
    will save it.
36 For what good does it do a man to gain
        the whole world
    yet forfeit his life?
37 For what would a man give
    in exchange for his life?

38 Anyone in this adulterous and sinful generation
        who is ashamed of me and my words,
Of him will the Son of Man also be ashamed
        when he comes in the glory of his Father
            with the holy angels."

9 1 And he said to them, "Amen, I say to you, there are some who are standing here who will not taste death until they see the Kingdom of God has come with power."

2 [n] Six days later Jesus took Peter and James and John along and led them up a high mountain all alone. He was transformed in front of them 3 and his clothes became an utterly glistening white, so white that no one on earth could bleach them that way. 4 Elijah appeared to them along with Moses, and they were talking together with Jesus. 5 So in response Peter said to Jesus, "Rabbi, it's good for us to be here; let's put up three dwellings, one for you, one for Moses, and one for Elijah." 6 For he didn't know what to say — they were terrified. 7 Then a cloud arose overshadowing them, and a voice came out of the cloud, "This is My

---

[n] Mt 17:1-13; Lk 9:28-36.

9:5   "Dwellings." This Greek word also means "tents," but was applied to the booths which the Jews constructed during the Feast of Tabernacles; they were meant to recall the way the Israelites lived during the Exodus.
9:7   Ex 40:34-35; 1 K 8:10.

Beloved Son, hear him!" **8** And suddenly as they looked around they no longer saw anyone but Jesus alone with them.

9 As they were descending the mountain he commanded them not to tell anyone what they'd seen until the Son of Man had risen from the dead. **10** So they kept what he'd said to themselves, arguing about what it meant to rise from the dead. **11** But they questioned him and said, "Why do the scribes say that Elijah must come first?" **12** But he said to them, "Elijah *will* come first and restore all things, yet how can it be written of the Son of Man that he'll suffer greatly and be rejected? **13** On the contrary, I say to you that Elijah *has* come, and they did whatever they wanted with him, just as it's written of him."

14 ° As they were coming toward the disciples they saw a large crowd around them and scribes arguing with them. **15** When they saw him the whole crowd was greatly surprised and at once ran up and greeted him. **16** And he asked them, "What are you arguing about with them?" **17** One of the crowd answered, "Teacher, I brought my son to you because he has a dumb spirit; **18** whenever it seizes him it throws him to the ground and he foams at the mouth and grinds his teeth and becomes stiff, and I told your disciples to drive it out but they couldn't." **19** But in answer to them he said,

> "O unbelieving generation!
> How long will I be with you?
> How long will I put up with you?

Bring him to me!" **20** So they brought him to Jesus, and when the spirit saw him it at once threw the boy into convulsions, and he fell down and kept rolling around, foaming at the mouth. **21** Jesus asked his father, "How long has it been like this for him?" "From childhood," he said, **22** "and it's often thrown him both into fire and into water in order to kill him, but if you can do anything, help us and take pity on us." **23** Jesus said to him, "'*If* you can?' — all things are possible for the believer!" **24** The father of the child cried out at once and said, "I believe; help my unbelief!" **25** When Jesus saw that a crowd was quickly rushing over he rebuked the unclean spirit and said to it, "Deaf and

---

° Mt 17:14-20; Lk 9:37-43.

9:11-13 Ml 3:23-24 (Ml 4:5-6). Jesus' words are a condemnation of Israel, for instead of repenting before the day of the Lord, John's call was not heeded, and now the day of the Lord is upon them in Jesus' ministry. Having failed to listen to John, Israel will, tragically, kill its Messiah.

dumb spirit, I command you, come out of him and may you go into him no more!" **26** And after crying out and convulsing violently it went out, and it was as if he were dead, leading many to say that he *had* died. **27** But Jesus took hold of his hand and roused him and he got up. **28** When he entered the house his disciples asked him privately, "Why couldn't *we* drive it out?" **29** And he said to them, "This kind can't be driven out by anything but prayer."

J. TRUE AUTHORITY

30 P After leaving there they went through Galilee, and he didn't want anyone to know **31** because he was teaching his disciples and telling them, "The Son of Man will be given over into the hands of men. They'll put him to death, and when he's been killed, after three days he'll rise." **32** But they couldn't understand what he meant and were afraid to ask him.

33 q Then they came to Capharnaum. When they were inside the house he asked them, "What were you arguing about on the way?" **34** But they were silent, because on the way they'd been arguing among themselves about who was the greatest. **35** He sat down and called the Twelve and said to them, "If anyone wishes to be first, he must be the last of all and the servant of all." **36** Then he took a child and stood it before them, and he put his arms around it and said to them,

37   "Whoever receives one such child in my name
              receives me;
        And whoever receives me,
              receives not me but the One who sent me."

38 r John said to him, "Teacher, we saw someone driving out demons in your name and we tried to stop him, because he wasn't following us." **39** But Jesus said, "Don't stop him — no one who does a mighty work in my name will be able to speak ill of me soon afterwards, **40** for whoever's not against us is for us. **41** Whoever gives you a cup of water in my name because you're of the Messiah, amen, I say to you, he will not lose his reward."

P Mt 17:22-23; Lk Lk 9:43-45. q Mt 18:1-5; Lk 9:46-48. r Lk 9:49-50.

---

42 ˢ "But whoever causes one of the least of these believers to sin, it'd be better for him if a donkey's millstone were tied around his neck and he were thrown into the sea.

43 If your hand causes you to sin,
    cut it off!
It's better for you to enter that life a cripple,
    than to go off with two hands to Gehenna,
        to the unquenchable fire. **[44]**
45 If your foot causes you to sin,
    cut it off!
It's better for you to enter that life lame,
    than to be thrown with two feet into Gehenna. **[46]**
47 If your eye causes you to sin,
    pull it out!
It's better for you to enter the Kingdom of God
      one-eyed,
    than to have two eyes and be thrown into Gehenna,
48 Where **Their worm does not die,**
    and the fire is not extinguished,
49 For each will be salted with fire.
50 Salt is good, but if the salt becomes unsalty,
    how will you season it?
Have salt within yourselves
    and be at peace with one another!"

K. OBSTACLES TO FAITH

10 **1** ᵗ When he went up from there he came to the region of Judea [and] beyond the Jordan. Once again crowds gathered around him, and again, as was his custom, he taught them. **2** Then the Pharisees came forward and asked him if it's lawful for a man to put his wife away,

---

ˢ Mt 18:6-9; Lk 17:1-2. ᵗ Mt 19:1-12.

9:43-45 "That life," i.e., the life of the Kingdom, as is made explicit in v. 47.
9:44 The best manuscript tradition omits this verse: "Where their worm doesn't die and the fire is not extinguished."
9:46 The best manuscript tradition omits this verse: "Where their worm doesn't die and the fire is not extinguished."
9:48 Is 66:24.

testing him. **3** In answer he said to them, "What did Moses command you?" **4** They said, "Moses permitted a bill of divorce to be written and to put her away." **5** Jesus said to them, "He wrote that commandment for you because of the hardness of your heart. **6** But from the beginning of creation

> **he made them male and female; 7 for this reason**
> **a man shall leave his father and mother and be united**
> **with his wife 8 and the two shall become one flesh.**

So, then, they're no longer two but one flesh. **9** Therefore,

> What God has joined together,
> Let man not separate."

10 In the house the disciples asked him about this again. **11** And he said to them, "Whoever puts his wife away and marries another commits adultery against her, **12** and if she, after putting her husband away, should marry another, *she* commits adultery."

13 ᵘ People were bringing children to him for him to touch, but the disciples rebuked them. **14** When Jesus saw this he became indignant and said to them, "Let the children come to me! Don't stop them! For of such as these is the Kingdom of God! **15** Amen, I say to you, whoever doesn't accept the Kingdom of God like a child shall not enter it!" **16** Then he put his arms around them and blessed them, laying his hands upon them.

17 ᵛ As he was setting out on the road a man ran up and knelt before him. "Good Teacher," he asked, "what should I do to gain eternal life?" **18** But Jesus said to him, "Why do you call me good? No one is good but God alone! **19** You know the commandments,

> **You shall not murder, you shall not commit**
> **adultery, you shall not steal, do not bear**
> **false witness, do not defraud, honor your**
> **father and mother."**

20 But he said to him, "Teacher, I've obeyed all these from my youth." **21** As Jesus gazed upon him he was moved with love for him and said,

---

ᵘ Mt 19:13-15; Lk 18:15-17. ᵛ Mt 19:16-30; Lk 18:18-30.

10:6   Gn 1:27.
10:7-8   Gn 2:24.
10:19   Ex 20:12-16.

"One thing is left for you; go sell what you have and give to the poor and you'll have treasure in Heaven, and come follow me." **22** But he was shocked by what Jesus had said and went off saddened, because he had many properties.

23 Then Jesus looked around and said to his disciples, "How hard it will be for those with wealth to enter the Kingdom of God!" **24** Now his disciples were astonished at his words. But Jesus, in answer, again said to them, "My children, how hard it is to come into the Kingdom of God; **25** it's easier for a camel to go through a needle's eye than for a rich man to go into the Kingdom of God." **26** They were even more amazed and said to each other, "Then who can be saved?" **27** Jesus gazed at them and said,

> "For men it's impossible,
> But not for God;
> All things are possible for God."

28 Peter spoke up and said, "You see we've left everything and followed you." **29** Jesus said to him, "Amen, I say to you, there's no one who has left his house or brothers or sisters or mother or father or children or fields for my sake and for the sake of the good news **30** who will not receive now, in this time, a hundredfold in houses and brothers and sisters and mothers and fields along with persecution, and in the coming age, life eternal.

31   But many who are first will be last,
        and the last, first."

L. TRUE AUTHORITY AND SPIRITUAL BLINDNESS

32 ᵂ Now they were on the road going up to Jerusalem and Jesus was leading them, and they were amazed, but those following were afraid. Once again he took the Twelve and began to tell them the things that were going to happen to him. **33** "Behold, we're going up to Jerusalem, and the Son of Man will be handed over to the chief priests and the scribes. They'll condemn him to death and hand him over to

---

ᵂ Mt 20:17-19; Lk 18:31-34.

the Gentiles; **34** they'll mock him and spit on him and scourge him and kill him, and after three days he'll rise."

35 ˣ Then James and John, the sons of Zebedee, approached him and said to him, "Teacher, we want you to do for us whatever we ask of you." **36** But he said to them, "What do you want me to do for you?" **37** They said to him, "Grant us that we may sit, one at your right hand and one at your left hand, in your glory." **38** But Jesus said to them, "You don't know what you're asking for!

> Can you drink the cup I am drinking,
> Or be baptized with the baptism with which
> I am being baptized?"

39 So they said to him, "We can." But Jesus said to them,

> "The cup I am drinking,
> *you* will drink,
> And with the baptism with which
> I am being baptized,
> *you* will be baptized,
> **40** But sitting at my right hand or left is not
> mine to give —
> it's for those for whom it's been prepared."

41 When the other ten heard about this they became indignant at James and John. **42** So Jesus called them together and said to them, "You know that

> Those considered rulers among the Gentiles
> lord it over them,
> And their leaders exercise authority over them.

43 But it won't be like that among you; instead,

> Whoever would be great among you,
> let him be your servant,
> **44** And whoever would be first among you,
> let him be the slave of all;
> **45** For even the Son of Man came, not to be served,
> but to serve,
> and to give his life as a ransom for many."

ˣ Mt 20:20-28.

46 y Then they came to Jericho. When he was leaving Jericho, with both his disciples and a considerable crowd, blind Bartimaeus — the son of Timaeus — was sitting by the road, begging. **47** And when he heard that it was Jesus of Nazareth he began to cry out, "Jesus, Son of David, have mercy on me!" **48** Many people were telling him to be quiet, but he cried out all the more, "Son of David, have mercy on me!" **49** Jesus stopped and said, "Call him!" They called the blind man and said to him, "Take courage! Get up! He's calling you!" **50** So he threw off his cloak, jumped up, and came to Jesus. **51** And in answer to him Jesus said, "What do you want me to do for you?" The blind man said to him, "Rabbi, I want to see again!" **52** Jesus said to him, "Go your way, your faith has saved you!" At once he regained his sight and followed him on the road.

M. JESUS' MINISTRY IN JERUSALEM

11 **1** z When they drew near to Jerusalem, to Bethphage and Bethany near the Mount of Olives, he sent two of his disciples **2** and told them, "Go into the village opposite you, and immediately upon entering it you'll find a colt tied up, which no one has ever sat on before; untie it and bring it. **3** And if anyone says to you, 'Why are you doing that?' say, 'The Lord has need of it and will send it back here again at once!'" **4** They went off and found the colt tied by the door out on the street, and they untied it. **5** Some of those standing there said to them, "What are you doing, untying the colt?" **6** They told them just what Jesus had said, and they let them go. **7** So they took the colt to Jesus and threw their cloaks over it for him to sit on. **8** Many people spread their

---

y Mt 20:29-34; Lk 18:35-43. z Mt 21:1-11; Lk 19:28-40; Jn 12:12-19.

10:45 Is 53:11-12.

11:1 Beginning with Jesus' entry into Jerusalem the fulfillment of Jesus' mission moves inexorably to its climax. As seen through the eyes of faith, all these events are "in accordance with the scriptures," and the account is punctuated with frequent references to scripture in order to underline this. All Jesus' words and actions are now seen in their full eschatological significance: the Kingdom has come and, following the Lord's atoning death, it will be proclaimed to all nations.

11:7 Significantly, the colt is the mount of the Prince of Peace *for all nations* at Zc 9:9. Jesus graphically indicates in his triumphal entry to the Holy City of the Jews that his mission is to all nations.

cloaks on the road, while others spread leafy branches cut from the fields. **9** Both those going ahead and those following kept shouting,

> "Hosanna!
> Blessed is he who comes in the name of the Lord!
> **10**   Blessed is the coming Kingdom of our father David!
> Hosanna in the highest!"

11 When he came into Jerusalem he went to the Temple and, after looking around at everything, since it was the evening hour he went out to Bethany with the Twelve.

12 [a] The next day as they were leaving Bethany Jesus was hungry. **13** And seeing from a distance a fig tree which had leaves on it, he went to see if he could find anything to eat, but when he came up to it he found it had nothing but leaves, because it wasn't the season for figs. **14** And in response he said to it, "May no one ever eat fruit from you ever again!" And his disciples heard it.

15 [b] When they came to Jerusalem he went into the Temple and began to drive out those who were selling and buying in the Temple. He overturned the tables of the moneychangers and the seats of those who sold the doves, **16** and he didn't let anyone carry anything through the Temple. **17** And he taught and said to them, "Is it not written,

> **My house shall be called a house of prayer**
> **for all the nations,**
> But you have made it a **robbers' den!**"

18 When the chief priests and scribes heard this they began to consider how they could do away with him, for they were afraid of him because all the people were astonished at his teaching. **19** And in the evening Jesus and his disciples would go away outside the city.

20 [c] As they were passing by early one morning they saw the fig tree shrivelled up from its roots. **21** Peter remembered and said to him, "Rabbi! Look! The fig tree you cursed has shrivelled up!" **22** In answer

---

a Mt 21:18-19. b Mt 21:12-17; Lk 19:45-48; Jn 2:13-22. c Mt 21:20-22.

11:15-17   The part of the Temple where this took place was the Court of the Gentiles and once again, this time verbally, Jesus lets it be clearly known that his is a mission to all nations. In quoting scripture Jesus combines Is 56:7 and Jr 7:11.

The basis for v. 16 is the Torah prohibition against using the Temple area as a short cut, and Jesus here insists on enforcement of the Torah.

Jesus said to them, "If you have faith in God, **23** amen, I say to you, whoever says to this mountain, 'Be taken away and thrown into the sea!' and doesn't doubt in his heart but believes that what he says will happen, it will come to be for him. **24** Therefore I say to you, pray for and ask for all things, believe that you've received it and it will be yours. **25** And whenever you stand in prayer, forgive whatever you have against anyone so that your Father in Heaven will also forgive *you* your offenses." **[26]**

N. CONFLICT WITH THE LEADERS OF ISRAEL

27 ^d They came to Jerusalem again, and as he was walking about in the Temple the chief priests and scribes and the elders came up to him **28** and said, "By what authority do you do these things? Who gave you the authority to do these things?" **29** But Jesus said to them, "I'll ask *you* one question; answer me and I'll tell you by what authority I do these things — **30** John's baptism, was it from Heaven or from men? Answer me!" **31** They began to argue among themselves, saying, "If we say, 'From Heaven,' he'll say, 'Then why didn't you believe him?' **32** but can we say, 'From men'?" — they were afraid of the people because they all held that John had, indeed, been a prophet. **33** So in answer to Jesus they said, "We don't know." And Jesus said to them, "Nor will I tell you by what authority I do these things."

12 **1** ^e Then he began to speak to them in parables. "A man planted a vineyard, and he placed a hedge around it, dug a trough for the wine press, and built a tower. Then he let it out to vinedressers and went off on a journey. **2** When the proper time came he sent a slave to the vinedressers so he could take some of the fruits of the vineyard, **3** but they took him and beat him and sent him away empty-handed. **4** Again he sent another slave to them, and they beat that one about the head and treated him shamefully. **5** He sent another, and they killed that one. And he sent many others, some of whom were beaten while

---

^d Mt 21:23-27; Lk 20:1-8. ^e Mt 21:33-46; Lk 20:9-19.

11:26   Some manuscript traditions include v. 26 here: "But if *you* don't forgive, neither will your Father in Heaven forgive you *your* trespasses."

12:1   Cf. Is 5:1-2.

others were killed. **6** He still had one, a beloved son; he sent him to them last, saying, 'They'll feel shame before my son.' **7** But these vinedressers said to each other, 'This is the heir; come on, let's kill him and the inheritance will be ours!' **8** So they took and killed him and threw him outside the vineyard. **9** What, then, will the lord of the vineyard do? He'll come and do away with the vinedressers and give the vineyard to others. **10** Haven't you read this passage?

> **The stone which the builders rejected**
> **has become the cornerstone;**
> **11   Through the Lord has this been done**
> **and it is wonderful in our eyes."**

12 They wanted to seize him but they were afraid of the people, because they knew he'd spoken the parable against them. So they left him and went off.

O. TRUE TORAH AND TRUE AUTHORITY

13 [f] Next they sent some of the Pharisees and Herodians to him to trap him in speech. **14** They came and said to him, "Teacher, we know that you're truthful and are influenced by no one, for you don't consider the person but truly teach the way of God; is it lawful to pay the tax to Caesar or not? Should we pay or should we not pay?" **15** But he realized their hypocrisy and said to them, "Why are you testing me? Bring me a *denarius* so I can look at it." **16** So they brought one. Then he said to them, "Whose image is this, and whose inscription?" "Caesar's," they said. **17** Then Jesus said,

> "Render to Caesar the things that are Caesar's,
>   and to God the things that are God's."

And they were amazed at him.

18 [g] Then the Sadducees came to him — those who say there's no resurrection — and they questioned him and said, **19** "Teacher, Moses

---

[f] Mt 22:15-22; Lk 20:20-26.   [g] Mt 22:23-33; Lk 20:27-40.

12:10-11   Ps 118:22-23.
12:19   Dt 25:5.

wrote for us that if a man's brother should die and leave a wife behind but not leave a child, the brother should take his wife and raise up offspring for his brother. **20** There were seven brothers, and the first took a wife and he died without offspring; **21** and the second took her and died without leaving offspring, and the third likewise; **22** and the seven left no offspring. Last of all the woman died, too. **23** When they rise at the resurrection whose wife will she be? — all seven brothers had her as wife." **24** Jesus said to them, "Isn't this the reason you go astray, that you understand neither the scriptures nor the power of God? **25** For when you rise from the dead you neither marry nor are given in marriage, but are like the angels in Heaven. **26** But as for the dead rising, haven't you read in the scroll of Moses, at the passage about the thorn bush, how God spoke to him, and said,

> **I am the God of Abraham and the God**
> **of Isaac and the God of Jacob?**

27 [h] He's not God of the dead but of the living; you've gone seriously astray."

28 [i] One of the scribes who had heard them arguing came forward when he saw that Jesus had answered them well and asked him, "What commandment is the first of all?" **29** Jesus answered, "The first is,

> **Hear, O Israel, the Lord your God is one,**
> **30 and you shall love the Lord your God**
> **with your whole heart and with your whole**
> **soul** and with all your understanding, **and**
> **with your whole strength.**

31 This is the second,

> **You shall love your neighbor as yourself.**

There is no other commandment greater than these." **32** And the scribe said to him, "Indeed, Teacher, you have spoken truly that

> **There is One and there is no other beside Him,**

---

h Mt 22:34-40; Lk 1:25-28. i Mt 22:41-46; Lk 20:41-44.

12:26   Ex 3:6, 15, 16.
12:29-30 Dt 6:4-5.
12:31   Lv 19:18.
12:32   Dt 4:35.

33 and,

> **Love Him with your whole heart and your**
> **whole mind and your whole strength,**

and,

> **Love your neighbor as yourself,**

are greater than all the burnt offerings and sacrifices." **34** Jesus, seeing that he had answered wisely, said to him, "You're not far from the Kingdom of God." And no one dared to question him any longer.

35 And in response, while teaching in the Temple, Jesus said, "Why do the scribes say that the Messiah is the son of David? **36** David himself says in the Holy Spirit,

> **The Lord said to my lord,**
> **'Sit at My right hand**
> **till I put your enemies under your feet.'**

37 David himself calls him 'lord,' so how can he be his son?" And a large crowd listened to him eagerly.

38 [j] And in his teaching he said,

> "Beware of the scribes,
> Who like walking about in long robes
> and greetings in the marketplaces,
> **39** And seats of honor in the synagogues
> and places of honor at the banquets;
> Eating up the houses of widows
> and saying long prayers as a pretense —
> These will receive the greater condemnation!"

41 [k] Then he took a seat opposite the offering box and watched the crowd throw money into the offering box. Many rich people threw in a great deal, **42** but when one poor widow came she threw in two small coppers, that is, about a penny. **43** He called his disciples together and said to them, "Amen, I say to you, this poor widow threw in more than

---

[j] Mt 23:1-36; Lk 20:45-47. [k] Lk 21:1-4.

12:33   Dt 6:5; Lv 19:18.
12:36   Ps 110:1.
12:38-40 The tendency for Pharisaism to degenerate into formalism and hypocrisy was well recognized in ancient times, cf. 7:5-13 and the note at Mt 23:1ff.

all the others who threw money into the offering box — **44** they all threw in from their abundance, but she from her want threw in all that she had, her whole livelihood."

P. PROPHECIES OF THE END TIME

13 **1**[1] When he was coming out of the Temple one of his disciples said to him, "Teacher, look at how wonderful the stones and the buildings are!" **2** Jesus said to him, "Do you see these great buildings? Not a stone will be left here upon a stone which will not be torn down."

3 [m] While he was sitting on the Mount of Olives, opposite the Temple, Peter and James and John and Andrew questioned him privately. **4** "Tell us when these things will happen, and what the sign will be that all these things are about to be fulfilled." **5** So Jesus spoke out and told them, "See that no one leads you astray; **6** many will come in my name saying, '*I'm* the one,' and they'll lead many astray. **7** But when you hear of wars and rumors of wars, don't be alarmed; this must happen, but it's not yet the end.

> **8**   For nation shall rise against nation,
> and kingdom against kingdom,
> There will be earthquakes in various places,
> there will be famines;

these things are the beginning of the birth pains. **9** But see to yourselves;

> They will hand you over to councils,
> and you'll be beaten in synagogues,
> Before rulers and kings
> you'll stand firm for my sake,
> as a witness to them.
> **10** But first to all the nations
> the good news must be proclaimed.
> **11** And when they lead you
> to hand you over,
> Don't worry ahead of time

---

[1] Mt 24:1-2; Lk 21:5-6. [m] Mt 24:3-14; Lk 21:7-19.

what you will say;
But whatever is given you in that hour,
    say it;
For it will not be you speaking,
    but the Holy Spirit.

12 Brother will hand brother over to death,
    and father, child,
Children will rebel against parents,
    and put them to death;

13 And you'll be hated by all
    because of my name.
But whoever holds out to the end,
    he shall be saved."

14 [n] "But when you see **the Abomination of Desolation** standing where he should not be — let the reader understand — then let those in Judea flee to the mountains, **15** let the man on his housetop not descend nor go in to take anything from his house, **16** and let the man in his field not turn back to get his cloak. **17** But woe to women who are with child and to those who are nursing in those days! **18** Pray that it won't happen in winter, **19** for in those days there will be **suffering such as has not been** since the beginning of the creation God created **up till now,** and *will* not be. **20** And if the Lord had not shortened those days no fleshly creature would be saved, but for the sake of those whom He has chosen He did shorten those days. **21** And then, if anyone says, 'Look, here's the Messiah!' or 'Look there!' don't believe it. **22** For false messiahs and false prophets will rise up and will produce signs and wonders to lead astray, if possible, the chosen ones. **23** But see to yourselves; I've told you everything ahead of time."

24 [o] "But in those days,
    after that suffering,
The sun will be darkened
and the moon will not give its light,

---

[n] Mt 24:15-28; Lk 21:20-24. [o] Mt 24:29-31; Lk 21:25-28.

13:14   Dn 9:27. "Abomination of Desolation." This phrase from Daniel envisions a Gentile, here a Roman, presence in the Temple, thus desecrating it.

13:19   Dn 12:1.

13:24-25 Is 13:10, 34:4, Ezk 32:7-8.

25 **And the stars will be falling** from the heavens,
    and the powers in the heavens
        will be shaken.
26 Then they'll see **the Son of Man**
    coming on clouds with great power
        and glory.
27 And then he'll send the angels
    and will gather the chosen
        from the four winds,
From the ends of earth
    to the ends of the heavens."

28 [P] "So learn the parable from the fig tree. As soon as its branch becomes tender and is putting out leaves, you know that summer is near. **29** So, too, when you see these things happening, you'll know that he's near, at the very gates. **30** Amen, I say to you, this generation will not pass away until all these things come to pass.

31 The heavens and the earth will pass away,
    But my words will not pass away."

32 [q] "But as for that day or hour, no one knows — not the angels in Heaven nor the Son, but only the Father. **33** See that you're watchful, for you don't know when the appointed time is. **34** It's like a man leaving on a journey. When he left his household he gave authority to his servants — each received a task — and ordered the doorkeeper to stay awake. **35** So stay awake, for you don't know when the lord of the household is coming, whether in the evening or in the middle of the night or at cock crow or in the morning. **36** You don't want him to come suddenly and find you sleeping! **37** But what I say to you I say to all — stay awake!"

Q. THE PASSION

14 **1** [r] Now the Passover and feast of Unleavened Bread was in two days and the chief priests and scribes were considering how

---

[p] Mt 24:32-35; Lk 21:29-33.   [q] Mt 24:36-44.   [r] Mt 26:1-5; Lk 22:1-2; Jn 11:45-53.

13:26   Dn 7:13-14.

14:1   The eight day period during which unleavened bread was eaten was closely linked to the Passover, but had its origins in a festival marking the beginning of the barley harvest.

they could seize Jesus on a pretext and kill him, **2** for they said, "If we wait till the festival there might be an outcry among the people."

3 ˢ While he was at Bethany, reclining at table in Simon the leper's house, a woman came with an alabaster jar of pure oil of nard, of great value; after breaking the alabaster jar she poured it over his head. **4** But there were some there who were indignant and said to themselves, "To what purpose was this waste of oil? **5** It could have been sold for more than three hundred *denarii* and given to the poor," and they spoke harshly to her. **6** But Jesus said, "Let her be! Why are you bothering her? She's done a beautiful thing for me.

7   For the poor you always have with you —

and whenever you want you can do good to them,

but me you will not always have.

8 She's done what she could; she's anointed my body in advance in preparation for burial. **9** Amen, I say to you, wherever the good news is proclaimed in all the world, what she did will also be told in memory of her."

10 ᵗ Then Judas Iscariot, one of the Twelve, went off to the chief priests in order to hand him over to them. **11** When they heard this they were overjoyed and promised to give him silver money, and he began to consider when the best time to hand Jesus over would be.

12 ᵘ On the first day of the Unleavened Bread, when they sacrificed the Passover lamb, his disciples said to him, "Where do you want us to go to prepare for you to eat the Passover?" **13** He sent two of his disciples and told them, "Go into the city, and a man carrying a clay jar of water will meet you; follow him, **14** and wherever he goes in, say to the householder, 'The Teacher says, "Where is my room where I'll eat the Passover with my disciples?"' **15** And he'll show you a large, furnished, upstairs room which has been prepared; make ready for us there." **16** So the disciples went away and came to the city and found it just as he told them, and they prepared the Passover.

ˢ Mt 26:6-13; Jn 12:1-8.   ᵗ Mt 26:14-16; Lk 22:3-6.   ᵘ Mt 26:17-25; Lk 22:7-14, 21-33; Jn 13:21-30.

14:2   Literally, "Not during the festival."

14:5   Since a *denarius* was equal to a laborer's daily wage, 300 *denarii* was a truly large amount of money.

17 When evening had come he came with the Twelve. **18** And while they were reclining and were eating, Jesus said, "Amen, I say to you, one of you will hand me over, **one eating with me**." **19** They became distressed and asked him, one by one, "Surely not me?" **20** but he said to them, "One of the Twelve, one who has dipped into the dish with me. **21** Because the Son of Man is going as it is written about him, but woe to that man by whom the Son of Man is handed over; it would be better for him if that man had not been born."

22 ᵛ And while they were eating he took bread, blessed it, broke it, gave it to them and said, "Take it; this is my body." **23** And taking the cup, he blessed it and gave it to them and they all drank from it. **24** Then he said to them, "This is my blood of the covenant, which will be poured out for many. **25** Amen, I say to you, I will not drink again of the fruit of the vine until that day when I drink it new in the Kingdom of God." **26** And after singing a hymn they went out to the Mount of Olives.

27 ʷ Then Jesus said to them, "All of you will lose your faith, because it is written,

> **I will strike the shepherd**
> **and the sheep will be scattered,**

28 but after I rise I'll go ahead of you into Galilee." **29** But Peter said to him, "Even if they all lose their faith, *I* won't!" **30** Jesus said to him, "Amen, I say to you, today, this very night, before the rooster crows twice, you'll deny me three times." **31** But Peter kept saying, "Even if it comes to dying with you, I won't deny you." And they all said the same, too.

32 ˣ When they came to a place named Gethsemane he said to his disciples, "Sit here while I pray." **33** He took Peter and James and John along with him and he became very distressed and troubled, **34** and he said to them, "My soul is greatly distressed, to the point of death; stay here and keep watch." **35** Then he went ahead a little, fell on the ground, and prayed that, if it were possible, this moment might pass away from him, **36** and he said, "*Abba*, Father, all things are possible for you; take this cup from me, but not what I wish, but what you do." **37** When he

---

ᵛ Mt 26:26-30; Lk 22:15-20. ʷ Mt 26:31-35; Lk 22:31-34; Jn 13:36-38. ˣ Mt 26:36-46; Lk 22:39-46.

14:18   Ps 41:9.
14:27   Zc 13:7.

came back he found them sleeping, and he said to Peter, "Simon, are you sleeping? Couldn't you stay awake for one hour? **38** Stay awake and pray that you won't come to the test,

> For the spirit is willing,
> But the flesh is weak."

39 Then he went off and prayed again, saying the same words. **40** When he came again he found them sleeping, for their eyes were very heavy, and they didn't know what to answer him. **41** He came the third time and said to them, "Are you going to keep sleeping and resting? It's settled; the hour has come; behold, the Son of Man will be handed over into the hands of sinners. **42** Get up! Let's be going! Behold, the one who will hand me over has come."

43 [y] And right then, while he was still speaking, Judas, one of the Twelve, arrived, and with him a crowd with swords and clubs from the chief priests and the scribes and the elders. **44** Now, the one handing him over had given them a sign, saying, "Whoever I kiss is the one; seize him and lead him away under guard." **45** Judas came right up to him and said, "Rabbi!" and kissed him. **46** So they laid hands on him and seized him. **47** Then one of those present drew his sword, struck the high priest's slave, and cut off his ear. **48** In answer Jesus said to them, "You came out with swords and clubs to seize me, as if you were after a robber? **49** I was among you daily, teaching in the Temple, yet you didn't seize me; but let the scriptures be fulfilled." **50** Then they all forsook him and fled.

51 A certain young man was following, wearing a linen cloth on his bare body, and they seized him, **52** but he left the linen behind and fled naked.

53 [z] So they led Jesus off to the high priest, and all the chief priests and elders and scribes came together. **54** Peter had followed him at a distance right inside into the courtyard of the high priest and was sitting among the Temple attendants, warming himself at the fire. **55** Now the chief priests and the whole Sanhedrin were seeking testimony against Jesus in order to put him to death, yet they found none; **56** although many gave false testimony against Jesus, the testimony was not the same. **57** Some had stood up and given false testimony against Jesus

---

[y] Mt 26:47-56; Lk 22:47-53; Jn 18:3-12. [z] Mt 26:57-68; Lk 22:54-55, 63-71; Jn 18:13-14, 19-24.

and said, **58** "We heard him saying, 'I'll tear down this sanctuary made by hands and in three days I'll build another not made by hands.'" **59** Yet their testimony wasn't the same in this, either. **60** Then the high priest stood up and questioned Jesus, saying, "You make no answer? Why are these men testifying against you?" **61** But he remained silent and made no answer. Again the high priest questioned him and said to him, "Are you the Messiah, the Son of the Blessed One?" **62** Then Jesus said, "I am, and

> **You will see the Son of Man**
> **seated at the right hand of Power**
> **and coming with the clouds of Heaven."**

63 At this the high priest tore his clothing and said, "What further need do we have for witnesses? **64** You heard the blasphemy! What's your opinion?" And they all judged him to be deserving of death. **65** Then some began to spit on him and cover his face and strike him, and to say, "Prophesy!" and the Temple attendants took him away, beating him as they went.

66 [a] While Peter was down in the courtyard one of the high priest's maidservants came, **67** and when she saw Peter warming himself she looked right at him and said, "You were with Jesus the Nazarene, too!" **68** But he denied it and said, "I neither know nor understand what you're saying!" And he went outside into the gateway and a rooster crowed. **69** When the maidservant saw him she again began to tell the bystanders, "This fellow's one of them!" **70** but he denied it again. After a little while the bystanders again said to Peter, "Surely you're one of them — you're a Galilean, too!" **71** And he put himself under a curse and swore an oath, "I don't know the man you're talking about!" **72** At that moment a cock crowed a second time. Then Peter remembered what had been said, how Jesus had told him, "Before a cock crows twice you'll deny me three times," and he stormed out weeping.

15 **1** [b] So early in the morning, when the chief priests had held a council with the elders and scribes and the whole Sanhedrin, they bound Jesus, sent him off, and handed him over to Pilate. **2** And Pilate asked him, "Are you the King of the Jews?" But in answer he said

---

[a] Mt 26:69-75; Lk 22:56-62; Jn 18:15-18, 25-27. [b] Mt 27:1-2, 11-14; Lk 23:1-5; Jn 18:28-38.

14:62   Dn 7:13.
14:65   "Beating him as they went." Literally, "with blows."

to him, "You say so." **3** And the chief priests kept making accusations against him. **4** But Pilate questioned him again and said, "Do you have no answer? Look how many accusations they're bringing against you!" **5** But Jesus made no further reply, to the amazement of Pilate.

6 ^c At the festival Pilate used to release to them any one prisoner they asked for. **7** Now there was a man called Barabbas who was imprisoned with the rebels who had committed murder in the revolt, **8** and when the crowd had grown it began to request [that he do] what he usually did. **9** But Pilate responded, "Do you want me to release to you the King of the Jews?" **10** for he was aware that the chief priests had handed Jesus over out of envy. **11** But the chief priests stirred up the crowd to get him to release Barabbas to them instead. **12** So in answer Pilate again said to them, "Then what shall I do with the King of the Jews?" **13** Again they cried out, "Crucify him!" **14** So Pilate said to them, "But what wrong has he done?" but they cried out all the more, "Crucify him!" **15** So Pilate, because he wanted to satisfy the crowd, released Barabbas to them, and after scourging Jesus he handed him over to be crucified.

16 ^d So the soldiers led him away inside the courtyard, that is, the praetorium, and called the whole cohort together. **17** They dressed him in a purple robe and put on him a crown of thorns they had woven, **18** and they began to greet him, "Hail, King of the Jews!" **19** and to hit his head with a reed, and they spat on him and knelt and worshipped him. **20** Then they stripped the purple robe off him, dressed him in his own clothes, and led him out to be crucified.

21 ^e They forced a passerby, one Simon of Cyrene, father of Alexander and Rufus, who was coming from the country, to take up his cross, **22** and they brought him to the place called *Golgotha*, which, translated, is, "the Place of the Skull." **23** They tried to give him wine mixed with myrrh, but he didn't take it. **24** Then they crucified him,

> and his **clothes were divided up,**
> **casting lots for them** to see
> who would take what.

---

^c Mt 27:15-26; Lk 23:13-25; Jn 18:39 - 19:16.   ^d Mt 27:27-31; Jn 19:2-3.   ^e Mt 27:32-44; Lk 23:26-43; Jn 19:17-27.

15:24   Ps 22:18.

25 Now it was the third hour when they crucified him. **26** The inscription of the charge against him was written, "The King of the Jews," **27** and they crucified two robbers with him, one on his right and one on his left. **[28] 29** The passersby blasphemed him, **shaking their heads** and saying, "Ha! You who would tear down the sanctuary and build it up in three days, **30** save yourself by coming down from the cross!" **31** The chief priests, likewise, made fun of him to each other to the scribes and said, "He saved others but can't save himself! **32** Let the Messiah, the King of Israel, come down now from the cross so we can see and believe!" Those crucified with him also derided him.

33 [f] Now when the sixth hour had come darkness came over the whole land until the ninth hour. **34** And at the ninth hour Jesus cried out with a loud voice, *"Eloi, Eloi, lema sabachthani?"* which, translated, is, **"My God, My God, why have You forsaken me?"** **35** Some of the bystanders heard it and said, "See? He's calling Elijah!" **36** But someone ran and, filling a sponge with sour wine, put it on a reed and gave it to him to drink, saying, "Let's see if Elijah is coming to take him down." **37** But Jesus let out a loud cry and died, **38** and the curtain of the sanctuary was torn in two from top to bottom. **39** Now when the centurion standing facing him saw that he'd died in this way he said, "Truly this man *was* the Son of God!" **40** There were also women there watching from a distance, among them Mary Magdalen and Mary mother of James the younger and Joses, Salome — **41** they had followed him when he was in Galilee and served him — and many other women who had come up with him to Jerusalem.

42 [g] Evening had now come. Since it was the Day of Preparation, that is, the day before the Sabbath, **43** Joseph of Arimathea, a respected Council member who himself was also awaiting the Kingdom of God, dared to go in to Pilate and ask for the body of Jesus. **44** But Pilate was amazed that he had already died, and he called in the centurion and asked if Jesus was already dead, **45** and after learning it from the

---

[f] Mt 27:45-46; Lk 23:44-49; Jn 19:28-30. [g] Mt 27:57-61; Lk 23:50-56; Jn 19:38-42.

15:28   The best manuscript tradition omits this verse: "And the scripture was fulfilled which says, **He was numbered among criminals.**" Is 53:12.

15:29   Ps 22:7.

15:34   Ps 22:1.

15:43   The bodies of executed criminals were not usually turned over for decent burial but were ignominiously disposed of in the Hinnom valley.

centurion he bestowed the corpse on Joseph. **46** So Joseph bought a linen shroud and took Jesus down, wrapped him in the linen shroud, and placed him in a tomb which had been hewn out of rock. Then he rolled a stone up against the door of the tomb. **47** But Mary Magdalen and Mary mother of Joses watched where he was laid.

R. THE RESURRECTION AND APPEARANCES OF JESUS

16 **1** [h] When the Sabbath was over Mary Magdalen and Mary the mother of James and Salome bought spices so they could go anoint him. **2** And very early in the morning of the first day of the week they came to the tomb when the sun had risen. **3** They were saying to each other, "Who will roll the stone away from the door of the tomb for us?" **4** but when they looked up they saw that the stone had been rolled away, for it was very large. **5** When they went into the tomb they saw a young man seated on the right hand side, dressed in a white robe, and they were astonished. **6** But he said to them, "Don't be alarmed; you're looking for Jesus the Nazarene who was crucified; he's risen, he's not here; look at the place where they laid him! **7** But go tell his disciples and Peter, 'He's going ahead of you into Galilee; you'll see him there just as he told you.'" **8** Then the women went out and fled the tomb, for trembling and amazement had seized them, and they said nothing to anyone because they were afraid.

9 [i] Now when he rose in the early morning of the first day after the Sabbath he appeared first to Mary Magdalen, from whom he had driven out seven demons. **10** She went to announce it to those who had been with him, who were mourning and weeping; **11** and when they heard that he was alive and had been seen by her they refused to believe.

12 [j] After this he appeared in a different form to two of them as they were walking into the countryside, **13** and when they went and told the rest they didn't believe them.

14 [k] But later he appeared to the Eleven themselves as they

---

[h] Mt 28:1-8; Lk 24:1-12; Jn 20:1-10. [i] Mt 28:9-10; Jn 20:11-18. [j] Lk 24:13-35. [k] Mt 28:16-20; Lk 24:36-49; Jn 20:19-23;

16:9-20   Some of the oldest manuscripts end the gospel at 16:8, while other manuscripts continue with 16:9-20. There is also a shorter ending attested to, which adds immediately after 16:8:

reclined at table and reproached them for their unbelief and hardness of heart, because they hadn't believed those who had seen him risen. **15** And he said to them, "Go into the whole world and proclaim the good news to all creation. **16** Whoever believes and is baptized will be saved, but whoever doesn't believe will be condemned. **17** But these signs will follow with those who believe — they'll drive out demons in my name, they'll speak in new tongues, **18** they'll pick up snakes in their hands, and if they drink poison it won't harm them; they'll lay their hands on the sick and they'll be well."

19 [1] So then the Lord, after speaking to them, was raised up to Heaven and took his seat at the right hand of God. **20** But they went out to proclaim the good news everywhere, the Lord working with them and confirming the word through the signs following upon it.

---

[1] Lk 24:50-53.

"And all these commands they told briefly to those around Peter. But after these things Jesus himself sent out through them, from the east until the west, the holy and undying message of eternal salvation. Amen."

THE GOSPEL ACCORDING TO
L U K E

INTRODUCTION TO LUKE

There is general agreement that Luke the physician, Paul's companion in Acts, was the author of the third Gospel. In contrast to the other evangelists, Luke had an excellent command of Greek. Whereas they usually confine themselves to simple constructions and reveal that Greek was an acquired language for them through their Semitic syntax and redundant use of certain phrases, Luke was clearly more at ease with Greek and had the ability to exploit far more of that language's potential. Nevertheless, Luke's Gospel also contains some of the most barbarous Greek in the Gospels, Greek which appears to be the most crudely literal translation of Semitic idioms. How are we to account for this?

The prologue to the Gospel clearly indicates that Luke was not an eyewitness of Jesus' ministry and that he relied upon a variety of sources in drawing up his account. It seems clear that some of these sources were influenced by an original Aramaic and many scholars believe that Luke felt compelled to adhere as strictly as possible to his sources out of respect for the tradition, in spite of his above average ability in Greek. On the other hand, many expressions are characteristic of Hebrew rather than Aramaic, as, for instance, his favorite introductory phrase: "And it happened..." For this reason many scholars have theorized that Luke, whose native language was Greek, deliberately imitated the translation Greek of the Greek Old Testament, the Septuagint, although he also improved on the style at times. Finally, many scholars are of the opinion that the Infancy Narratives may well be direct translations from a Semitic original, thus accounting for their strongly Semitic flavor.

In the prologue Luke states that his purpose in writing the Gospel is to assure Theophilus that the teaching he has received is, in fact, a reliable account of the meaning and message of Jesus. It would be wrong to assume from this, however, that Luke intended to write a critical biography. For one thing, Luke is noticeably lacking in geographical and chronological detail and, in the second place, although Luke is faithful to his sources and may at times place the sayings of Jesus in a more original context than Matthew, he also feels free to group stories from Jesus' ministry in a logical rather than a chronological manner. On the other hand, Luke does not impose an overall pattern on his sources. Instead, he basically follows the order of Mark, inserting other material where he deems it appropriate.

Luke shares many of the same concerns that we have already seen in Matthew and Mark but, in addition, there is an emphasis that is unique in degree to Luke alone. This is his emphasis on God's loving forgiveness and the need for self-renunciation on the part of disciples. In addition, in this Gospel we see Jesus, time after time, reaching out to and championing the weak, the outcast, and the underdog, challenging shallow prejudices and presuppositions. Luke clearly had a flair for storytelling and many of the best loved Gospel stories (the Prodigal Son, the Good Samaritan, the Sinful Woman, etc.) are found in his Gospel, precisely in the context of God's, and Jesus', mercy and loving forgiveness and radical openness to all sinners. As in Mark, however, the unifying theme is Jesus' mission to all nations and his rejection by his own people, whose truest hopes he had fulfilled.

A.   1:1-4   Prologue.

B.   1:5-80   The origins of the Baptist and Jesus; the fulfillment of Israel's hopes is imminent.

C.   2:1-52   Birth and early years of Jesus; Jesus to be a light to the Gentiles and glory to Israel.

D.   3:1-20   Ministry of the Baptist: the stage is set for Jesus.

E.   3:21-4:13   Beginning of Jesus' ministry: baptism and the descent of the Spirit, genealogy of Jesus, his temptation.

F.   4:14-9:50   Ministry in Galilee: teaching, healing, and mighty works.

G. 9:51-18:30   Jesus journeys toward Jerusalem, healing and teaching.

H. 18:31-21:38   Jesus begins his ascent: triumphant entry into Jerusalem, cleansing of the Temple, controversy with the Jewish authorities and teaching, prophecies concerning the destruction of the Temple, the end of the world, and coming of the Son of Man.

I. 22:1-23:49   Last Supper and Passion.

J. 23:50-24:53   Resurrection and appearances of Jesus, Ascension and mandate to teach all nations.

THE GOSPEL ACCORDING TO
L U K E

A. PROLOGUE

1 **1** Inasmuch as many others have undertaken to draw up an account of the events which have been accomplished among us — **2** just as those who were eyewitnesses and servants of the word from the beginning have handed them down to us — **3** it seemed proper that I, too, after carefully examining everything anew, should write you an orderly account, most excellent Theophilus, **4** so that you may recognize the certainty of the words concerning which you have been instructed.

B. ORIGINS OF THE BAPTIST AND JESUS

5 In the days of Herod, King of Judea, there was a priest named Zechariah from the division of Abijah, and he had a wife from among the daughters of Aaron whose name was Elizabeth. **6** They were both

---

1:2   "Servants of the word." Elsewhere, the word translated "servant" is translated "attendant." The exact meaning is, unfortunately, unclear. The word has two principal uses in the Gospels, in the context of contemporary Judaism: (1) It refers to members of the temple police force, and (2) it also refers to the synagogal official who had custody of the scriptures, cf. Lk 4:20. In both uses the idea of a custodian or guardian is present. Presumably the word had a similar meaning in the early Church, but whether such persons had custody of the Old Testament writings only or also of early Christian writings cannot be pinpointed, nor can the full extent of their duties. It is interesting to note that John Mark (probably the Evangelist Mark) accompanied Saul and Barnabas as their "attendant."

1:2   The expression "handed down" most probably refers to oral tradition, although it is entirely possible that by the time Luke began to compose his Gospel some of the early traditions had been committed to a written form.

1:5   So that all priests could participate in the Temple services in an orderly fashion, the Judaic priesthood was divided into twenty-four "divisions." Each division served in the Temple twice a year, for a week at a time.

righteous before God, blamelessly following all the commandments and regulations of the Lord 7 yet they had no child because Elizabeth was barren, and they were both on in years. 8 Now it happened that when he was doing his priestly service before God when his division was on duty, 9 according to the custom of the priestly office, he was chosen by lot to go into the sanctuary of the Lord to offer incense. 10 All the multitude of the people were outside praying at the hour of the incense offering 11 when an angel of the Lord appeared to him, standing to the right of the incense altar. 12 Zechariah was terrified when he saw him and fear fell upon him, 13 but the angel said to him,

> "Fear not, Zechariah —
>> your petition has been heard.
> Your wife Elizabeth will bear you a son,
>> and you shall name him John.

14 Joy and gladness will be yours,
>> and many will rejoice at his birth.

15 For he'll be great before the Lord
>> and shall drink neither wine nor strong drink.
> He'll be filled with the Holy Spirit
>> even from his mother's womb,

16 And he'll bring back many of the sons of Israel
>> to the Lord their God.

17 He'll go before Him
>> in the spirit and power of Elijah,
> **To bring back the hearts of fathers to the children**
>> and the rebellious to the wisdom of the upright,
> To make ready for the Lord
>> a people made perfect."

18 Zechariah said to the angel, "How can I be sure of this? — I'm elderly and my wife is advanced in years." 19 And in answer the angel said to him,

> "I am Gabriel
>> who stands before God,
> I was sent to speak to you
>> and bring you these good tidings,

1:7   "Years"; literally, "days." Cf. also 2:36.
1:17   Ml 3:23-24 (Ml 4:5-6).

20   Now, behold, you shall be silent
        and unable to speak until the day
           these things happen,
    Because you did not believe my words,
        which will be fulfilled in their proper time."

21 Meanwhile the people were waiting for Zechariah and wondering at how long he was staying in the sanctuary. **22** When he came out he was unable to speak to them and they realized that he'd seen a vision in the sanctuary, because he kept making signs to them but remained mute. **23** And it happened that when the days of his liturgical service were fulfilled he went off to his home. **24** Now after these days his wife Elizabeth became pregnant, and she secluded herself for five months, saying, **25** "Thus has the Lord dealt with me in the days he deigned to take away my disgrace before men."

26 Now in the sixth month the angel Gabriel was sent from God to a city of Galilee named Nazareth, **27** to a virgin who was betrothed to a man of the house of David named Joseph, and the virgin's name was Mary. **28** And when he came into her presence he said, "Hail, full of grace, the Lord is with you!" **29** She was perplexed by this saying and wondered what sort of greeting this could be. **30** Then the angel said to her,

    "Fear not, Mary —
        you have found grace before the Lord.
31   And, behold, you will conceive in your womb
        and will bear a son,
        and you shall name him Jesus.
32   He'll be great and will be called
        Son of the Most High,
        and the Lord God will give him the throne
           of his father, David.
33   He'll reign over the house of Jacob forever,
        and his Kingdom will have no end."

34 So Mary said to the angel, "How will this come about, since I do not know man?" **35** And in answer the angel said to her,

---

1:28 "Full of grace." This more traditional translation has been preferred as communicating the Greek more economically than such phrases as "highly favored one." The one Greek word carries the meaning: "You (woman) who have received and retained the favor of God freely given."

"The Holy Spirit will come upon you,
And the power of the Most High
　　will overshadow you;
Therefore, the holy child to be born
　　will be called Son of God.

36　　And, behold, your kinswoman Elizabeth, even she
　　　　conceived a son in her old age,
And this is the sixth month for her who was
　　called barren.

37　　For **nothing will be impossible for God**."

38 And Mary said,

"Behold, the handmaid of the Lord;
　　let it be done to me according to your word."

Then the angel went away from her.

39 Now in those days Mary set out and went with solicitude into the hill country to a city of Judah, 40 and when she came into the house of Zechariah she greeted Elizabeth.　41 And it happened that when Elizabeth heard Mary's greeting the baby leapt in her womb and Elizabeth was filled with the Holy Spirit, 42 and she exclaimed with a loud cry, "Blessed are you among women, and blessed is the fruit of your womb! 43 And how is it that the mother of my Lord should come to *me*? 44 For, behold, when the sound of your greeting came into my ears, the baby in my womb leapt with a great joy. 45 Blessed is she who believed that there would be a fulfillment of what was spoken to her by the Lord."

46 And Mary said,

"My soul gives praise to the Lord,
47　　　　and my spirit rejoices in God my Savior;
48　　Because He had regard for the lowliness
　　　　　　of His handmaid,
　　　　behold, henceforth all generations shall
　　　　　　call me blessed,

1:37　Gn 18:14.

1:42　The hymns which follow are replete with allusions to the Old Testament. Mary's hymn, the Magnificat, in particular shows a number of marked similarities to the hymn at 1 S 2:1-10.

1:48　1 S 1:11.

49	For the Mighty One has done great things for me,
	and holy is His name,
50	And His mercy is from generation to generation
	toward those who fear Him.
51	He has shown might with His arm,
	scattered the arrogant in the conceit
	of their heart,
52	He has pulled down the mighty from their thrones,
	and exalted the lowly,
53	The hungry He has filled with good things,
	and has sent the rich away empty.
54	He has come to the aid of His servant, Israel,
	mindful of His mercy,
55	Just as He promised our fathers,
	Abraham and his descendants forever."

56 Mary remained with her for three months and then returned to her home.

57 Now the time for Elizabeth to give birth was fulfilled, and she bore a son. **58** And when the neighbors and her relatives heard that the Lord had manifested His mercy to her they rejoiced for her. **59** And it happened that on the eighth day they went to circumcise the child, and they were going to call him by his father's name, Zechariah. **60** His mother answered, "No! He shall be called John, instead!" **61** And they said to her, "None of your relatives is called by that name!" **62** So they asked the father by signs what *he* wanted the child to be called. **63** And after asking for a writing tablet he wrote, "His name is John." And they were all amazed. **64** Then his mouth was immediately opened as well as his tongue, and he spoke, blessing God. **65** Fear came upon all their neighbors and in all the Judean hill country they discussed all these events, **66** and all those who heard kept it in their hearts and said, "What, then, will this child be?" For the hand of the Lord was with him as well.

67 And his father Zechariah was filled with the Holy Spirit and prophesied, saying,

| 68 | "Blessed be the Lord God of Israel— |
| | He has visited and set His people free, |

1:68 Ps 41:13.

145

69 And He has raised up a horn of salvation for us
in the house of His servant David,

70 Just as He promised through the mouths of His
holy prophets from of old:

71 to save us from our enemies and from the hand
of all who hate us;

72 To show mercy to our fathers
and to be mindful of His holy covenant,

73 Of the oath He swore to our father Abraham,
to grant us, 74 saved from the hand
of enemies,
That we might worship Him without fear,

75 in holiness and righteousness,
in His presence all our days.

76 And you, child, will be called a prophet
of the Most High,
for you will go before the Lord to prepare
His ways,

77 To give knowledge of salvation to His people
by forgiving their sins,

78 Through the tender mercy of our God,
whereby the Shining Light from on high
will visit us,

79 To give light to those in darkness and
in the shadow of death,
to guide our feet into the way of peace."

80 Now the child grew and became strong in spirit, and he was in the deserts until the day of his manifestation before Israel.

C. BIRTH AND EARLY YEARS OF JESUS

2 1 ᵃ Now it happened that in those days a decree went out from Caesar Augustus that all the world should be registered. 2 This first registration took place when Quirinius was governor of Syria. 3 So

---

ᵃ Mt 1:18-25.

1:76 Is 40:3, Ml 3:1.
1:78 Ml 4:2; Is 60:1-2. The Shining Light was understood to be the Messiah.
1:79 Is 9:2, 60:1-2.

everyone went to be registered, each to his own city. **4** Since Joseph was of the house and family of David he went up from Nazareth in Galilee to Bethlehem of Judea, the city of David, **5** to be registered with Mary, who was betrothed to him and who was pregnant. **6** Now it happened that while they were there the days for her to give birth were fulfilled. **7** She gave birth to her firstborn son, wrapped him in swaddling clothes, and laid him in a manger, because there was no room for them in the inn.

8 There were shepherds in the same region, living out of doors and keeping guard at night over their flock. **9** An angel of the Lord appeared to them and the glory of the Lord shone around them, and they were greatly afraid. **10** And the angel said to them, "Fear not! for, behold, I bring you good news which will give joy to the whole nation, **11** because this day a savior has been born for you in the city of David who is the Messiah, the Lord, **12** and this will be the sign for you — you will find a baby, swaddled and lying in a manger." **13** And, suddenly, with the angel was an assembly of the heavenly host, praising God and saying,

14 "Glory to God in high Heaven,
and, on earth, peace to those on whom
his favor rests."

15 And it happened that when the angels had departed from them to Heaven the shepherds said to one another, "Come on! Let's go over to Bethlehem and see this thing that happened, which the Lord has made known to us." **16** They hurried off and located Mary and Joseph and the baby, which was lying in the manger. **17** Now when they saw they let them know what had been told them about this child, **18** and when they all heard it they were amazed at what the shepherds told them. **19** Mary remembered all this and pondered it in her heart, **20** and the shepherds returned, glorifying and praising God for all they had heard and seen, just as they had been told.

21 And when eight days had passed for his circumcision they gave him the name Jesus, the name given him by the angel before he was conceived in the womb.

2:8   As always, Luke emphasizes Jesus' openness to the outcasts of society. Shepherding was considered an unclean occupation by the Pharisees.

2:13   "Host." The Greek word means "army."

22 When the days of their purification according to the Torah of Moses had passed they took the child up to Jerusalem to present him to the Lord — **23** as it is written in the Torah of the Lord, **every firstborn male shall be called holy to the Lord,** — **24** and to offer a sacrifice according to what is said in the Torah of the Lord, **a pair of turtle doves or two young pigeons.**

25 And, behold, there was a man in Jerusalem named Simeon. He was an upright and devout man who awaited the liberation of Israel and the Holy Spirit was upon him; **26** moreover it had been revealed to him by the Holy Spirit that he would not see death before he saw the Messiah of the Lord. **27** He was led by the Spirit to come to the Temple, and when the parents brought the child Jesus in to do for him according to the custom of the Torah **28** he, too, took him in his arms and blessed God, saying,

> **29** "Now You send Your servant away in peace, O Master,
> according to Your word,
> **30** Because my eyes have seen Your salvation
> **31** prepared in the presence of all the peoples,
> **32** A light of revelation to the Gentiles
> and glory to Your people Israel."

33 His father and mother were amazed at what was said about Jesus. **34** And Simeon blessed them and said to his mother, Mary,

> "Behold, he's destined to bring about the fall
> and rise of many in Israel,
> and to be a sign which will be opposed;
> **35** And a sword shall pierce your own soul,
> so that the thoughts of many hearts
> may be revealed."

2:22   "Torah," or "law," referred to the totality of God's revelation which could serve as a guide for one's life. Torah was, therefore, quintessentially, the Decalogue, but it also extended far beyond the confines of the Pentateuch to areas which we would never characterize as "law," as can be seen in several New Testament passages.

2:23   Ex 13:2, 12, 15.

2:24   Lv 12:8.

2:25, 38   The nationalist hopes of Simeon and Anna are raised once again by the two disciples on the road to Emmaus (24:21), but Jesus explains the true meaning of the liberation which has come to Israel.

2:32   Here at his birth Jesus is proclaimed to be "a light of revelation to the Gentiles," and at the end of the Gospel (24:47), when Jesus appears to the disciples in Jerusalem, he sends them forth to bring the light to "all nations."

36 The prophetess Anna was there, too, the daughter of Phanuel from the tribe of Asher; she was greatly advanced in years, having lived seven years with her husband from her virginity **37** and alone as a widow up to eighty-four years, worshipping night and day with fasts and prayers. **38** And she came up at that very hour and began to give thanks to God and spoke about him to all who were awaiting the liberation of Israel.

39 When they had carried out everything according to the Torah of the Lord they returned to Galilee to their own city, Nazareth. **40** Now the child grew and became strong and was filled with wisdom, and the grace of God was on him.

41 His parents used to go to Jerusalem every year for the festival of the Passover. **42** And when he was about to turn twelve — they had gone up to Jerusalem in accordance with the custom of the feast **43** and had fulfilled the days, while they were returning — the child Jesus remained in Jerusalem, and his parents didn't know. **44** But since they thought he was in their group of travellers they went a day's journey and then looked for him among their relatives and acquaintances, **45** and when they didn't find him they returned to Jerusalem in search of him. **46** And it happened that after three days they found him in the Temple, seated in the midst of the teachers, both listening to them and asking them questions, **47** and all those listening to him were amazed at his intelligence and his answers. **48** When his parents saw him they were amazed, and his mother said to him, "Son, why did you do this to us? You see your father and I have been looking for you and worrying!" **49** And he said to them, "Why were you looking for me? Didn't you know that I have to concern myself with my Father's affairs?" **50** And they didn't understand what he was telling them. **51** Then he went down with them and went to Nazareth, and he was subject to them. His mother kept all these things in her heart, **52** and Jesus **progressed** in wisdom and age **and grace before God and men.**

2:37 This could mean either that Anna lived as a widow for eighty-four years or that she lived as a widow up to the age of eighty-four, when this episode, presumably, takes place.

2:42 Twelve was the age when Jewish boys began scriptural studies, so Jesus would have just been beginning those studies.

2:52 1 S 2:26.

D. THE MINISTRY OF THE BAPTIST

3 1 [b] Now in the fifteenth year of the reign of Tiberius Caesar, when Pontius Pilate was governing Judea and Herod was Tetrarch of Galilee, while his brother Philip was Tetrarch of the region of Iturea and Trachonitis and Lysanias was Tetrarch of Abilene, 2 during the high priesthood of Annas and Caiaphas, the word of God came to John son of Zechariah in the desert. 3 And he came to the whole region around the Jordan, proclaiming a baptism of repentance for the forgiveness of sins, 4 as it is written in the book of the words of the prophet Isaiah,

> **The voice of one crying out in the desert,**
> **'Prepare the way of the Lord,**
> **make straight his paths.'**
> 5 **Every valley shall be filled in**
> **and every mountain and hill brought low,**
> **The crooked ways shall be made straight,**
> **and the rough ways made into smooth ways,**
> 6 **And all flesh shall see the salvation of God.**

7 So he said to the crowds that were coming out to be baptized by him, "You brood of vipers! Who warned you to flee from the coming wrath? 8 Produce fruit that shows you've repented, then, and don't go saying to yourselves, 'Abraham is our father!' for I say to you that God can raise up children to Abraham from these stones. 9 Already now the axe is laid at the root of the trees; any tree, then, not producing good fruit will be cut down and thrown into the fire." 10 So the people questioned him and asked, "Then what should we do?" 11 In answer he told them, "Let whoever has two tunics share with the one who has none, and let whoever has food do likewise." 12 Now tax collectors came to be baptized as well, and they asked him, "Teacher, what should *we* do?" 13 So he told them, "Collect nothing more than what has been designated for you." 14 And soldiers questioned him as well, saying, "What

---

b Mt 13:1-12; Mk 1:1-8; Jn 1:19-28.

3:4-6 Is 40:3-5 (Septuagint).

3:7-9 Of particular interest in the Baptist's indictment of the Jewish leaders is v. 8, in which he states that descent from Abraham merits no special consideration from God and will not save them from God's wrath. In chapter 13 Jesus takes this theme up (v. 28) and concludes that the Gentiles will be admitted to the Kingdom before the descendants of Abraham.

about us, what should *we* do?" "Don't rob or cheat anyone," he told them, "and be satisfied with your wages."

15 Now the people were in suspense and were all wondering in their hearts whether John might be the Messiah. **16** John answered by telling everyone, "I baptize you with water, but one more powerful than I am is coming, the strap of whose sandal I'm not worthy to untie; he'll baptize you with the Holy Spirit and fire — **17** his winnowing shovel is in his hand to clean out his threshing floor and gather his grain into the barn, but he'll burn up the chaff with unquenchable fire." **18** And so he proclaimed the good news to the people with many other words of encouragement; **19** but Herod the Tetrarch, who had been rebuked by John on account of Herodias, his brother's wife, and on account of all the evil things Herod had done, **20** added this to them all — he shut John up in prison.

E. THE BEGINNINGS OF JESUS' MINISTRY

21 ᶜ Now it happened that when all the people were being baptized, and when Jesus had been baptized and was in prayer, the sky was opened **22** and the Holy Spirit descended upon Jesus in bodily form like a dove, and a voice came from Heaven, "You are My Beloved Son; in you I am well pleased!"

23 ᵈ And Jesus himself, when he started out, was about thirty years old, being the son, as was supposed, of Joseph the son of Heli, **24** the son of Matthat, the son of Levi, the son of Melchi, the son of Jannai, the son of Joseph, **25** the son of Mattathias, the son of Amos, the son of Nahum, the son of Esli, the son of Naggai, **26** the son of Maath, the son of Mattathias, the son of Semein, the son of Josech, the son of Joda, **27** the son of Joanan, the son of Rhesa, the son of Zerubbabel, the son of Shealtiel, the son of Neri, **28** the son of Melchi, the son of Addi, the son of Cosan, the son of Elmadan, the son of Er, **29** the son of Joshua, the son of Eliezer, the son of Jorim, the son of Matthat, the son of Levi, **30** the son of Simeon, the son of Judah, the son of Joseph, the son of Jonam, the

---

ᶜ Mt 3:13-17; Mk 1:9-11. ᵈ Mt 1:1-17.

3:22 Is 42:1.

son of Eliakim, **31** the son of Melea, the son of Menna, the son of Mattatha, the son of Nathan, the son of David, **32** the son of Jesse, the son of Obed, the son of Boaz, the son of Sala, the son of Nahshon, **33** the son of Amminadab, the son of Admin, the son of Arni, the son of Hezron, the son of Perez, the son of Judah, **34** the son of Jacob, the son of Isaac, the son of Abraham, the son of Terah, the son of Nahor, **35** the son of Serug, the son of Reu, the son of Peleg, the son of Eber, the son of Shelah, **36** the son of Cainan, the son of Arphaxad, the son of Shem, the son of Noah, the son of Lamech, **37** the son of Methuselah, the son of Enoch, the son of Jared, the son of Mahalaleel, the son of Cainan, **38** the son of Enos, the son of Seth, the son of Adam, the son of God.

4 **1** ᵉ Now Jesus returned from the Jordan full of the Holy Spirit and was led by the Spirit through the desert **2** for forty days, while being tempted by the Devil. He ate nothing during those days, and when they were completed he was hungry. **3** Then the Devil said to him, "If you're the Son of God, tell this stone to become a loaf of bread." **4** Jesus answered him, "It is written, **Not by bread alone shall man live.**" **5** Then he led Jesus up and showed him all the kingdoms of the world in an instant of time, **6** and the Devil said to him, "I can give you all this power and glory, because it's been given to me and whoever I want to give it to. **7** So, if you'll worship before me, it'll all be yours." **8** And in answer Jesus said to him, "It is written,

> **The Lord your God shall you worship,**
> **and Him alone shall you adore."**

9 Then he led Jesus to Jerusalem and set him on the parapet of the Temple and said to him, "If you're the Son of God, throw yourself down from here, **10** for it's written,

> **He will give His angels orders concerning you,**
> **to protect you.**

11 and,

> **On their hands they will carry you**
> **lest you strike your foot against a stone."**

ᵉ Mt 4:1-11; Mk 1:12-13.

4:4   Dt 8:3.
4:8   Dt 6:13-14.
4:10   Ps 91:11.
4:11   Ps 91:12.

12 In answer Jesus said to him, "It is said, **You shall not tempt the Lord your God.**" **13** And when the Devil had finished all his tempting he left him until an opportune time.

F. THE GALILEAN MINISTRY

14 [f] When Jesus returned to Galilee in the power of the Spirit, word of him went out through all the surrounding region. **15** And he taught in their synagogues, praised by all.

16 [g] He went to Nazareth, where he'd been brought up, and as was his custom he went into the synagogue on the Sabbath day, and he stood up to read. **17** They handed him the scroll of the prophet Isaiah, and when he unrolled the scroll he found the place where it was written,

> **18** **The Spirit of the Lord is upon me,**
> **because he has anointed me**
> **to bring the good news to the poor,**
> **He has sent me to proclaim release to captives**
> **and recovery of sight to the blind,**
> **to set at liberty the oppressed,**
> **19** **To proclaim the acceptable year of the Lord.**

20 When he had rolled up the scroll and handed it back to the attendant he sat down, and the eyes of everyone in the synagogue were fixed on him. **21** Then he began to tell them, "Today this scripture has been fulfilled in your hearing." **22** All the people bore witness against him and were amazed at the words of mercy which came from his mouth, and they said, "Isn't this fellow Joseph's son?" **23** So he said to them, "No doubt you'll quote me this parable, 'Physician, heal thyself!' 'Do here, too, in your hometown, what we heard was done in Capharnaum.'" **24** Then he said, "Amen, I say to you, no prophet is acceptable in his hometown. **25** But I tell you in truth,

---

[f] Mt 4:12-17; Mk 1:14-15. [g] Mt 13:53-58; Mk 6:1-6.

4:12 Dt 6:16.

4:18 Is 61:1-2 (Septuagint).

4:22 Jesus had outraged his listeners by breaking off the quote in mid-sentence, omitting all reference to Divine vengeance against the Gentiles.

> There were many widows in Israel in the days
> of Elijah,

when the sky was shut up for three years and six months while there was a severe famine over all the land,

26   yet Elijah was sent to none of them except to
         Zarephath of Sidon, to a woman, a widow.
27   And there were many lepers in Israel in the time
         of Elisha the prophet,
         yet none of them was cleansed except Naaman
         the Syrian."

28 All the people in the synagogue who heard these things were enraged. **29** They rose up and threw him out of the city and took him to the brow of the hill on which their city was built in order to throw him over the edge, **30** but he passed through the middle of them and went away.

31 [h] Then he went down to Capharnaum, a city of Galilee. He was teaching them on the Sabbath, **32** and they were amazed at the way he taught because he spoke on his own authority. **33** Now in the synagogue was a man who had the spirit of an unclean demon, and he cried out with a loud voice, **34** "Ah! What do you want with us, Jesus of Nazareth? Have you come to destroy us? I know who you are — the Holy One of God!" **35** Jesus rebuked him and said, "Be silenced and come out of him!" Then the demon threw the man down in their midst and came out of him without harming him. **36** All the people were overcome with wonder and kept saying to one another, "What sort of word is this? — he gives orders to the unclean spirits with authority and power, and they go out!" **37** And news of him went out to every place in the surrounding region.

38 [i] When he left the synagogue he went into Simon's house. Now Simon's mother-in-law was suffering from a high fever, and they appealed to him on her account. **39** And when he stood over her he rebuked the fever and it left her; immediately she got up and began to serve them. **40** Now when the sun was setting all those who had people

---

[h] Mk 1:21-28. [i] Mt 8:14-17; Mk 1:29-34.

4:25-26   1 Kg 17.
4:27   2 Kg 5.

sick with various diseases brought them to him, and he laid his hands on each one of them and healed them. 41 Demons also came out of many people, shouting and saying, "You are the Son of God!" And when he rebuked them he wouldn't let them speak, because they knew he was the Messiah.

42 j At daybreak he slipped out and went to a desert place. The people began to search for him and when they came to where he was they tried to keep him from leaving them. 43 But he said to them, "I must give the good news of the Kingdom of God to the other cities, too, because I was sent for them." 44 And he preached in the synagogues of Judea.

5 1 k It happened that the people were pressing in on him as they listened to the word of God. Now he was standing by the Lake of Gennesaret 2 and he saw two boats pulled up on the shore, while the fishermen had gotten out and were washing the nets. 3 So he got into one of the boats — it was Peter's — and asked him to put out from land a little, and when he had seated himself he taught the crowds from the boat. 4 When he finished speaking he said to Simon, "Put out to the deep and lower your nets for a catch." 5 In answer Simon said, "We've been at it all night, working hard, and have caught nothing, but at your word I'll lower the nets." 6 And when they did this they took in a tremendous number of fish, but it began to rip their nets. 7 So they signalled to their companions in the other boat to come help them, and they filled both boats to the point that they began to sink. 8 Now when Simon Peter saw this he fell down on his knees before Jesus and said, "Leave me, because I'm a sinful man, Lord!" 9 For wonder at the catch of fish they had taken in seized him and all those with him, 10 and likewise James and John the sons of Zebedee, who were partners with Simon. Jesus said to Simon, "Don't be afraid; from now on you'll be catching men." 11 And when they pulled the boats onto the land they left everything and followed him.

---

j Mk 1:35-39. k Mt 4:18-22; Mk 1:16-20.

4:44 The best manuscript tradition states: "in the synagogues of Judea." However, this is somewhat confusing, since there has been no mention of Jesus leaving Galilee and the very next sentence refers to action in Galilee, as if Jesus had never left. Perhaps because of this confusion, some textual traditions amended "Judea" to "Galilee," which fits better logically. Others have suggested that "Judea" is used in a very general sense for "Israel." While this would be unusual, there is a possible similar use at Mk 10:1: "Judea [and] beyond the Jordan."

12[1] It happened that he was in one of the cities and a man was there who was full of leprosy, and when he saw Jesus he fell on his face and begged him, saying, "Lord, if you wish to, you can make me clean!" **13** So he reached out his hand and touched him and said, "I *do* wish it, be made clean!" At once the leprosy left him. **14** And he ordered the man to tell no one, but "go show yourself to the priest and make an offering for your cleansing as Moses commanded, as a witness to them." **15** But, instead, word of him kept spreading and many people gathered to listen and be healed of their illnesses, **16** but he used to withdraw into the deserts to be in prayer.

17 [m] It happened that on one of the days he was teaching, Pharisees were seated there as well as teachers of the Torah who had come from every village of Galilee and Judea and Jerusalem, and the power of the Lord was in his healing. **18** There were some men carrying a paralyzed man on a bed and they were trying to bring him in and set him in front of him. **19** And since they couldn't find a way, they carried him in through the crowd by taking him onto the roof and lowering him through the tiles of the roof with the bed into the middle, in front of Jesus. **20** When he saw their faith he said, "Man, your sins are forgiven you!" **21** Then the scribes and Pharisees began to question and say, "Who is this fellow who speaks blasphemies? Who can forgive sins but God alone?" **22** Now Jesus, realizing their questionings, said to them in response, "Why are you questioning in your hearts? **23** What's easier, to say, 'Your sins are forgiven you,' or to say, 'Get up and walk'? **24** But so you'll know that the Son of Man has authority on earth to forgive sins —" he said to the paralytic, "I say to you, get up, pick up your bed and go to your house!" **25** Immediately he got up in front of them, picked up what he was lying on, and went off to his house, glorifying God. **26** Amazement seized them all, and they glorified God and were filled with fear and said, "We've seen incredible things today!"

27 [n] After this he went out and he noticed a tax collector named Levi seated at the tax stand, and he said to him, "Follow me!" **28** He left everything, got up, and followed him. **29** Later Levi held a big banquet for him in his house, and there was a large crowd of tax collectors and others who were reclining with them. **30** The Pharisees and their scribes

---

[l] Mt 8:1-4; Mk 1:40-45. [m] Mt 9:1-8; Mk 2:1-12. [n] Mt 9:9-13; Mk 2:13-17.

complained to his disciples and said, "Why do you eat and drink with tax collectors and sinners?" **31** In answer Jesus said to them, "Those in good health are not in need of a doctor — the sick are; **32** I've come to call, not the righteous, but sinners to repentance!"

33 ° Then they said to him, "John's disciples often fast and offer prayers, and likewise the disciples of the Pharisees, but yours eat and drink." **34** So Jesus said to them,

> "Can you make the groomsmen fast
> while the bridegroom is with them?
> **35** But the days will come, and when the groom
> is taken from them,
> then they'll fast in those days."

36 He also told them a parable.

> "No one tears a patch from a new cloak
> and puts it on an old cloak,
> Otherwise, both the new one will tear
> and the patch from the new one won't match the
> old.
> **37** And no one puts new wine
> into old skins,
> Otherwise, the new wine bursts the skins,
> and it spills out and the skins are ruined;
> **38** On the contrary,
>
> 'new wine in new skins.'

39 No one drinking old wine wants new wine, for he says, 'The old wine is good.'"

6 **1** ᴾ Now it happened on a Sabbath as he was going through some grainfields that his disciples were plucking and eating the heads of grain, after rubbing them in their hands. **2** Some of the Pharisees said, "Why are you doing what's unlawful on the Sabbath?" **3** And in answer he said to them, "Haven't you read what David did when *he* was hungry, as well as those with him? **4** He went into the house of God and took and ate the Loaves of Offering and gave them to those with him,

---

° Mt 9:14-17; Mk 2:18-22. ᴾ Mt 12:1-8; Mk 2:23-28.

---

which it wasn't lawful for them to eat but only for the priests." **5** And
he said to them, "The Son of Man is Lord of the Sabbath."

6 [q] It happened on another Sabbath that he went into the
synagogue and taught, and there was a man there whose right hand
was withered. **7** Now the scribes and Pharisees were watching him
closely to see whether he healed on the Sabbath, so they could find
something to accuse him of. **8** Jesus knew their thoughts, so he said to
the man with the withered hand, "Get up and stand in the middle." So
he got up and stood there. **9** Then Jesus said to them, "I ask you,

> Is it lawful on the Sabbath to do good or do evil,
> to save a life or to kill?"

10 And after looking around at them all he said to him, "Hold out your
hand." So he did, and his hand was healed. **11** Now they were filled
with rage and began to discuss among themselves what they could do
about Jesus.

12 [r] It happened in those days that when he went out to the
mountain to pray he spent the night in prayer to God. **13** When day
came he called his disciples to him and he chose twelve of them, whom
he also called apostles — **14** Simon, whom he also named Peter, and
Andrew his brother, and James and John and Philip and Bartholomew
15 and Matthew and Thomas and James son of Alpheus and Simon,
who was called the Zealot, **16** and Judas son of James and Judas Iscariot,
who became a traitor.

17 [s] When he went down with them he stood on a level place, and
a large crowd of his disciples as well as a great number of the people
from all Judea and Jerusalem and the coastal district of Tyre and Sidon
18 came to hear him and be healed of their diseases, and those troubled
by unclean spirits were cured. **19** All the people kept trying to touch
him, because power kept coming out from him and healing them all.

20 [t] Then he raised his eyes to his disciples and said,

> "Blessed are you poor,
> for yours is the Kingdom of God.

---

[q] Mt 12:9-14; Mk 3:1-6. [r] Mt 10:1-4; Mk 3:13-19. [s] Mt 4:23-25. [t] Mt 5:1-12.

6:15 Literally, "Simon the Canaanite." This is generally considered to be a designation for the ultranationalist (and, therefore, anti-Roman) Zealots, but some scholars maintain that the Zealots did not become an organized movement until after the time of Jesus.

21 Blessed are you who hunger now,
for you shall be satisfied.
Blessed are you who weep now,
for you shall laugh.
22 Blessed are you when men hate you

and exclude you and insult you and reject your name as evil on account
of the Son of Man; **23** rejoice on that day and leap for joy — behold, your
reward will be great in Heaven,

because their fathers did the same to the prophets.
24 But woe to you rich,
for you *have* your delights!
25 Woe to you who are full now,
for you shall be hungry!
Woe, you who laugh now,
for you shall mourn and wail!
26 Woe, when all men speak well of you,
for their fathers did the same
to the false prophets!"

27 [u] "But to you who are listening, I say,

Love your enemies,
do good to those who hate you,
28 Bless those who curse you,
pray for those who insult you.
29 To the one who strikes you on one cheek,
offer the other cheek as well,
And from the one who takes your cloak,
don't hold back your tunic.
30 Give to all who ask of you,
and don't demand what's yours
from the one who took it.
31 And as you wish others to do for you,
do likewise for them.

---

[u] Mt 5:38-48, 7:12.

6:27 It was a common teaching of the rabbis that "neighbor" referred only to fellow Jews. Non-Jews were in opposition to God and therefore "enemies." Other currents of rabbinic thought, however, did manifest a more conciliatory view toward Gentiles.

32 And if you love those who love you,
    what kindness is that in you?
        For sinners also love those who love them.

33 And if you do good to those who do good to you,
    what kindness is that in you?
        Sinners also do the same.

34 And if you lend to those from whom you
        expect to receive,
    what kindness is there in you?
Sinners also lend to sinners,
    to get back equal amounts.

35 But love those who hate you,
    do good, and lend expecting nothing,
And your reward will be great,
    and you'll be sons of the Most High,
Because He's kind to the ungrateful
    and the evil.

36 Be merciful,
    as your Father is merciful.

37 [v] Don't judge,
    and you won't be judged;
Don't condemn,
    and you won't be condemned.
Forgive,
    and you will be forgiven,

38 Give,
    and it will be given to you.
Good measure,
    pressed down, shaken together,
Overflowing,
    they shall give into your bosom,
For with the measure you measure
    it will be measured out to you in return."

39 He also told them a parable.

---

[v] Mt 7:1-5.

"Can a blind man lead a blind man?
Won't they both fall into a ditch?

40 A disciple is not above his teacher but, when fully trained, each disciple will be like his teacher.

41   But why do you see the speck in your brother's eye,
              yet don't notice the log in your own eye?
42   Or how can you say to your brother, 'Brother, let me
                    take the speck from your eye!'
              while you don't see the log in your own eye?
          You hypocrite!
          First take the log out of your own eye,
              and *then* you'll see clearly to take the speck
                    from your brother's eye."

43 ᵂ "For a good tree isn't one
              which bears rotten fruit,
          Nor, again, is a rotten tree one
              which bears good fruit;
44   For each tree is known
              by its own fruit.
          For you don't gather figs from thorn bushes,
              nor pick grapes from brambles.
45   The good man brings forth good
              from the good treasure of his heart,
          And the evil man brings forth evil
              from his evil treasure,
          For the mouth speaks
              from the abundance of the heart."

46 ˣ "But why do you address me, 'Lord, Lord,' yet don't do the things I say? **47** Everyone who comes to me both hearing my words and doing them, I'll show you what he's like. **48** He's like a man building a house, who dug and went deep and placed a foundation on rock; now when a flood came the river burst upon that house, yet it wasn't able to shake it because it had been well built. **49** But the one who heard but didn't act is like a man who built a house on the ground without a foundation, and when the river burst upon it, it collapsed at once, and great was the ruin of that house.

ᵂ Mt 7:17-20, 12:34-35. ˣ Mt 7:24-27.

7 1 ʸ After he finished everything he had to say in the hearing of the people he went into Capharnaum. 2 Now a certain centurion had a servant who was dear to him and the servant was sick and about to die. 3 When the centurion heard about Jesus he sent Jewish elders to him and asked him to come save his servant. 4 When they appeared before Jesus they began to beg him earnestly, saying, "He's worthy that you should do this for him — 5 he loves our nation and built our synagogue for us." 6 So Jesus set out with them. While he was still some distance away from the house the centurion sent friends to say to him, "Lord, don't put yourself to the trouble — I'm not worthy to have you come under my roof. 7 Nor, therefore, did I consider myself worthy to come before you; just say a word, and my servant will be healed! 8 For I, too, am subject to authority, with soldiers under me, and when I tell this one, 'Go!' he goes, and if I tell another, 'Come!' he comes, and if I say to my servant, 'Do this!' he does it." 9 When Jesus heard these things he was amazed at him, and he turned to the crowd following him and said, "I tell you, not even in Israel have I found such faith!" 10 And when those who had been sent got back home they found the servant in good health.

11 It happened that on the next day he entered a city called Nain, and his disciples and a large crowd entered with him. 12 Now as he approached the city gate, behold, a dead man was being carried out for burial. He was the only son of his mother, who was a widow, and a considerable crowd from the city was with her. 13 The Lord was moved with pity when he saw her and said, "Don't weep!" 14 Then he went forward and touched the bier and the bearers stood still, and he said, "Young man, I say to you, arise!" 15 Then the dead man sat up and began to speak, and Jesus gave him to his mother. 16 Now fear seized them all and they glorified God and said, "A great prophet has risen among us! God has visited his people!" 17 And word about him went out through all Judea and the whole surrounding region.

18 ᶻ John's disciples informed him of all these things. So John summoned two of his disciples and 19 sent them to the Lord to ask, "Are you he who is to come or are we to expect another?" 20 Now when they came to him the men said, "John the Baptist sent us to you to ask, 'Are

---

ʸ Mt 8:5-13; Jn 4:43-54. ᶻ Mt 11:2-19.

you he who is to come or are we to expect another?'" **21** At that moment he was curing many people from diseases and illnesses and evil spirits, and he was bestowing sight on many blind people. **22** So in answer he said to them, "Go tell John what you saw and heard,

> **The blind can see again,** the lame walk,
>> lepers are made clean and the deaf hear,
> The dead are raised, **the poor are given**
>> **the good news,**
> **23** and blessed is whoever is not scandalized by me."

24 Now when John's messengers had gone off he began to speak to the crowds about John.

> "What did you go out to the desert to see?
>> A reed, shaken by the wind?
> **25** But what did you go out to see?
>> A man in luxurious robes?
> Behold, those in expensive and luxurious clothing
>> live in palaces.
> **26** But what did you go out to see?
>> A prophet?
> Yes, I tell you, and one greater than a prophet.
> **27** He it is of whom it is written,
> **Behold, I'm sending my messenger before your face,**
>> **who will prepare your way before you.**
> **28** I say to you, among those born of women
>> none is greater than John,
> Yet whoever is least in the Kingdom of God
>> is greater than he is."

29 When they heard this all the people as well as the tax collectors praised the righteousness of God's plan because they had been baptized with John's baptism, **30** but the Pharisees and lawyers had rejected God's will for them, since they hadn't been baptized by him.

> **31** "To what shall I compare the men of this generation,
>> and to what are they similar?

7:22 Is 35:5, 61:1.

7:23 Jesus again omits all reference to Divine vengeance against the Gentiles.

7:27 Ml 3:1.

32 They're like the children who sit in the marketplace and call to each other,

> 'We piped for you and you didn't dance,
>> we wailed and you didn't weep.'

33   For John the Baptist came neither eating bread
>> nor drinking wine, and you said,
>> 'He has a demon';

34   The Son of Man came eating and drinking,
>> and you said,
>>> 'Look at him, a glutton and a drunkard, a friend
>>> of tax collectors and sinners!'

35   Yet wisdom is justified by all her children."

36 Now one of the Pharisees asked Jesus to eat with him, so he went into the Pharisee's house and reclined at table. **37** There was a woman who was a sinner in the city, and when she learned that "he's reclining at table in the Pharisee's house!" she bought an alabaster jar of perfumed oil **38** and stood behind by his feet, weeping, and she began to wet his feet with her tears and to wipe them with the hair of her head, and she kissed his feet repeatedly and anointed them with the oil. **39** Now when the Pharisee who had invited him saw this he said to himself, "If this fellow were a prophet he'd have realized who and what kind of woman it is who's touching him — she's a sinner!" **40** In response Jesus said to him, "Simon, I have something to say to you." And he said "Teacher, say it." **41** "Two men were debtors of a certain moneylender; the one owed five hundred *denarii,* the other, fifty. **42** When they were unable to repay, he forgave them both. Which of them, then, will love him more?" **43** In answer Simon said, "I suppose the one he forgave the most." So he said to him, "You've judged correctly." **44** And turning to the woman he said to Simon, "You see this woman?

> I came into your house —
>> you gave me no water for my feet,
> But she wet my feet with her tears
>> and dried them with her hair.

45   You gave me no kisses,
>> but she, from the moment she came in,
>>> has not stopped kissing my feet.

46 You didn't anoint my head with olive oil,
  but she anointed my feet with perfumed oil.
47 Therefore I tell you: her sins, many as they are,
    have been forgiven,
  and so she has shown great love;
  But whoever is forgiven little,
    loves little."

48 Then he said to her, "Your sins are forgiven." **49** And those reclining at table began to say to themselves, "Who is this fellow who even forgives sins?" **50** Then he said to the woman, "Your faith has saved you, go in peace!"

8 **1** It happened next that he went travelling through city and village, preaching and proclaiming the good news of the Kingdom of God, and the Twelve were with him **2** as well as some women who had been healed from evil spirits and illnesses — Mary, who was called the Magdalen, from whom seven demons had gone out, **3** and Joanna, the wife of Chuza, Herod's steward, and Susanna, and many others who provided for them out of their possessions.

4 [a] Now when a large crowd had gathered, as well as those who had come to him from every city, he said in a parable, **5** "The sower went out to sow his seed. And as he sowed some fell along the footpath, and it was trampled underfoot and the birds of the sky ate it up. **6** And other seed fell on rock, and when it grew up it was scorched because it had no moisture. **7** And other seed fell among the thorns, and when the thorns grew up with it they choked it. **8** And other seed fell on the good earth, and when it grew up it gave fruit a hundredfold." When he had said these things he called out,

  "Whoever has ears to hear,
    let them hear!"

9 [b] Now his disciples asked him what this parable could mean. **10** So he said, "To you it's given to know the secrets of the Kingdom of God, but to the rest of them it's given in parables, so that

---

a Mt 13:1-9; Mk 4:1-9.

7:47 "Have been forgiven"; this is an example of the so-called Divine Passive, occasioned by the Jewish desire to avoid using the name of God. The meaning is: "her sins... have been forgiven *by God.*"

> **Seeing they may not see,**
> **And hearing they may not understand.**

11 [c] "This is the parable. The seed is the word of God. **12** Now those on the footpath are those who hear, and then the Devil comes and takes the word from their heart, so they won't believe and be saved. **13** Those on the rock are those who, when they hear, accept the word joyfully, yet these have no root; they believe for a time but forsake it in time of trial. **14** Now the seed that fell among the thorns, these are those who hear but are choked by the worries and wealth and pleasures of life as they proceed, and they don't mature. **15** But the seed on the good earth, these are those who listen to the word with an honest and good heart, hold fast to it, and bear fruit with perseverance."

16 [d] "No one, after lighting a lamp, covers it with something or puts it under a bed; on the contrary, he puts it on a lampstand so those who enter will see the light.

> **17**   For nothing is hidden that will not be revealed
>   Nor secret that will not be made known
>   and brought into the open.

18 Therefore, watch how you listen;

> For whoever has, it will be given to him,
> And whoever does not have, even what he thinks he has
>   will be taken from him."

19 [e] Now his mother and brothers showed up where he was, but they couldn't get near him because of the crowd.   **20** So he was informed, "Your mother and your brothers are standing outside and wish to see you." **21** But in answer he said to them, "My mother and my brothers are those who hear the word of God and do it."

22 [f] Now it happened that on one of those days both he and his disciples got into a boat, and he said to them, "Let's go over to the other

---

[b] Mt 13:10-17; Mk 4:10-12. [c] Mt 13:18-23; Mk 4:13-20. [d] Mk 4:21-25. [e] Mt 12:46-50; Mk 3:31-35.

8:10 Is 6:9-10 (Septuagint).

8:19 Church tradition has consistently maintained that the "brothers" of Jesus referred to here were merely close relatives, not sons of the same mother. It is instructive to compare this passage to 23:49-24:10 (and parallel passages in the other Gospels, esp. Mk 15:40-16:1 and Mt 27:60) where these brothers are again referred to as sons of "Mary," but this time it is unambiguously clear that *this* Mary was not Mary the mother of Jesus. Such usage was typically Semitic.

side of the lake," and so they set sail. **23** While they were sailing he fell asleep and a wind squall descended on the lake, and they were being swamped and were in danger. **24** So they came and woke him and said, "Master, master, we're going to die!" He woke up and rebuked the wind and the waves of water, and they stopped and there was a calm. **25** Then he said to them, "Where's your faith?" But they were amazed and fearful and said to each other, "Who *is* he, then? When he rebukes the winds and the water even *they* obey him!"

26 ᵍ Then they sailed to the region of the Gerasenes, which is opposite Galilee. **27** Now as he was coming ashore a certain man from the city who had a demon confronted him. This man hadn't worn a cloak for a long time; he didn't live in a house but instead lived among the tombs. **28** When he saw Jesus he cried out and fell down before him and said in a loud voice, "What do you want with me, Jesus, Son of the Most High God? I beg you, don't torment me!" **29** because he'd been commanding the unclean spirit to come out of the man. Many times it had seized him, and he was kept under guard and bound with chains and leg irons, and when he'd break the chains he was driven into the deserts by the demon. **30** So Jesus asked him, "What's your name?" "Legion," he said, because many demons had gone into him. **31** And they begged him not to order them to go off to the abyss.

32 Now there was a herd there of a considerable number of swine, feeding on the hillside, and when they begged him to let them go into them he let them. **33** When the demons went out of the man they went into the swine, and the herd rushed down the slope into the lake and drowned. **34** Now when the herdsmen saw what had happened they fled and told those who were in the city and the fields. **35** When the people went out to see what had happened and came to Jesus they found the man from whom the demons had gone out — clothed and in his right mind — seated at Jesus' feet, and they became frightened. **36** Then those who had seen [what happened] told them how the demon-possessed man had been saved. **37** And the whole crowd from the district of the Gerasenes asked him to go away from them, because they were seized with a great fear. So he got into a boat and returned. **38** Now the man from whom the demons had gone out begged to stay with Jesus, but he sent him off and said, **39** "Return to your house and

---

ᶠ Mt 8:23-27; Mk 4:35-41. ᵍ Mt 8:28-34; Mk 5:1-20;

announce what God has done for you." And he went off through the whole city, proclaiming what Jesus had done for him.

40 [h] Now when Jesus returned the crowd welcomed him, because they'd all been looking for him. **41** And, behold, a man named Jairus came — he was a ruler of the synagogue — and he fell at Jesus' feet and begged him to come to his house, **42** because he had an only daughter about twelve years old who was at the point of death.

Now as he was going the crowd kept pressing in on him. **43** A woman was there who had had a heavy flow of blood for twelve years that couldn't be cured by anyone. **44** She came up and touched the hem of his cloak from behind, and immediately the flow of blood stopped. **45** And Jesus said, "Who was it that touched me?" When everyone denied it Peter said, "Master, the crowd is pressing in on you and crowding around!" **46** But Jesus said, "Someone touched me — I could feel power going out from me." **47** When the woman saw that she couldn't hide she came, trembling, and fell down before him and, in the presence of all the people, she told why she'd touched him and how she'd been immediately cured. **48** So he said to her, "Daughter, your faith has saved you; go in peace!"

49 While he was still speaking someone came from the ruler of the synagogue's and said, "Your daughter has died; don't trouble the teacher further." **50** But Jesus heard this and told him, "Don't be afraid! Just believe and she'll be saved!" **51** When he came to the house he didn't allow anyone to go in with him except Peter, John, and James, and the mother and father of the child. **52** Now everyone was weeping and mourning for her, but he said, "Don't weep — she hasn't died, she's sleeping!" **53** And they laughed at him because they knew she *had* died. **54** Then he grasped her hand and called out, "Child, arise!" **55** Her spirit returned and she immediately sat up, and he gave instructions that she be given something to eat. **56** Her parents were beside themselves, but he ordered them to tell no one what had happened.

9 **1** [i] Then he called the Twelve together and gave them power and authority over all the demons and to cure all diseases, **2** and he sent them to proclaim the Kingdom of God and to heal, **3** and he said to them,

---

[h] Mt 9:18-26; Mk 5:21-43.

"Take nothing for your journey,
  neither staff nor bag,
Nor bread nor silver,
  nor two tunics.

4   And whatever house you go into,
      stay there and go on from there.

5   And whoever doesn't receive you,
      when you go out of that city,
    Shake off its dust from your feet
      as a witness against them."

6 So when they went out they went through the villages, proclaiming the good news and healing everywhere.

7 ʲ Now Herod the Tetrarch heard everything that was going on, and he was confused because some were saying, "John has risen from the dead!" 8 while some said, "Elijah has appeared!" and others, "One of the prophets of old has risen!" 9 But Herod said, "John, I beheaded! Who is this, then, I hear so much about?" And he tried to see him.

10 ᵏ When the apostles returned they told him what they'd done. Then he took them along and withdrew privately to a city called Bethsaida, 11 but when the crowds found out they followed him. After greeting them he spoke to them about the Kingdom of God and cured those who were in need of healing. 12 Now as day was coming to an end the Twelve came up to him and said, "Send the crowd away so they can go to the surrounding villages and farms and find food and lodging, because here we're in a desert place." 13 But he said to them, "*You* give them something to eat." They said, "We have no more than five loaves and two fish, unless we go buy food for all these people!" 14 There were about five thousand men. Then he said to his disciples, "Have them recline in groups of fifty." 15 They did so and they had them all recline. 16 Then he took the five loaves and the two fish and, after looking up to heaven, he blessed them and broke them into pieces and kept giving them to the disciples to distribute to the crowd. 17 And they all ate and were filled, and they picked up what was left over — twelve baskets of fragments.

18 ˡ And it happened that while he was praying alone the disciples were with him, and he asked them, "Who do the crowds say I am?" 19

ⁱ Mt 10:5-15; Mk 6:7-13. ʲ Mt 14:1-12; Mk 6:14-29. ᵏ Mt 14:13-21; Mk 6:30-44; Jn 6:1-14.

But in answer they said, "Some say, 'John the Baptist,' while others say, 'Elijah,' and others say, 'One of the prophets of old has risen.'" **20** So he said to them, "But *you* — who do *you* say I am?" And in answer Peter said, "The Messiah of God!"

21 [m] But he gave them orders and commanded them to tell no one this **22** and said, "The Son of Man must suffer greatly and be rejected by the elders and chief priests and scribes and be put to death and rise on the third day." **23** Then he said to everyone,

> "If anyone would come after me,
>> let him deny himself,
> And let him take up his cross daily
>> and follow me.

24   For whoever would save his life
>> will lose it,
> While whoever loses his life for my sake,
>> he'll save it.

25   For what good is there in a man gaining
>> the whole world,
>> but losing or forfeiting his life?

26   For whoever is ashamed of me and my words,
>> of him will the Son of Man be ashamed
> When he comes in his glory and in the glory
>>> of his Father,
>> and of the holy angels.

27 But I tell you truly, there are some who are standing here who will not taste death until they see the Kingdom of God."

28 [n] Now it happened that about eight days after he spoke these words he took Peter, John, and James and went up the mountain to pray. **29** And it happened that while he was praying the appearance of his face was altered, and his clothing became a dazzling white. **30** And, behold, two men were speaking with him, Moses and Elijah, **31** who were seen in glory speaking about his Exodus, which he would bring to completion in Jerusalem. **32** Now Peter as well as those with him had been overcome by sleep, but when they were fully awake they saw his glory and the two men standing with him. **33** And it happened that as Moses

---

[l] Mt 16:13-19; Mk 8:27-29. [m] Mt 16:20-28; Mk 8:30 -9:1. [n] Mt 17:1-8; Mk 9:2-8.

and Elijah were leaving him Peter said to Jesus, "Master, it's good for us to be here; let's put up three dwellings, one for you, one for Moses, and one for Elijah" — he didn't really know what he was saying. **34** Now as he was saying this a cloud arose and overshadowed them; then they were afraid when they went into the cloud. **35** And a voice came from the cloud and said, "This is My Son, My Chosen; hear him!" **36** After the voice had spoken Jesus was found alone, and they kept silent and told no one in those days anything they'd seen.

37 ᵒ Now it happened that on the next day when they were coming down from the mountain a large crowd met him. **38** And, behold, a man from the crowd called out and said, "Teacher, please look at my son — he's my only child **39** and, behold, a spirit takes hold of him and cries out suddenly, then it throws him into convulsions with foam at the mouth and will hardly stop battering him. **40** I asked your disciples to drive it out, but they weren't able to." **41** In answer Jesus said, "O unbelieving and perverse generation, how long will I be with you and put up with you? Bring your son here." **42** But while he was coming the demon threw the boy to the ground and convulsed him, so Jesus rebuked the unclean spirit and healed the child and gave him back to his father. **43** And they were all amazed at God's greatness.

ᵖ But while they were marvelling at all the things he was doing he said to his disciples, **44** "Listen closely to what I'm going to tell you: the Son of Man is going to be handed over into the hands of men." **45** But they didn't understand this saying and it was hidden from them so they wouldn't ask about it, and they were afraid to ask him about this saying.

46 ᑫ Now an argument arose among them as to which of them was the greatest. **47** Jesus, aware of the argument in their hearts, took a child and stood it next to himself, **48** and he said to them,

---

ᵒ Mt 17:14-18; Mk 9:14-27. ᵖ Mt 17:22-23; Mk 9:30-32.

9:31 "Exodus"; this expression is difficult to render adequately in English. The word has as its basic meaning a departure or going out but is also used to signify a departure from this life, i.e. decease. It clearly has this last meaning in this passage, but just as clearly retains all the connotations associated with the word Exodus as referring to the Israelites' departure from their slavery in Egypt. Jesus, through his death, leads the New Israel out of slavery and into the Promised Kingdom.

9:33 Cf. the note to Mt 17:4. Luke specifically states (v. 31) that Jesus was discussing "his Exodus."

9:35 Dt 18:15.

9:44 Lit., "Put these words into your ears."

"Whoever receives this child in my name
    receives me,
And whoever receives me
    receives the One who sent me,
For the least of all of you —
    he's the one who is great."

49 [r] In response John said, "Master, we saw someone driving out demons in your name, and we stopped him because he doesn't follow with us." **50** But Jesus said to him, "Don't stop him, for

Whoever isn't against you
    is with you."

G. HEALING AND TEACHING
ON THE ROAD TO JERUSALEM

51 Now it happened that as the days were drawing near for Jesus to be taken up he set his face to go to Jerusalem, **52** and he sent messengers ahead of him. They came and entered a Samaritan village to prepare for him, **53** but the people didn't welcome him because his face was set on going to Jerusalem. **54** When his disciples James and John saw this they said, "Lord, do you want us to call down **fire from Heaven to consume** them?" **55** But he turned and rebuked them, **56** and they went to the next village.

57 [s] As they were going along the road someone said to him, "I'll follow you wherever you go." **58** And Jesus said to him,

"Foxes have holes,
And the birds of the sky have nests,
But the Son of Man has nowhere to lay his head."

---

q Mt 18:1-5; Mk 9:33-37. r Mk 9:38-40. s Mt 8:19-22.

9:51, 53   "Set his face"; i.e., "he resolved."
9:54   2 K 1:10, 12.
9:58   Manson has suggested that the "foxes," of proverbial cunning, are Herod and his hated Edomite followers who played one side off against the other to their own advantage. The "birds of the air" were the Roman overlords. Jesus would then be warning his followers about what to expect: his kingdom would be very different.

59 Then he said to another, "Follow me!" but he said, "Let me first go bury my father." **60** Jesus said to him,

> "Let the dead bury their own dead,
> But *you*, go proclaim the Kingdom of God!"

61 Then another said, "I'll follow you, Lord, but first let me take leave of those at home." **62** But Jesus said,

> "No one who puts his hand to the plow
> And looks behind
> Is fit for the Kingdom of God."

10 **1** Now after this the Lord appointed seventy-two others and sent them in twos ahead of him to every town and place he was going to come to. **2** Then he said to them,

> "The harvest is great,
> But the laborers are few,

so implore the Lord of the harvest to send out laborers to his harvest. **3** Go now! Behold, I'm sending you like sheep in among wolves. **4** Don't carry a purse or a bag or sandals, and greet no one along the way. **5** And to whatever house you go into, first say, 'Peace be to this house.' **6** If there's a son of peace there your peace will rest upon him, but, if not, your peace will return to you. **7** Stay, then, in that house and eat and drink what they have, for the laborer is worthy of his reward. Don't move from house to house. **8** And in whatever town you go into and they receive you, eat what's set before you, **9** heal the sick in it, and say to them, 'The Kingdom of God has come upon you!' **10** But whatever town you go into and they *don't* receive you, go out into its streets and say, **11** 'Even the dust of your town sticking to our feet we wipe off against you, but know this, the Kingdom of God has come!' **12** I say to you,

> It will be more tolerable for Sodom on that day
> Than it will be for that town."

13 [t] "Woe to you, Chorazin! Woe to you, Bethsaida! because if the mighty works that took place in you had taken place in Tyre and Sidon,

---

10:1 Gn 10:1-32. Seventy-two is the number of the nations of the world. The symbolism indicates that Jesus' mission is to all nations. When taken in conjunction with Jesus' instruction to eat what was placed before them, contrary to Jewish dietary laws, some authors, among them B. Reicke, have suggested that this particular mission was to an area where large numbers of Gentiles lived, perhaps Transjordan.

they would have repented long ago and sat in sackcloth and ashes.
14 But it will be more tolerable for Tyre and Sidon at the judgment than
for you. **15** And you, Capharnaum,

> **You'll be exalted to Heaven, will you?**
> **You'll be brought down to Hell!**

16   Whoever hears you,
>   hears me,
> And whoever rejects you,
>   rejects me.
> And whoever rejects me,
>   rejects the one who sent me."

17 Now the seventy-two returned joyfully and said, "Lord, even
the demons are subject to us in your name!" **18** And he said to them,
"I saw Satan falling like lightning from Heaven. **19** Behold, I've given
you the power to step on snakes and scorpions and to trample on all the
power of the Enemy, and nothing can harm you. **20** But don't rejoice in
the fact that the spirits are subject to you — rejoice because your names
are recorded in Heaven."

21 ᵘ At that very hour he rejoiced in the Holy Spirit and said,

> "I praise you, Father,
>   Lord of Heaven and earth,
> Because You hid these things from the wise
>   and intelligent
>   and revealed them to babes;
> Yes, Father,
>   for such was Your desire.

22   All things have been given to me by my Father,
>   and no one knows who the Son is
>   except the Father,
> Nor who the Father is except the Son,
>   and whoever he chooses to reveal it to."

23 And when he turned to the disciples in private he said,

> "Blessed are the eyes that see
>   what you're seeing,

ᵗ Mt 11:20-24. ᵘ Mt 11:25-27; Mk 13:16-17.

10:15   Is 14:13-15.

24 For I tell you,

> Many prophets and kings wished to see
> > what you're seeing,
> > yet didn't see,
> And to hear what you're hearing,
> > yet didn't hear."

25 And, behold, a certain lawyer stood up to put Jesus to the test and said, "Teacher, what must I do to gain eternal life?" **26** Jesus said to him, "What's written in the Torah? How do *you* read it?" **27** In answer he said, **"You shall love the Lord your God with your whole heart and with your whole soul and with your whole strength** and with your whole understanding, and **you shall love your neighbor as yourself."** **28** Then Jesus said to him, "You've answered correctly; do this and you'll live." **29** But he wished to find favor with God and so he said to Jesus, "But who *is* my neighbor?" **30** After considering, Jesus said, "A certain man was going down from Jerusalem to Jericho and ran into robbers who, after stripping and beating him, went off leaving him half dead. **31** Now by chance a priest was going down by that road, yet when he saw him he passed by on the other side of the road. **32** Now likewise a Levite was also going past the spot, and when *he* saw him *he* passed by on the other side of the road. **33** But a certain Samaritan who was on a journey came upon him, and when he saw him he took pity. **34** He came up to him and bandaged his wounds, poured oil and wine on them, set him on his own mount, brought him to an inn, and took care of him. **35** The next day when he left he gave the innkeeper two *denarii* and said, 'Look after him, and whatever you spend in addition I'll repay you upon my return.' **36** Which of these three, do you think, was a neighbor to the man who ran into the robbers?" **37** The lawyer said, "The one who had mercy on him." Then Jesus said to him, "Go, and *you* do likewise."

38 Now in their journeying he came into a certain village where a woman named Martha received him. **39** She had a sister named Mary who seated herself at the Lord's feet and listened to his teaching. **40** But Martha was distracted with all the serving, so she came up and said,

---

10:27   Dt 6:5.

10:29   Cf. the note at 6:27.

10:35   "Two *denarii*." Silver coins, each worth a laborer's daily wage.

"Lord, doesn't it matter to you that my sister has left me to serve alone?" **41** In answer the Lord said to her, "Martha, Martha! You're anxious and upset over many things, **42** but one thing is necessary. Mary has chosen the better part, which will not be taken from her."

11 **1** ᵛ It happened that Jesus was praying at a certain spot, and when he was done one of his disciples said to him, "Lord, teach us to pray, like John taught *his* disciples." **2** So he said to them, "When you pray, say,

> Father, Your name be blessed;
> > may Your Kingdom come;
> **3** Give us today our daily bread
> **4** And forgive us our sins,
> > for we also forgive all who are indebted to us,
> And lead us not into temptation."

5 Then he said to them, "If any of you had a friend and you went to him at midnight and said to him, 'Friend, lend me three loaves — **6** my friend has arrived on a journey to me and I haven't a thing to set before him,' **7** would he answer from inside, 'Don't bother me! The door's already locked and my children are with me in the bed; I can't get up and give you anything.' **8** I tell you, even if he doesn't get up and give you something because he's your friend, he'll get up and give you whatever you need out of a sense of shame. **9** And to you I say,

> Ask! and it shall be given to you;
> Seek! and you shall find;
> > Knock! and it shall be opened to you.

> **10** For everyone who asks, receives;
> > And whoever seeks will find;
> > > And to those who knock it shall be opened.

> **11** But is there a father among you who,
> > if his son asks for a fish,
> > > instead of a fish will hand him a snake?
> **12** Or if he asks for an egg,
> > will hand him a scorpion?

ᵛ Mt 6:9-15; Mk 7:7-11.

11:8 The Greek word translated "sense of shame" has often been translated "shameless persistence." K. Bailey's explanation has been followed here.

13 So if you who are evil know how
  to give good gifts to your children,
  How much more will the Father from Heaven
  give the Holy Spirit to those who ask him!"

14 ᵂ And he was driving out a dumb demon; now it happened that when the demon had gone out the dumb man spoke. The crowds were amazed, 15 but some of them said, "He drives out demons by Beelzebul, the prince of demons," 16 while others demanded that he show them a sign from Heaven, as a test. 17 But he knew their thoughts and so he said to them,

  "Every kingdom divided against itself is laid waste,
    and house divided against house falls.

18 Now if Satan, too, is divided against himself—because *you* say I drive out demons by Beelzebul— how will his kingdom stand? 19 But if I *do* drive out demons by Beelzebul, by whom do *your* followers drive them out? Therefore, they'll be your judges. 20 But if I drive out demons by the finger of God, then the Kingdom of God has come upon you. 21 When the strong man guards his own palace fully armed his possessions are safe; 22 but when someone stronger than he is comes he'll conquer him, take away the armor on which he relied, and they'll distribute his spoils.

23 Whoever isn't with me is against me,
  And whoever doesn't gather with me scatters."

24 ˣ "When the unclean spirit comes out of the man it goes about through waterless places seeking relief, and when it finds none it says, 'I'll return to the house I came from,' 25 and when it comes it finds it swept and decorated. 26 Then it goes and brings along seven other spirits worse than itself, and it goes in and settles there, and the last state of that man becomes worse than the first."

27 Now it happened that while he was saying these things a woman in the crowd raised her voice and said to him,

---

ᵂ Mt 12:22-30; Mk 3:20-27. ˣ Mt 12:43-45.

11:19   "Followers"; literally, "sons."

11:21-22 Here Jesus compares Satan to a "strong man" and the present age to Satan's house. It is Jesus who has entered Satan's house, bound him, and freed those in Satan's power. Jesus' power over demons is a sign of this mastery and of the coming of the Messianic age.

"Blessed is the womb that bore you,
and the breasts that you nursed at!"

28 But he said, "Rather,

Blessed are those who hear the word of God
and keep it!"

29 ^y Now as the crowds pressed around he said,

"This generation is a wicked generation;
it seeks a sign,
Yet no sign will be given it but the sign of Jonah.

30 For just as Jonah became a sign for the Ninevites,
So also will the Son of Man be for this generation.

31 The Queen of the South will rise up at the judgment
against the men of this generation
and will condemn them,
Because she came from the ends of the earth
to hear the wisdom of Solomon,
And, behold, one greater than Solomon is here.

32 The Ninevite men will stand up at the judgment
against this generation and will condemn it,
Because they repented at the preaching of Jonah,
And, behold, one greater than Jonah is here!"

33 ^z "No one, after lighting a lamp, puts it in the cellar — he puts it on the lampstand so those who enter will see the light.

34 Your eye is the lamp of the body.
When your eye is generous,
Your whole body is full of light, too,
But when it's grudging,
Your body, too, is full of darkness.

35 Take care, then, lest the light within you
be darkness.

36 So if your whole body is full of light, having no part darkened, it will be full of light, like when the lamp flashes its light on you."

---

y Mt 12:38-42; Mk 8:12. z Mt 5:15, 6:22-23.

11:29   Cf. the note at Mt 12:39.

37 [a] While he was speaking a Pharisee asked him to eat with him, so he went and sat down. **38** Now when the Pharisee saw, he was amazed that Jesus didn't first wash before the meal. **39** But the Lord said to him, "Now you Pharisees, you cleanse the outside of the cup and the dish, but your inside is full of greed and wickedness. **40** You fools! Didn't He Who made the outside make the inside as well? **41** But give what's within as alms and then everything will be clean for you.

42   But woe to you Pharisees!
     You tithe mint and rue and every herb,
          and neglect the justice and love of God;
     These are the things that should be done,
          and what should not be neglected.
43   Woe to you Pharisees!
     You love the first seat in the synagogues,
          and greetings in the marketplaces.
44   Woe to you!
     You're like unmarked tombs,
          and those who walk over them don't know it."

45 In response one of the lawyers said to him, "Teacher, you insult us, too, by saying these things!" **46** But he said,

          "And woe to you lawyers!
     You load men down with heavy burdens,
          yet you don't touch the burdens
               with one of your fingers.
47   Woe to you!
     You build the monuments of the prophets,
          but your fathers killed them.
48   So you're witnesses,
          and you approve of your fathers' works —

---

a Mt 23:1-36; Mk 12:38-40.

11:37-52 The tendency for Pharisaism to degenerate into formalism and hypocrisy was well recognized in ancient times, cf. Mt 23:1ff.

11:41 Several authors have suggested that "give what's within as alms" is a mistranslation of an Aramaic original and that Mt 23:26 renders this passage correctly.

11:44 Contact with a dead body or a tomb was a serious matter for the Pharisees, since it made them ritually unclean. Here, Jesus compares the Pharisees *themselves* to the cause of uncleanness. As the lawyer's response shows, this was a grave insult, indeed.

> They killed them,
>> while you build their tombs.

49 Therefore the Wisdom of God also said, 'I will send them prophets and apostles and they will kill and persecute some of them,' **50** so that this generation might be responsible for the blood of all the prophets that was shed from the creation of the world, **51** from the blood of Abel to the blood of Zechariah, who was killed between the altar and the sanctuary; yes, I tell you, this generation will be responsible.

52 Woe to you lawyers!
>> because you've taken the key of knowledge;
> You wouldn't go in,
>> and you hindered those who *were* going in."

53 When he went out from there the scribes and Pharisees became hostile and began to press him with questions about many things, **54** lying in wait for him to pounce on something he said.

12 **1** When the countless thousands of the crowd had gathered, so that they were trampling on each other, he said to his disciples first, "Guard against the leaven of the Pharisees, which is hypocrisy.

2 But nothing is concealed
>> that will not be revealed,
> Nor hidden
>> that will not be made known.
3 Therefore, what you have said in the darkness
>> will be heard in the light,
> And what you whispered in inner rooms
>> will be proclaimed from the roof tops."

4 [b] "But I say to you, my friends,

> Fear not those who kill the body,
>> and after that can do no more.

5 But I'll let you know whom to fear!

> Fear the One Who, after killing,
>> has power to thrust into Gehenna.

---

b Mt 10:28-31.

11:51 Gn 4:8, 1 Ch 24:20-21.

Yes, I tell you, fear *Him!* 6 Aren't five sparrows sold for a few cents? Yet not one of these is overlooked in the presence of God! 7 Moreover, even the hairs of your head are all numbered. Fear not! You're worth far more than sparrows."

8 ^c "But I tell you,

> Everyone who acknowledges me before men,
> > the Son of Man will acknowledge him, too,
> > > before God's angels;

9   But whoever denies me before men
> > will be denied before God's angels.

10   And everyone who utters a word against the Son of Man,
> > he'll be forgiven,
> But whoever blasphemes the Holy Spirit
> > will not be forgiven.

11 But when they bring you before the synagogues and rulers and officials, don't worry how to speak your case or what to say — 12 the Holy Spirit will teach you what to say at that very hour."

13 Then someone from the crowd said to him, "Teacher, tell my brother to share the inheritance with me!" 14 But he said to him, "Man, who made me judge or arbitrator over you?" 15 Then he said to them, "Watch out for and guard against all greed, because your life doesn't consist in the abundance of your possessions." 16 Then he told them a parable and said, "The land of a certain rich man produced good crops. 17 So he considered to himself, 'What shall I do — I have nowhere to gather my grain!' 18 Then he said, 'This is what I'll do! I'll pull down my barns and build bigger ones, and I'll gather all my grain and my goods there, 19 and I'll tell my soul, "Soul, you have many goods laid up for many years. Relax; eat, drink, be merry!"' 20 But God said to him, 'You fool! This night they'll demand your soul of you. But the things you prepared, whose will *they* be?' 21 That's how it will be for whoever accumulates treasure for himself, yet is not generous toward God."

22 ^d Then he said to his disciples, "Therefore I say to you,

---

^c Mt 10:32-33; 12:32, 10:19-20.

12:6   Lit., "an *assarion*," a Roman copper coin worth 1/16 of a *denarius*, which was worth the daily wage of a laborer.

Don't worry about your life,
    what you will eat,
Or about your body,
    what you will wear.

23   For life is more than food,
    and the body more than clothing.

24   Consider the ravens —
    they neither sow nor reap,
Nor have either storeroom or barn,
    yet God feeds them;
How much more does He value *you*
    than *birds!*

25   But which of you can add
    any time to his life by worrying?

26   So if you can't even do such a little thing,
    why do you worry about the rest?

27   Consider how the lilies grow —
    they neither work nor spin,
But I tell you, not even Solomon in all his glory
    was arrayed like one of them!

28   If God so clothes the grass in the field,
    which is here today and thrown
        into the oven tomorrow,
How much more you,
    O you of little faith!

29   And *you* — don't ask what you'll eat
    and what you'll drink,
    and don't get upset.

30   All the nations of the world seek these things,
    but your Father knows that you need them.

31   Instead, seek His Kingdom
    and these things will also be given to you.

32   Fear not, little flock,
    for it pleased your Father
        to give you the Kingdom.

---

d Mt 6:25-34, 19-20.

33 Sell your possessions and give alms;
>> make yourselves purses that don't grow old,
> An inexhaustible treasure in the heavens,
>> where no thief approaches nor moth destroys;
34 For where your treasure is,
>> there will your heart be, too!"

35 e "Let your loins be girt
>> and your lamps burning,
36 And you like men awaiting their lord,
>> when he at last returns from the wedding feast,
> So when he comes and knocks
>> they can open up for him at once.

37 Blessed those servants who, when he comes,
>> the lord will find still awake!
> Amen I say to you, he'll get himself dressed
>>> and have them recline at table,
>> and he'll come wait on them
38 And if he comes in the middle of the night
>> and finds them thus,
>>> they are blessed!

39 But know this — if the householder had known
>> at what hour the thief was coming
>>> he wouldn't have let his house be broken
>>>> into.
40 You be ready, too,
>> because you don't know the hour
>>> when the Son of Man is coming!"

41 Then Peter said, "Lord, are you telling this parable for us or for everyone?" 42 And the Lord said,

> "Who, then, is the faithful steward,
>> the wise one,
> Whom the lord will set over his staff
>> to give them their ration at the proper time?

---

e Mt 24:45-51.

12:38   Lit., "at the second or third watch."

43   Blessed that servant who, when his lord comes,
        he finds doing so!

44   Surely, I tell you,
        he'll set him over all his possessions.

45   But if that servant says in his heart,
        'My lord is long in coming,'
   And begins to beat the servants and maids,
        eating and drinking and getting drunk,

46   The lord of that servant will come
           on a day he doesn't expect,
        and at an hour he doesn't know,
   And he'll cut him in pieces
        and assign him the lot of the unbelievers.

47   But that servant who knew his lord's will,
        yet didn't prepare or act according to his will,
        will be severely beaten,

48   Whereas, the one who didn't know,
        but did what deserved a beating,
        will receive fewer blows.

   But to whomever much has been given,
        much shall be required of him,
   And to whomever much was entrusted,
        they will ask more of him."

49 [f]   "I came to spread fire on the earth,
        and would that it were already kindled!

50   But I have a baptism to be baptized with,
        and how apprehensive I am until it is
           accomplished!

51   Do you think I came to bring peace to the earth?
        no, I tell you, but division instead!

52   For from now on five in one house will be divided,
        three against two and two against three,

53   Father against son will be divided
        and son against father,
   Mother against daughter

---

[f] Mt 10:34-36.

12:53   Mi 7:6.

and daughter against mother,
Mother-in-law against daughter-in-law
and daughter-in-law against mother-in-law."

54 Then he said to the crowds, "When you see a cloud rising in the west you say at once, 'A rainstorm is coming!' and so it is, **55** and when a south wind blows you say, 'There will be scorching heat!' and it happens. **56** You hypocrites! You know how to interpret the face of the earth and the sky, so how is it you don't know how to interpret these times?"

57 ᵍ "Why, then, don't you judge for yourselves what's right? **58** While you're going with your opponent to the official, make an effort to settle with him on the way, lest he drag you before the judge, and the judge will hand you over to the officer, and the officer will throw you into prison. **59** I tell you, you won't come out of there until you pay back the very last penny."

13 **1** Now some people came at that very time and told him about the Galileans whose blood Pilate mixed with their sacrifices. **2** And in response he said to them,

"Do you think these Galileans
were worse sinners
than all the other Galileans were
because they suffered these things?

3   No, I tell you,
but unless you repent
you'll all die the same way.

4   Or those eighteen on whom the tower fell in Siloam —
do you think they were guiltier
than everyone else living in Jerusalem?

5   No, I tell you,
but unless you repent
you'll all die the very same way."

---

g Mt 5:25-26.

12:58   "Officer." Literally, *praktor*, a Roman term for an officer of the court.
12:59   Lit., "a *lepton*," a copper coin worth 1/2 *quadrans* or 1/128 *denarius*.

6 Then he told them this parable. "A man had a fig tree planted in his vineyard, and he came looking for fruit on it and found none. **7** So he said to the vinedresser, 'For three years now I've come looking for fruit on this fig tree and I haven't found any. Cut it down—why should it use up the land, after all?' **8** But in answer the vinedresser said, 'Lord, let it be for this year, too, until I dig around it and put down manure, **9** and it may produce fruit in the future — but, if it doesn't, have it cut down.'"

10 Now he was teaching in one of the synagogues on the Sabbath. **11** And, behold, a woman was there who for eighteen years had had a crippling spirit, and she was bent over double and unable to straighten herself up fully. **12** When Jesus saw her he called out to her and said, "Woman, you've been set free from your illness!" **13** Then he laid his hands on her and she straightened up immediately and glorified God. **14** Now the ruler of the synagogue was indignant that Jesus had healed on the Sabbath, so in response he said to the crowd, "There are six days on which it's proper to perform work, so come be healed on them and not on the Sabbath day!" **15** But the Lord answered him and said, "You hypocrites! Don't each of you untie your ox or donkey and lead it off to water it on the Sabbath? **16** Wasn't it proper for this daughter of Abraham, whom Satan had bound for all these eighteen years, to be released from this bond on the Sabbath day?" **17** And when he said these things all those who were opposed to him were ashamed, and the whole crowd rejoiced at all the glorious things that were done by him.

18 ^h So he said,

> "What is the Kingdom of God like,
> and to what shall I compare it?

19 It's like a grain of mustard seed which a man took and threw into his garden, and it grew and became a tree, and the birds of the sky nested in its branches."

20 And again he said, "To what shall I compare the Kingdom of God? **21** It's like yeast that a woman took and mixed into a bushel of wheat flour until all of it was leavened."

---

h Mt 13:31-33; Mk 4:30-32.

13:21   "A bushel." Lit., "a *saton*," a dry measure of 21.6 pints.

22 [i] And he travelled around the cities and villages, teaching and journeying toward Jerusalem. **23** Now someone said to him, "Lord, will only a few be saved?" So he said to them,

24 "Strive to come in
through the narrow gate,
Because many, I tell you, will try to come in,
but won't be able to.

25 Once the householder has risen
and locked the door,
You'll stand outside
and knock on the door,
Saying, 'Lord, open up for us!'
and in answer he'll say to you,
'I don't know you,
where you're from!'

26 Then you'll try to say,
'We ate and drank in your presence
and you taught in our streets!'

27 And he'll say to you,
'I don't know you,
where you're from!
Get away from me,
all you evildoers!'

28 There there will be wailing
and gnashing of teeth,
When you see Abraham and Isaac and Jacob
and all the prophets in the Kingdom of God,
while you're thrown outside.

29 They'll come from east and west
and from north and south
and recline at table in the Kingdom of God.

30 And, behold, some who are last shall be first,
and some who are first shall be last."

---

[i] Mt 7:13-14, 21-23.

13:28   Cf. note at 3:7-9.

31 [j] At that very time some Pharisees came and said to him, "Go out and leave here—Herod wants to kill you!" **32** And he said to them, "Go tell that fox, 'Behold, I'll drive out demons and do cures today and the next day, and on the third day I'll be done with my work.' **33** But I must keep travelling today and tomorrow and the next day, because it's unacceptable for a prophet to be killed outside Jerusalem.

34   Jerusalem, Jerusalem,
       Who killed the prophets
          and stoned those sent to her!
       How often I wished
          to gather your children,
       Like a hen gathers her brood
          under her wings,
       But you would not!
35   Behold, there remains to you
       your desolate house.
       I tell you, you shall not see me
          until you say,
          **Blessed is he who comes
          in the name of the Lord!**"

14 **1** It happened that when he went to the house of one of the rulers of the Pharisees on the Sabbath to eat bread they were watching him closely. **2** And, behold, a man with dropsy was before him. **3** In response Jesus spoke to the lawyers and Pharisees and said, "Is it lawful to heal on the Sabbath or not?" **4** But they remained silent. So he took hold of him, cured him, and sent him away. **5** Then he said to them, "Can any of you imagine having a son or ox fall into a well, and not at once pulling him out on the Sabbath day?" **6** And they were unable to respond to these things.

7 Then he told a parable to those who had been invited, having noted how they had selected the places of honor for themselves, and he said to them, **8** "When you're invited by someone to a wedding feast, don't recline at the place of honor, lest someone more eminent than you

---
[j] Mt 23:37-39.

13:32   "That fox"; cf. 9:58, note. Under Manson's interpretation Jesus would be referring to Herod's fox-like cunning in playing off various competing powers against each other.
13:35   Ps 118:26.

was invited by him, **9** and the man who invited you and him will come say to you, 'Give the place to this man!' and then you'll shamefacedly proceed to take the last place. **10** Instead, when you're invited and arrive, sit at the last place, so that when the one who invited you comes he'll say to you, 'Friend, move up higher!' Then you'll receive glory before all those reclining with you.

11   Because everyone who exalts himself will be humbled,
        And whoever humbles himself will be exalted."

12 He also said to the one who invited him, "When you give a meal or a feast, call neither your friends, nor your brothers, nor your kinsmen, nor rich neighbors, lest they also invite you in turn and repay you. **13** Instead, when you give a banquet, invite the poor, crippled, lame, and blind, **14** and you'll be blessed because they won't have anything to repay you with — you'll be repaid at the resurrection of the righteous!"

15 ᵏ Now one of those reclining with him heard these things, and said to him, "Happy is he who eats bread in the Kingdom of God!" **16** But he said to him, "A man gave a big banquet and invited many people, **17** and he sent his servant at the time of the banquet to tell those who had been invited, 'Come — everything's ready now!' **18** But they one and all began to make excuses. The first said, 'I bought a field and I have to go see it; I beg you, consider me excused.' **19** Another said, 'I bought five yoke of oxen and I'm setting out to examine them; I beg you, consider me excused.' **20** And another said, 'I married a wife and therefore can't come.' **21** And when the servant appeared he told this to his lord. The householder was furious and said to his servant, 'Go quickly to the streets and alleys of the city and bring the poor and crippled and blind and lame here.' **22** The servant said, 'Lord, your commands have been carried out, but there's still room.' **23** Then the lord said to the servant, 'Go out along the roads and hedges and force them to come in, so my house may be filled — **24** I tell you, not one of those men I invited will taste my banquet!'"

25 ˡ Now large crowds were travelling with him, and he turned and said to them, **26** "If anyone comes to me and doesn't hate his own father and mother and his wife and children and his brothers and sisters, even his own life, he cannot be my disciple. **27** Whoever doesn't

---

ᵏ Mt 22:1-10. ˡ Mt 10:37-38.

pick up his cross and follow me cannot be my disciple. **28** After all, wouldn't any of you who wanted to build a tower first sit down and figure out if you had enough to complete it? **29** lest, after laying the foundation but not being able to finish it, all the onlookers begin to make fun of you **30** and to say, 'This man began to build but he couldn't finish.' **31** Or wouldn't a king setting out to meet another king in war first sit down and consider if he's able to oppose with ten thousand the one who's coming against him with twenty thousand? **32** If he can't he sends an envoy to request peace terms while his enemy is still a long way off. **33** So in the same way, no one who doesn't part with all his possessions can be my disciple."

34 [m] "Therefore, salt is good, but if the salt, too, has lost its taste, what can it be seasoned with? **35** It's good neither for the land nor for manure — they throw it out.

> Whoever has ears to hear,
> let them hear!"

15 **1** [n] Now the tax collectors and sinners were all drawing near to listen to him, **2** and the Pharisees and scribes complained, "This fellow welcomes sinners and eats with them!" **3** So he told them this parable, **4** "What man of you who had a hundred sheep and lost one of them wouldn't leave the ninety-nine in the desert and set out after the lost one until he found it? **5** And when he finds it he puts it on his shoulders, rejoicing, **6** and when he comes home he calls his friends and neighbors together and says to them, 'Rejoice with me — I've found my lost sheep!' **7** I say to you that, likewise, there will be more joy in Heaven at the repentance of one sinner than at ninety-nine of the righteous who had no need of repentance."

8 "Or a woman who has ten *drachmas* — if she loses one *drachma*, won't she light a lamp and sweep her home and search thoroughly until she finds it? **9** And when she finds it she calls her friends and neighbors and says, 'Rejoice with me, because I've found the *drachma* I lost!' **10** Likewise, I tell you, there is more joy among God's angels at one sinner who repents."

---

[m] Mt 5:13; Mk 9:50. [n] Mt 18:12-14.

15:8 A *drachma* was a Greek silver coin worth about the same as a *denarius*, i.e., the daily wage of a laborer.

11 Then he said, "A man had two sons, **12** and the younger of them said to his father, 'Father, give me the share of the property that falls to me.' Now he divided his living between them. **13** Not many days later the younger son gathered up everything and left home for a far off country, and there he squandered his property, leading a dissolute life. **14** Now when he had spent everything a severe famine came to that country and he was reduced to poverty, **15** so he went and attached himself to one of the citizens of that country, who sent him to his fields to feed pigs. **16** And he longed to fill himself with the carob pods the pigs were eating, but no one gave him anything. **17** Then, when he came to himself, he said, 'How many of my father's hired men have more than enough bread, while I'm dying here of hunger. **18** I'll get up and go to my father and I'll say to him, "Father, I've sinned against Heaven and before you; **19** I'm no longer worthy to be called your son; treat me like one of your hired men."' **20** So he got up and went to his father. Now while he was still far away his father saw him and took pity, and he ran and fell upon his neck and kissed him repeatedly. **21** His son said to him, 'Father, I've sinned against Heaven and before you; I'm no longer worthy to be called your son.' **22** But his father said to his servants, 'Quick, bring out the best robe and clothe him in it, and put a ring on his hand and sandals on his feet, **23** and bring the fatted calf — slaughter it and let's eat and celebrate —

24   This son of mine was dead,
           and has come back to life,
       He was lost,
           and has been found.'

And they began to celebrate.

25 "Now his older son was in the field, and when he had come and was approaching the house he heard music and dancing, **26** and he called one of the servants over and asked what these things meant. **27** So he told him, 'Your brother has come and your father has slaughtered the fatted calf, because he's gotten him back in good health.' **28** Then he became furious and refused to go in. So his father came out and appealed to him. **29** But in answer he said to his father, 'I've worked all these years for you now and never went against your command, and you never gave me a kid goat so I could celebrate with my friends, **30** but when this son of yours who devoured your living with whores came, you slaughtered the fatted calf for him!' **31** But he said to him, 'My child, you're always with me and everything of mine is yours, **32** but we *had* to celebrate and rejoice —

> This brother of yours was dead,
> > and has come back to life,
> He was lost,
> > and has been found!'"

16

1 He also said to his disciples, "There was a rich man who had a steward, and a report came to him that this steward had been squandering his possessions. **2** So he summoned him and said to him, 'What's this I hear about you? Turn in the accounts of your stewardship — you can no longer be steward!' **3** The steward said to himself, 'What can I do? — my lord is taking the stewardship away from me! I can't dig; I'm ashamed to beg. **4** I know what I can do so when I'm removed from the stewardship people will welcome me into their homes!' **5** So he called his lord's debtors in one by one and said to the first, 'How much do you owe my lord?' **6** He said, 'Eight hundred gallons of oil.' So he told him, 'Take your bills, sit down, and quickly write four hundred.' **7** Next he said to another, 'You now, how much do *you* owe?' So he said, 'A thousand bushels of wheat.' He said to him, 'Take your bills and write eight hundred.' **8** And the lord commended the steward for his wrongdoing because he'd acted wisely, for the sons of this age are wiser than the sons of light are in their own generation. **9** And to you I say, make friends for yourselves with unrighteous mammon so that when it runs out they'll receive you into the eternal dwellings.

> **10** Whoever is faithful in very little
> > is also faithful in much,
> And whoever is dishonest in very little
> > is also dishonest in much.
> **11** So if you haven't been faithful with
> > unrighteous mammon,
> Who will entrust you with the true riches?
> **12** And if you haven't been faithful
> > with what's another's,
> Who will give you what's his own?

16:6 "Eight hundred gallons." Lit., "a *batos*." A *batos* was a liquid measure of 8.1 gallons.
16:8 "A thousand bushels." Lit., "a *cor*." A *cor* was a dry measure of about 10-12 bushels.

13   No steward can serve two lords,
      For either he'll hate the one and love the other,
      Or be loyal to one and despise the other.
      You cannot serve God and Mammon!"

14 ° The Pharisees, who loved money, heard all these things and made fun of him. 15 And he said to them, "You're the ones who hold yourselves out as righteous before others, but God knows your hearts, because

> What is exalted among men
> Is an abomination before God.

16 The Torah and the Prophets lasted until John; from then on

> The Kingdom of God is proclaimed in the good news,
> And everyone forces his way into it.

17   But it's easier for the heavens and the earth to pass away
      Than for one letter or stroke of the Torah to fall.

18   Anyone who puts his wife away and marries another
              commits adultery,
      And whoever marries a woman put away by her
              husband
      commits adultery."

19 "There was a rich man who used to dress in purple and fine linen and who feasted splendidly every day. 20 Now a poor man named Lazarus used to lay at his gate, covered with sores, 21 and he longed to fill himself with what fell from the rich man's table; why, even the dogs came and licked his sores! 22 Now it happened that the poor man died and was carried away by the angels to the bosom of Abraham, but the rich man also died and was buried. 23 And in Hades when he lifted his eyes — he was in torments — he saw Abraham from a great distance, and Lazarus in his bosom. 24 So he called out and said, 'Father Abraham! Have mercy on me and send Lazarus to dip the tip of his finger in water and cool my tongue — I'm in great pain in these flames!' 25 But Abraham said, 'My child, remember that you got your good things during your lifetime, and Lazarus, likewise, his bad things, but now he's being comforted while you're in pain. 26 And in any case, there's a deep chasm which has been placed between you and us, so that

---

° Mt 11:12-13.

---

those who wish to cross over from here to you are unable, nor can they cross over from there to us.' **27** Then he said, 'Then I beg you, father, to send him to my father's house — **28** for I have five brothers — so he can solemnly warn them so they won't come to this place of torment, too.' **29** But Abraham said, 'They have Moses and the prophets; let them listen to *them!*' **30** But he said, 'Oh no, Father Abraham! but if someone came to them from the dead, they'd repent.' **31** But Abraham said to him, 'If they won't listen to Moses and the prophets, they won't be convinced if someone rises from the dead, either.' "

17 **1** ᴾ Then he said to his disciples, "For scandal not to come is impossible, but woe to the one through whom it comes! **2** It would be better for him to have a millstone placed around his neck and be thrown into the sea, rather than to scandalize one of these little ones. **3** Watch out for each other.

> If your brother sins,
>> rebuke him,
> And if he repents,
>> forgive him,

4 and if he sins against you seven times in a day and turns to you seven times, saying, 'I repent,' you shall forgive him."

5 And the apostles said to the Lord, "Increase our faith!" **6** So the Lord said, "If you have faith like a grain of mustard seed you could say to this mulberry tree, 'Be uprooted and be planted in the sea,' and it would obey you."

7 "But would any of you who had a slave who was plowing or tending sheep say to him when he came in from the field, 'Go sit down at the table at once.' **8** On the contrary, wouldn't you say to him, 'Prepare something for me to eat and dress yourself and serve me while I eat and drink. After that, you can go eat and drink.' **9** The servant is owed no thanks because he did what he was commanded, is he? **10** Likewise, you, too, when you do everything you were commanded, should say, 'We're servants of no special merit; we only did what we should have done.'"

ᴾ Mt 18:6-7, 21-22; Mk 9:42.

17:10   "Servants of no special merit" has been preferred to the more usual "worthless servants," following K. Bailey.

11 It happened during his journey to Jerusalem that he was crossing the border of Samaria and Galilee. **12** As he was entering a village he was met by ten lepers who stood at a distance, **13** and they raised their voices and cried out, "Jesus, master, have mercy on us!" **14** When he saw them he said, "Go show yourselves to the priests!" And it happened that they were made clean while they were on their way. **15** Now one of them, when he saw he'd been cured, returned, glorifying God in a loud voice, **16** and he fell face down and thanked him. And he was a Samaritan. **17** In response Jesus said, "Weren't ten made clean? Where, then, are the other nine? **18** Did no one return to give glory to God except this foreigner?" **19** Then he said to him, "Arise and go; your faith has saved you."

20 ꝗ Now when he was asked by the Pharisees, "When is the Kingdom of God coming?" he answered them and said, "The Kingdom of God is not coming in a way that can be observed, **21** nor will they say, 'Look, here it is!' or, 'There it is!' — behold, the Kingdom of God is in your midst!" **22** Then he said to his disciples, "The days will come when you'll long to see one of the days of the Son of Man, but you *won't* see it. **23** And they'll say to you, 'Look, it's there!' 'Look, it's here!' Don't go off and don't follow them, **24** because just as the lightning, when it flashes, lights up from one side of the sky to the other side of the sky, so will the Son of Man be. **25** But first he must suffer many things and be rejected by this generation. **26** Just as it happened in the days of Noah, so, too, will it be in these days of the Son of Man. **27** They ate, they drank, they married, they gave in marriage, until the day Noah went into the ark and the deluge came and destroyed them all. **28** Likewise, it happened like that in the days of Lot; they ate, they drank, they bought, they sold, they planted, they built; **29** but on the day Lot came out of Sodom, fire and brimstone rained down from Heaven and destroyed them all. **30** It will be the same on the day the Son of Man is revealed. **31** On that day let whoever is on his roof and has his things in the house not go down to get them, and, likewise, let whoever is in his field not return. **32** Remember Lot's wife!

ꝗ Mt 24:23-28, 37-41.

17:21 "In your midst." This phrase has often been translated as "within you," but both the context and the most obvious meaning of the Greek are against such a translation. Here, Jesus appears to be telling the Pharisees that the Kingdom has already arrived and is right there among them, if they have eyes to see it.

33   Whoever tries to save his life will lose it,
        While whoever loses it will save his life.

34   I tell you,

        On that night there will be two men in one bed —
            one will be taken and the other will be left.

35   There will be two women grinding together —
            one will be taken while the other will be left." [36]

37 In response they asked him, "Where, Lord?" But he said to them,

            "Where the body is,
            There, too, will the vultures be gathered."

18 1 Then he told them a parable about the need for them to pray
always and not become discouraged 2 and he said, "There was
a judge in a certain city who neither feared God nor felt shame before
men. 3 Now there was a widow in that city and she kept coming to him
and saying, 'Do me justice against my adversary!' 4 For a while he didn't
want to, but later he said to himself, 'Even though I neither fear God nor
feel shame before men, 5 still, because of the way this widow keeps
bothering me, I'll do her justice so she won't keep coming and finally
wear me out.'" 6 Then the Lord said, "Listen to what the unjust judge
says! 7 Won't God, then, vindicate His chosen ones when they cry out
to Him day and night? and He'll be patient with them. 8 I tell you, He'll
do them justice with all speed. But, nevertheless, when the Son of Man
comes, will he find faith on earth?"

9 He also told this parable to some of those who self-confidently
believed in their own righteousness and looked down on others. 10
"Two men went up into the Temple to pray, one a Pharisee and the other
a tax collector. 11 The Pharisee stood by himself and made these
prayers. 'O God, I give You thanks because I'm not like other men,
greedy, unjust, adulterers — or even like this tax collector. 12 I fast twice
a week, I tithe everything I get.' 13 But the tax collector stood at a

---

17:36   The best manuscript tradition omits v. 36: "Two in the field — one will be taken and the
            other will be left."

18:7   "be patient"; i.e., God will bear with the human failings of "His chosen ones," who are
            also not perfect.

8:9-14   Bailey's explanation for this parable's setting is as follows. The two men went up to the
            temple to pray at the most common time for offering prayers in the temple — during one of
            the twice a day atonement sacrifices. Thus, the tax collector is not simply making a general
            plea for mercy; he is specifically begging that the atonement sacrifice being offered may be
            applied to the forgiveness of his sins. Moreover, the beating of his breast was more than a

distance and didn't want to even lift his eyes up to Heaven; instead, he beat his breast and said, 'O God, forgive me, a sinner!' **14** I tell you, *he* went down to his house pardoned and reconciled [with God] rather than the other one, because

> Everyone who exalts himself shall be humbled,
> While whoever humbles himself shall be exalted."

15[r] Now they were even bringing babies to him so he could touch them, but when his disciples saw this they rebuked them. **16** But Jesus called the children over and said,

> "Let the children come to me,
> And don't stop them,
> For of such as these is the Kingdom of God.

17 Amen, I say to you, whoever doesn't accept the Kingdom of God like a child shall not come into it."

18[s] Then a ruler asked him, "Good Teacher, what should I do to gain eternal life?" **19** But Jesus said to him, "Why do you call me good? No one is good but God alone! **20** You know the commandments — **you shall not commit adultery, you shall not murder, you shall not steal, you shall not bear false witness, honor your father and mother."** **21** But he said, "I've obeyed all these from my youth." **22** Now when Jesus heard that he said to him, "You still lack one thing. Sell everything you have and give to the poor and you'll have treasure in Heaven, and come follow me." **23** When he heard this he became very sad, for he was extremely rich.

24 Now when Jesus saw him so saddened he said,

> "How hard it is
> for those who are wealthy
> to enter the Kingdom of God!

25   It's easier for a camel to go through
>   a needle's eye

---

[r] Mt 19:13-15; Mk 10:13-16.   [s] Mt 19:16-30; Mk 10:17-31.

pro forma expression of humility — it was quite an extreme expression of sorrow and repentance which was normally used only by women. Bailey's interpretation is borne out by the use of the phrase "forgive me" (*hilastheti*). Normally translated "have mercy on me" (*eleeson*), this expression almost certainly has the sense of atonement or forgiveness of sins.

18:20   Ex 20:13-16.

> than for a rich man
>> to go into the Kingdom of God!"

26 Those who were listening said, "Then who can be saved?" **27** But he said,

> "What is impossible for men
>> is possible for God."

28 Then Peter said, "You see we've left our homes and followed you." **29** So he said to them, "Amen, I say to you, there's no one who has left his house or wife or brothers or parents or children for the sake of the Kingdom of God **30** who will not receive many times more in this time, and in the coming age, life eternal."

H. THE MINISTRY IN JERUSALEM

31 ᵗ Then he took the Twelve and said to them, "Behold, we're going up to Jerusalem where all the things written by the prophets about the Son of Man will be brought to completion, **32** for he'll be handed over to the Gentiles and he'll be mocked and insulted and spit upon. **33** Then they'll scourge him and put him to death, and on the third day he'll rise." **34** But they understood none of this and the saying was kept hidden from them, and they didn't realize what had been said.

35 ᵘ Now it happened that when he was approaching Jericho a blind man was seated beside the road, begging. **36** When he heard the crowds going by he asked what was going on, **37** and they told him, "Jesus of Nazareth is passing by." **38** So he cried out and said, "Jesus, Son of David, have mercy on me!" **39** Those who were going ahead ordered him to be silent, but he kept crying out all the more, "Son of David, have mercy on me!" **40** Jesus stopped and ordered the man to be brought to him, and when he approached he asked him, **41** "What do you want me to do for you?" And he said, "Lord, that I might see again!" **42** Jesus said to him, "Regain your sight! Your faith has saved you!" **43** Immediately he could see again and followed Jesus, glorifying God. And all the people, when they saw this, gave praise to God.

ᵗ Mt 20:17-19; Mk 10:32-34. ᵘ Mt 20:29-34; Mk 10:46-52.

19

1 Then he went in and passed through Jericho. 2 And, behold, a man named Zacchaeus was there; he was chief tax collector and he was rich. 3 He was trying to see who Jesus was, but he wasn't able to because of the crowd, because he was short of stature. 4 So he ran on ahead to the front and climbed up into a sycamore in order to see him, because he was going to be passing by there. 5 When Jesus came to that place he looked up and said to him, "Zacchaeus! Hurry on down — today I must stay at your house!" 6 So he hurried down and welcomed him joyfully. 7 When everyone saw this they complained and said, "He went in as the guest of a sinful man!" 8 But Zacchaeus stood up and said to the Lord, "Look, Lord, I'm giving half of my possessions to the poor, and if I've cheated anyone of anything I'm paying back fourfold." 9 Then Jesus said to him, "Today salvation has come to this house, because he's a son of Abraham, too. 10 For the Son of Man came to seek out and save what was lost."

11 ᵛ Now after they'd listened to these things he continued and told them a parable, because he was near Jerusalem and they thought the Kingdom of God was going to appear immediately. 12 So he said, "A noble born man departed for a distant country to receive a kingdom for himself and then return. 13 So he summoned ten of his servants and gave them ten gold coins and said to them, 'Do business till I come.' 14 But his citizens hated him and sent a representative after him to say, 'We don't want this man to reign over us.' 15 And it happened that when he returned after receiving the kingdom he ordered the servants to whom he'd given the money to be called to him so he could find out what profit they'd made. 16 So the first one appeared and said, 'Lord, your one coin made ten more.' 17 And he said to him, 'Well done, good servant! Because you've been faithful in very little, may you have authority over ten cities!' 18 The second came and said, 'Your one coin made five.' 19 So to this one he said, 'And *you* be over *five* cities.' 20 Then the other came and said, 'Lord, behold your coin, which I had tucked away in a handkerchief — 21 I feared you, because you're a stern man — you take what you didn't set down and reap what you didn't sow.' 22 He said to him, 'I'll judge you from your own mouth, wicked servant! You knew that I'm a stern man, taking what I didn't set down and

---

ᵛ Mt 25:14-30.

19:13   A *mina* was a Greek coin worth 100 *denarii* or 1/60 *talent*.

reaping what I didn't sow? **23** And why didn't you give my money to a bank? Then when I came I would have collected it with interest!' **24** And he said to those standing by, 'Take the coin from him and give it to the one who has the ten. **[25] 26** I say to you,

> To the one who has, it will be given,
> But from the one who doesn't have,
>   even what he has will be taken.

27 But bring those enemies of mine here who didn't want me ruling over them, and slaughter them in front of me.'"

28 ^w And after saying these things he went on ahead, going up to Jerusalem. **29** It happened that when he drew near to Bethphage and Bethany at the mount called Olivet he sent two of his disciples **30** and said, "Go into the opposite village. When you enter it you'll find a colt tied up on which no man has ever sat; untie it and bring it. **31** And if anyone asks you, 'Why are you untying the colt?' this is what you'll say, 'The Lord has need of it.'" **32** When they went off, those who were sent found it just as he'd told them. **33** Now when they were untying the colt its owners said to them, "Why are you untying the colt?" **34** So they said, "The Lord has need of it." **35** And they led it to Jesus and after spreading their cloaks on the colt they had Jesus mount it. **36** Then as he proceeded they spread their cloaks out on the road.

37 Now by this time he was approaching the descent from the Mount of Olives and the whole crowd of the disciples began to praise God in a loud voice, rejoicing at all the mighty works they had seen and **38** saying,

> "Blessed is the king
>   who comes in the name of the Lord;
> Peace in Heaven
>   and glory in the highest!"

---

^W Mt 21:1-11; Mk 11:1-11; Jn 12:12-19.

19:25   The best manuscript tradition omits v. 25: "And they said to him, 'Lord, he *has* ten coins!'"

19:28f   Beginning with Jesus' entry into Jerusalem the fulfillment of Jesus' mission moves inexorably to its climax. As seen through the eyes of faith, all these events are "in accordance with the scriptures," and the account is punctuated with frequent references to scripture in order to underline this. All Jesus' words and actions are now seen in their full eschatological significance: the Kingdom has come and, following the Lord's atoning death, it will be proclaimed to all nations.

19:38   Ps 118:26.

39 And some of the Pharisees from the crowd said to him, "Teacher, rebuke your disciples!" **40** He answered and said, "I tell you, if *they* were silent the *stones* would cry out!"

41 When Jesus drew near and caught sight of the city he began to weep over it **42** and said, "If only you had realized on this day what leads to peace — but now it's been hidden from your eyes. **43** Because days will come upon you,

> And your enemies will set up a siege wall
> > around you,
> They'll surround you and close you in
> > on all sides,
> **44** And level you to the ground, and your children
> > within you,
> And they will not leave a stone upon a stone
> > within you,

because you didn't recognize the appointed time of your visitation."

45 ˣ And when he went into the Temple he began to drive out those who were selling **46** and he said to them, "It has been written,

> **And my house shall be a house of prayer,**
> > but you have made it a **robbers' den!"**

47 And he taught daily in the Temple. Now the chief priests and the scribes as well as the leaders of the people sought to do away with him, **48** yet they couldn't find anything to do, because the whole people hung upon him, listening.

20 **1** ʸ It happened that on one of the days when he was teaching the people in the Temple and proclaiming the good news the chief priests and scribes along with the elders came up **2** and said to him, "Tell us by what authority you do these things, or who it is who gave you this authority." **3** In answer he said to them, "I'll ask a question, too, and *you* tell *me!* **4** John's baptism — was it from Heaven or from men?" **5** They conferred with each other, saying, "If we say, 'From Heaven,' he'll say 'Then why didn't you believe him?' **6** But if we say, 'From men,' the whole people will stone us because they're convinced John was a

---

ˣ Mt 21:12-17; Mk 11:15-19; Jn 2:13-22.

19:46   Is 56:7; Jr 7:11.

prophet." **7** So they answered that they didn't know where it was from. **8** And Jesus said to them, "Nor will I tell you by what authority I do these things."

9 ᶻ Then he went and told the people this parable. "A man planted a vineyard and let it out to vinedressers and left home on a journey for a considerable time. **10** And at the proper time he sent a servant to the vinedressers so they'd give him some of the fruit of the vineyard, but the vinedressers sent him away empty handed after beating him. **11** Again he sent another servant, but after beating that one and treating him shamefully they sent him away empty handed. **12** And again he sent yet a third, but after injuring this one, too, they threw him out. **13** Then the owner of the vineyard said, 'What can I do? I'll send my beloved son; maybe they'll feel shame before him.' **14** But when the vinedressers saw him they conferred with one another and said, 'This is the heir — let's kill him so the inheritance will be ours!' **15** Then they threw him out of the vineyard and killed him. What will the owner of the vineyard do to them? **16** He'll come and destroy these vinedressers and give the vineyard to others." Those who were listening said, "God forbid!" **17** But he gazed at them and said, "What, then, is this that is written,

The stone which the builders rejected
has become the cornerstone.
18   Everyone who falls on that stone
                    will be broken to pieces,
              while whoever it falls upon it will crush."

19 The scribes and chief priests wanted to get their hands on him at that very hour, yet they feared the people because they knew he'd spoken this parable against them.

20 ᵃ Then they kept him under observation and sent spies who pretended to be upright men so they could seize on what he said in order to hand him over to the authority and power of the governor. **21** And they put this question to him, "Teacher, we know you speak and teach plainly and without regard for the person; instead, you truly teach the way of God. **22** Is it lawful for us to pay the tax to Caesar or not?" **23**

ʸ Mt 21:23-27; Mk 11:27-33. ᶻ Mt 21:33-46; Mk 12:1-12.

20:9   Is 5:1.
20:17   Ps 118:2.

Now he realized their deceit and said to them, **24** "Show me a *denarius;* whose image and inscription does it have?" So they said, "Caesar's." **25** Then he said to them,

> "Then render to Caesar the things that are Caesar's
> and to God the things that are God's."

26 And they weren't able to catch him in what he said before the people, and they remained silent, amazed at this answer.

27 [b] Then some of the Sadducees came forward — those who say there's no resurrection — and they put this question to him, **28** "Teacher, Moses wrote for us, if a brother with a wife should die, and he should be childless, then his brother should take the wife and raise up offspring for his brother. **29** So then, there were seven brothers, and the first, after taking a wife, died childless; **30** the second **31** and the third also took her and, likewise, the seven, too, left no children and died. **32** Finally the woman died, too. **33** So at the resurrection, whose wife will the woman be? — all seven had her as wife." **34** Jesus said to them, "The children of this age marry and are given in marriage, **35** but those counted worthy of *that* age and resurrection from the dead neither marry nor are given in marriage, **36** because they are no longer able to die — they're angel-like and are children of God, since they've attained the resurrection. **37** But that the dead rise Moses, too, made known at the passage about the thorn bush, when he calls the Lord **God of Abraham and God of Isaac and God of Jacob.** **38** Now He's not God of the dead but of the living — for Him they're all alive." **39** In answer some of the scribes said, "Teacher, you spoke well," **40** and no one dared to question him any longer.

41 [c] Then he said to them, "How can they say the Messiah is the son of David? — **42** David himself says in the Book of Psalms,

> **The Lord said to my lord,**
> **'Sit at My right hand**
> **43**　　　**till I make your enemies a footstool**
> 　　　　**for your feet.'**

---

a Mt 22:15-22; Mk 12:13-17. b Mt 22:23-33; Mk 12:18-27.

20:24　　A *denarius* was a Roman silver coin equal to the daily wage of a laborer.
20:34　　"Children." Lit., "sons."
20:37　　Ex 3:6.
20:42-43　Ps 110:1.

44 If David calls him 'lord,' how can he be his son?"

45 ^d Then with the whole people listening he said to the disciples,

46   "Beware of the scribes,
        Who like to walk about in long robes,
           and love greetings in the markets,
        And seats of honor in the synagogues,
           and places of honor at the banquets,
47   Who eat up the houses of widows,
           and as a pretense make long prayers —
        These will receive the greater condemnation!"

21 1 ^e Then he looked up and saw the rich throwing their offerings into the offering box. 2 Now he saw a poor widow throwing two small coins there 3 and he said, "Truly, I say to you, this poor widow threw in more than all of them. 4 All the others threw in offerings from their abundance, while she from her want threw in all the livelihood she had."

5 ^f And when some of them were talking about the Temple, that it had been decorated with beautiful stones and votive offerings, he said, 6 "These things you see — the days will come in which not a stone will be left upon a stone which will not be torn down."

7 ^g Then they asked him, "Teacher, when will these things be, and what will be the sign when they're about to happen?" 8 But he said, "See that you're not led astray, for many will come in my name, saying, 'I am he!' and, 'The time has come!' Don't follow them. 9 But when you hear of wars and insurrections, don't be terrified — these things must happen first, but the end will not come at once." 10 Then he said to them,

    "Nation will rise against nation,
        and kingdom against kingdom,
11   There will be powerful earthquakes
        and famines and plagues in various places,
    There will be dreadful sights
        and great signs from Heaven.
12   But before all this they'll lay hands on you

---

^c Mt 22:41-46; Mk 12:35-37. ^d Mt 23:1-36. ^e Mt 12:41-44. ^f Mt 24:1-2; Mk 13:1-2. ^g Mt 24:3-14; Mk 13:3-13.

21:2 "small coins." Literally, *lepta.*

and they'll persecute you —
Handing you over to the synagogues and prisons,
having you brought before kings and governors
for the sake of my name;

13 this will lead to you giving witness. **14** So resolve in your hearts not to prepare ahead of time how to defend yourselves — **15** I'll give you eloquence and wisdom which all those opposing you will not be able to resist or refute. **16** But you'll be handed over by parents and brothers and kinsmen and friends. They'll kill some of you **17** and you'll be hated by all because of my name, **18** yet not a hair on your head will be destroyed. **19** You'll gain your lives by your endurance."

20 [h] "But when you see Jerusalem surrounded by an army,
know, then, that its desolation has come.

21 Then let those in Judea flee to the mountains, and
let those inside it leave,
and let those in the countryside not go into it.

22 Because these are days of retribution,
of the fulfillment of everything
that has been written.

23 Woe to women who are with child,
and to those who are nursing in those days,
For there will be great distress over the land,
and wrath to this people,

24 And they will fall by the edge of the sword,
and be made captive in all nations,
And Jerusalem will be trampled by the Gentiles
until the times of the Gentiles are fulfilled."

25 [i] "And there will be signs in the sun
and moon and stars,
and distress of nations on the earth in despair
at the roaring of the sea and waves,

26 Men fainting from fear and foreboding of what
is coming upon the world,
for **the powers of the heavens** will be shaken.

---

[h] Mt 24:15-21; Mk 13:14-19.

21:26   Hg 2:6,11.

27   And then they'll see **the Son of Man**
              coming on a cloud with power and great glory.
28   Now when these things begin to happen, stand up
              and raise your heads,
         because your deliverance is at hand."

29 [j] And he told them a parable. "Look at the fig tree and all the trees. **30** When they put out leaves you see for yourselves and know that spring is near. **31** So, too, you, when you see these things happening, you'll know that the Kingdom of God is near. **32** Amen, I say to you, this generation will not pass away until all these things come to pass.

33   Heaven and earth will pass away,
        But my words will *not* pass away."

34 "But take care for yourselves lest your hearts be weighed down with dissipation and drunkenness and everyday cares, and that day come upon you unexpectedly, **35** like a trap, for it will come upon all those living on the face of the whole earth. **36** But be alert at all times, and pray that you'll have the strength to escape all these things that are going to happen, and to stand before the Son of Man."

37 Now during the days he taught in the Temple, while at night he'd go out and spend the night on the mount called Olivet, **38** and all the people came early in the morning to listen to him in the Temple.

I. LAST SUPPER AND PASSION

22   **1** [k] Now the feast of Unleavened Bread was approaching, which is called the Passover, **2** and the chief priests and scribes kept considering how they could do away with him, because they feared the people. **3** Then Satan went into Judas — the one called Iscariot — who was numbered among the Twelve, **4** and he went off and spoke

---

[i] Mt 24:29-31; Mk 13:24-27. [j] Mt 24:32-35; Mk 13:28-31. [k] Mt 26:1-5; Mk 14:1-2; Jn 11:45-53.

21:27   Dn 7:13.

22:1   The eight day period during which unleavened bread was eaten was closely linked to the Passover, but had its origins in a festival marking the beginning of the barley harvest.

22:2   The meaning is probably that they kept considering but could come to no decision because of their fear of the people.

with the chief priests and officers as to how he should hand him over to them. **5** They were overjoyed and agreed to give him silver, **6** and he agreed and sought the right time to hand Jesus over to them away from the crowd.

7[l] Now the day of Unleavened Bread came, on which the paschal lamb was supposed to be sacrificed. **8** And Jesus sent Peter and John and said, "Go prepare the Passover for us so we can eat it." **9** So they said to him, "Where do you want us to prepare it?" **10** Then he said to them, "Behold, when you go into the city a man carrying a clay jar of water will meet you; follow him to the house he enters. **11** Tell the master of the house, 'The Teacher says to you, "Where's the room where I'll eat the Passover with my disciples?"'" **12** He'll show you a large, furnished, upstairs room; make ready there." **13** Now when they went off they found it just as he'd told them, and they prepared the Passover.

14[m] When the hour came he sat down at table with the apostles. **15** And he said to them, "With what longing have I longed to eat this Passover with you before I suffer, **16** for I tell you that I will not eat it until it's fulfilled in the Kingdom of God." **17** Then he took a cup, blessed it, and said, "Take this and divide it among yourselves, **18** for I tell you I will not drink the fruit of the vine from this moment until the Kingdom of God comes." **19** Then he took bread, blessed it, broke it, and gave it to them and said, "This is my body which is given up for you — do this in my remembrance." **20** Likewise he took the cup after supper and said, "This cup is the new covenant in my blood which is poured out for you. **21** But, behold, the hand of the one who will hand me over is on the table with me, **22** because the Son of Man is going as it has been decided, but woe to the man through whom he's handed over!" **23** And they began to argue among themselves as to which of them it could be who intended to do this.

24 Now a dispute also arose among them as to which of them should be considered the greatest. **25** But he said to them,

---

[l] Mt 26:17-25; Mk 14:12-21; Jn 13:21-30. [m] Mt 26:26-30; Mk 14:22-26.

22:15   "With longing"; a typically Semitic intensifying idiom meaning, "I have greatly longed."
22:20   Ex 24:8; Zc 9:11.

"The kings of the Gentiles lord it over them,
And those who exercise authority over them
are called 'benefactors.'

26 But not so with you! Instead,

Let the greatest among you be like the youngest,
and the ruler like the one who serves.

27 For who is greater, the one reclining at table or the one serving? Isn't it the one reclining at table? But I'm among you like the one who serves. **28** You're the ones who stayed with me in my trials **29** and I grant to you dominion, just as my Father granted it to me, **30** so you can eat and drink at my table in my Kingdom, and you can sit on thrones judging the Twelve Tribes of Israel."

31 [n] "Simon, Simon! Behold, Satan has been demanding you, to sift you like wheat, **32** but I've prayed for you so that your faith may not fail, and you, when you return, strengthen your brothers." **33** Peter said to him, "Lord, I'm ready to go with you even to prison and to death." **34** But he said, "I tell you, Peter, the cock will not crow today until you deny you know me three times."

35 And he said to them, "When I sent you without a purse and bags and sandals you didn't lack for anything, did you?" "Nothing," they said. **36** Then he said to them,

"But now, let whoever has a purse take it,
and likewise a bag,
And let whoever is without one
sell his cloak and buy a sword.

37 For I tell you that this scripture must
come to completion in me,
And he was counted among the outlaws,
for that, too, which was written about me,
has its completion."

---

[n] Mt 26:31-35; Mk 14:27-31; Jn 13:36-38.

22:27   This may possibly be an allusion to the foot washing mentioned in John.
22:30   Dn 7:9, 22.
22:31-32   In v. 31 "you" is plural and refers to all the disciples, but in v. 32 it is singular and refers to Peter, clearly giving primacy to Peter.
22:37   Is 53:12.

38 Then they said, "Lord, look, we have two swords here." But he said
to them, "That's enough."

39 [o] And he went out and left for the Mount of Olives, as was his
custom, and the disciples followed him, too. **40** Now when he'd come
to the place he said to them, "Pray that you won't come into temptation." **41** Then he withdrew about a stone's throw away from them,
knelt down, and began to pray, **42** and he said, "Father, if it's Your will,
take this cup away from me, but not my will but Yours be done." **[43]**
[44] 45 When he rose from his prayer and came to the disciples he found
them sleeping, out of grief, **46** and he said to them, "Why are you
sleeping? Get up and pray that you won't come to the test."

47 [p] While he was still speaking a crowd came with the one called
Judas, one of the Twelve, at the head of them, and he approached Jesus
to kiss him. **48** But Jesus said to him, "Judas, would you hand over the
Son of Man with a kiss?" **49** Now when those around him saw what was
coming they said, "Lord, shall we strike with the sword?" **50** And one
of them struck the high priest's servant and cut off his right ear. **51** But
in response Jesus said, "Enough of this!" and he picked up the ear and
cured him. **52** Then Jesus said to those who had come out after him, chief
priests and Temple officers and elders, "You came out with swords and
clubs as if after a robber? **53** When I was with you daily in the Temple
you didn't lay hands on me, but this is your hour and the power of
darkness."

54 [q] After they seized him they led him away and brought him into
the high priest's house, while Peter followed at a distance. **55** Now
when they'd lit a fire in the middle of the courtyard and had sat down
together Peter sat down with them. **56** A maidservant who saw him as
he sat in the light stared at him and said, "This fellow was with him,
too!" **57** But he denied it and said, "I don't know him, woman!" **58** A
little later someone else saw him and said, "You're one of them, too!"
But Peter said, "Man, I'm not!" **59** And when an hour or so had passed,
still another insisted and said, "Of course this fellow was with him —
he's a Galilean, too!" **60** But Peter said, "Man, I don't know what you're

---

[o] Mt 26:36-46; Mk 14:32-42. [p] Mt 26:47-56; Mk 14:43-50; Jn 18:3-11. [q] Mt 26:57-58, 69-75; Mk 14:53-54, 66-72; Jn 18:12-18, 25-27.

22:43-44 The best manuscript tradition omits vv. 43-44: "Then there appeared to him an angel from heaven to strengthen him, and in his anguish he prayed more earnestly, and his sweat became like drops of blood falling to the ground."

talking about!" Immediately, while he was still speaking, a cock crowed. **61** And the Lord turned and looked right at Peter, and Peter remembered the Lord's saying, when he said to him, "Before a cock crows today you'll deny me three times." **62** And he went outside and wept bitterly.

63 ʳ Then the men guarding him began to make fun of him and beat him. **64** After blindfolding him they asked him, "Prophesy! Who was it that struck you?" **65** And they spoke many other blasphemies against him.

66 ˢ When day came the Body of Elders of the people was gathered, both chief priests and scribes, and they led him away to their Sanhedrin **67** and said, "If you *are* the Messiah, tell us!" But he said to them,

> "If I speak to you, you won't believe,
> **68** But if I ask, you won't answer.

69 But from this moment **the Son of Man will be seated at the right hand of the power of God."** **70** Then they all said, "Then you *are* the Son of God?" But he said to them, "You say it because I am." **71** Then they said, "What further need do we have for testimony? — we heard it from his own mouth!"

23 **1** ᵗ Then their whole assembly rose and led him to Pilate. **2** They began to accuse him and said, "We found this fellow misleading our nation — forbidding payment of taxes to Caesar and calling himself Messiah, a king." **3** Then Pilate questioned him and said, "Are you the King of the Jews?" But in answer he said, "You say so." **4** Pilate said to the chief priests and the crowds, "I find no case against this man." **5** But they insisted and said, "He's inciting the people, teaching throughout all of Judea, starting from Galilee as far as here."

6 Now when Pilate heard this he asked if the man was a Galilean, **7** and when he found out that he was from Herod's jurisdiction he sent him to Herod, who was himself also in Jerusalem at that time. **8** Herod was extremely pleased when he saw Jesus — he'd been wanting to see

---

ʳ Mt 26:67-68; Mk 14:65. ˢ Mt 26:59-66; Mk 14:55-64; Jn 18:19-24. ᵗ Mt 27:1-2, 11-14; Mk 15:1-5; Jn 18:28-38.

22:69 Ps 110:1.

22:70 "You say it because I am." This seemingly noncommittal reply is a tacit acceptance of the truth of what was said, but not necessarily as it was understood by Jesus' interrogators.

him for a considerable time because he'd heard about him and was hoping to see some sign performed by him. 9 He questioned Jesus at some length, but Jesus gave him no answer. 10 Then the chief priests and scribes stood up and accused him vehemently. 11 But after Herod and his soldiers had treated him with contempt and mocked him he had him dressed in fine apparel and sent him back to Pilate. 12 On that very day Herod and Pilate became friends — previously they'd been hostile to each other.

13 [u] Now when Pilate had called together the chief priests and the rulers and the people 14 he said to them, "You brought me this man as one who was misleading the people and, behold, after examining him in your presence, I've found no case against this man concerning what you alleged against him; 15 moreover, neither has Herod — *he* sent him back to *us*. And, behold, nothing deserving of death has been done by him. 16 Therefore, I'll release him after having him scourged." [17] 18 But they all cried out together and said, "Take this fellow away and release Barabbas to us!" — 19 who had been thrown into prison during a riot in the city and for murder. 20 So Pilate called them forward again, wanting to release Jesus, 21 but they kept shouting and saying, "Crucify him, crucify him!" 22 Then for a third time he said to them, "But what wrong has the fellow done? I've found no charge against him deserving death, so I'll scourge him and release him." 23 But they were insistent, demanding with loud cries that he be crucified, and their outcries prevailed. 24 Pilate decided that their demand should be carried out. 25 So he released the one they were asking for, who had been thrown in prison for rioting and murder, while Jesus he handed over to their will.

26 [v] As they were leading him away they seized Simon of Cyrene, who was coming from the country, and laid the cross on him to carry behind Jesus. 27 Now a large crowd of the people was following him, as well as women who were lamenting and wailing for him. 28 But Jesus turned to them and said, "Daughters of Jerusalem, don't weep for me; weep, instead, for yourselves and for your children, 29 because, behold, the days are coming in which they'll say,

---

[u] Mt 27:15-26; Mk 15:6-15; Jn 18:39 - 19:16.

23:17   The best manuscript tradition omits this verse: "By custom he released one prisoner to them during the festival."

'Blessed are those who are barren,
    and the wombs that did not give birth,
    and the breasts that did not nurse!'
30   Then **they will say to the mountains, 'Fall on us!'
    and to the hills, 'Cover us!'**

31 Because if they do these things when the wood is green, what will happen when it's dry?"

32 They also led away two other criminals with him to be killed, **33** and when they came to the place called "the Skull" they crucified him there as well as the criminals, one on his right and one on his left. **34** Then Jesus said, "Father, forgive them, for they don't know what they're doing." Then they divided his clothes and cast lots for them. **35** And the people stood there watching while the rulers made fun of him, saying, "He saved others, let him save himself, if this fellow *is* God's Messiah, the Chosen One!" **36** The soldiers who had come also mocked him, offering him sour wine **37** and saying, "If you're the King of the Jews, save yourself!" **38** There was also an inscription above him which read, "This is the King of the Jews."

39 One of the criminals who was hanging blasphemed him and said, "Aren't you the Messiah? Save yourself and us!" **40** But in response the other rebuked him and said, "Don't you fear God? — you're under the same sentence! **41** And we justly, for we're being paid back fittingly for what we did, while this fellow has done nothing wrong." **42** And he said, "Jesus, remember me when you come into your Kingdom!" **43** Jesus said to him, "Amen, I say to you, this day you'll be with me in Paradise."

44 ᵂ It was already about the sixth hour and darkness came over the whole land until the ninth hour, **45** the sun having failed, while the sanctuary curtain was torn down the middle. **46** And Jesus called out

---

ᵛ Mt 27:32-44; Mk 15:21-32; Jn 19:17-27. ᵂ Mt 27:45-46; Mk 15:33-41; Jn 19:28-30.

23:30   Ho 10:8.

23:31   This seemingly enigmatic statement is believed to have the following meaning: if "they" (the Romans) react so violently against Jesus, who opposed the extreme nationalists (and thus was "green," not ready for the fire), what will be the result when those who were pushing for confrontation with the Romans get their way? The result will be the tragic conflagration prophesied in the preceding verse.

23:34   Ps 22:18.

23:35-36 Ps 22:7-8, 69:21.

with a loud voice and said, "Father, into Your hands I entrust my spirit!" And after saying this, he died. **47** When the centurion saw what had happened he glorified God and said, "This man really was innocent!" **48** And all the crowds who had assembled for this spectacle, when they saw what had happened, returned, beating their breasts. **49** But all those who had known him stood there at a distance, and the women who had followed with him from Galilee watched these things.

J. RESURRECTION, APPEARANCES, AND ASCENSION OF JESUS

50 ˣ There was a man named Joseph who was a Council member, a good and upright man from the Judean city of Arimathea — **51** he had not agreed with their plan and deed — who looked forward to the Kingdom of God; **52** he came to Pilate and asked for Jesus' body, **53** and after taking it down he wrapped it in a linen shroud and placed it in a tomb hewn out of rock in which no one had yet been laid. **54** And it was the Day of Preparation and the Sabbath was about to begin. **55** Now the women had followed along, those who had come with him from Galilee, and they saw the tomb and how his body was laid, **56** then they returned and prepared aromatic spices and perfumed oils.

24 **1** ʸ On the first day of the week, at early dawn, the women came to the tomb bringing the aromatic spices they had prepared. **2** They found the stone rolled away from the tomb **3** and when they went in they didn't find Jesus' body, **4** and it happened that when they were at a loss over this, behold, two men in dazzling clothes stood near them. **5** The women were terrified and bowed their faces to the ground, and the men said to them, "Why are you looking for He Who Lives among the dead? **6** He isn't here — he's risen. Remember — he spoke to you when he was still in Galilee, **7** and said that the Son of Man would have to be handed over into the hands of sinners and be crucified and rise on the third day." **8** Then they remembered what he had said, **9** and when they returned from the tomb they told all these things to the Eleven and

---

ˣ Mt 27:57-61; Mk 15:42-47; Jn 19:38-42. ʸ Mt 28:1-10; Mk 16:1-8; Jn 20:1-10.

23:46   Ps 31:5.

to all the rest. **10** Now it was Mary Magdalen and Joanna and Mary mother of James and the rest with them who told these things to the apostles. **11** And it all seemed like nonsense to them, and they didn't believe the women. **12** But Peter got up and ran to the tomb, and when he stooped down he saw only the linen cloths, and he went away wondering to himself at what had happened.

13 ᶻ And, behold, two of them were travelling the same day to a village seven miles away from Jerusalem named Emmaus, **14** talking to each other about all these events. **15** And it happened while they were talking and discussing these things that Jesus himself approached and began to walk with them, **16** but their eyes were kept from recognizing him. **17** So he said to them, "What are these words you're exchanging with each other as you walk?" They stopped, gloomily, **18** and in answer one named Cleopas said to him, "Are you the only person staying in Jerusalem who's unaware of what happened there in these days?" **19** "What things?" he said. So they told him, "Those concerning Jesus of Nazareth, who was a prophet mighty in word and deed before God and all the people, **20** how the chief priests and our rulers handed him over under sentence of death and had him crucified. **21** We were hoping that he was the one who was coming to liberate Israel, but with all these things it's now the third day since this happened. **22** Moreover, some women from among us have amazed us. They were at the tomb early in the morning **23** and didn't find his body, and they came and said they'd even seen a vision of angels, who said he was alive. **24** Some of those with us went off to the tomb, and they, too, found it just as the women said, but they didn't see him." **25** He said to them, "How dense you are, and how slow of heart to believe all the prophets said! **26** Didn't the Messiah have to suffer all these things and go into his glory?" **27** And starting from Moses and all the prophets he interpreted for them what was in all the scriptures about himself.

28 They were approaching the village to which they were travelling, and when he made as if to travel further **29** they urged him and said, "Stay with us, because it's near evening and the day has

---

ᶻ Mk 16:12-13.

24:13   "Seven miles." Lit., "sixty *stadious*," each *stadioi* being about 607 feet.
24:21   Cf. note at 2:25, 38.

already come to a close." So he went in to stay with them. **30** And it happened that when he reclined at table with them he took the bread and blessed it, broke it, and gave it to them. **31** Then their eyes were opened and they recognized him, and he disappeared from them. **32** And they said to each other, "Weren't our hearts burning within us while he spoke to us on the road, as he opened up the scriptures to us?" **33** They got up and returned to Jerusalem that very hour, and they found the Eleven and those with them gathered together, **34** saying, "The Lord has really risen and has been seen by Simon!" **35** And they related what had happened on the road, and how they recognized him in the breaking of the bread.

36 [a] Now as they were speaking of these things Jesus stood among them and said to them, "Peace be with you!" **37** But they were startled and terrified, thinking they were seeing a spirit. **38** And he said to them, "Why are you frightened, and why are doubts arising in your hearts? **39** Look at my hands and my feet—it's me! Touch me and see, because a spirit doesn't have flesh and bones, as you see I do!" **40** And as he said this he showed them his hands and feet. **41** But since they were still incredulous and wondering for joy, he said to them, "Do you have anything to eat here?" **42** So they gave him a piece of broiled fish **43** and he took it and ate it in front of them.

44 Then he said to them, "These are my words which I spoke to you while I was still with you, that everything written about me in the Torah of Moses and in the Prophets and in the Psalms had to be fulfilled." **45** Then he opened their minds to understand the scriptures. **46** And he said to them, "So it is written, that the Messiah would suffer and rise from the dead on the third day, **47** and repentance and forgiveness of sins for all nations would be proclaimed in his name — starting from Jerusalem.

48 You are witnesses of these things. **49** And, behold, I'm sending the promise of my Father upon you, so stay in the city until you're clothed with power from on high."

50 [b] Then he led them out to Bethany, and he lifted up his hands and blessed them. **51** And it happened that as he was blessing them he

---

a Mt 28:16-20; Mk 16:14-18; Jn 20:19-23. b Mk 16:19-20.

passed away from them and was carried up to Heaven. **52** After they worshipped him they returned to Jerusalem with great joy, **53** and they were constantly in the Temple, blessing God.

THE GOSPEL ACCORDING TO
J O H N

INTRODUCTION TO JOHN

The last several decades have seen a drastic reevaluation of the Gospel of John. Whereas previously it was held by many to have been written late, c. 130-150 A.D., it is now generally believed that John's Gospel was completed by 100 A.D. at the latest. Once regarded as the product of a Hellenistic mind and environment, it is now recognized that this Gospel's roots are deep within Palestine and the Judaism of our Lord's time. Once considered to be primarily a theoretical theological creation only tenuously linked to the Jesus of history, modern scholarship has established that, in fact, the sources behind the Gospel of John embody some of the oldest and most reliable of all Gospel traditions. Finally, it is now realized that the Johannine portrait of Jesus is in fundamental harmony with that of the Synoptic Gospels.

What has prompted this reevaluation? Primarily, it has been the progress of modern archaeology, historical studies, and linguistics which have greatly expanded and deepened our knowledge of the many divergent religious and cultural currents in first century Judaism. For example, John places more stress on the role of the Sadducaic priesthood and also uses liturgically oriented symbolism more frequently than the Synoptic tradition, which is more concerned with the Pharisees, who stressed interpretation of the Law. Likewise, much of what was thought to be original in John's vocabulary is now seen to have been common currency in some circles of first century Judaism. There is still considerable controversy concerning the authorship of this Gospel — was it substantially the work of the Apostle John or did it undergo many decades of development and editing at the hands of several generations of John's disciples — and some scholars are also questioning whether it may not have been written several decades earlier than usually supposed, but all are in agreement concerning the high degree of reliability now to be accorded to John's historical tradition.

But if this is how modern scholarship has come to regard John's Gospel, what may we suppose his intent was in writing it? The intent is clearly stated: "...these things have been written so you may believe that Jesus is the Messiah, the Son of God, and so that by believing you may have life in his name." (20:31) What is this life? Eternal life, says John, is to know God, and this knowledge is gained through belief in Jesus, His Son, who was sent into the world for the very purpose of bringing us to knowledge of the Father. John's chosen method for communicating this knowledge was not to construct a systematic theology in a deductive fashion, but to plumb the mystery of the Christ through a loving meditation on the events of his ministry and their continuance in the sacramental life of the Church, so that their full truth and significance might be realized. Again and again he raises the same themes, but in new and different contexts so that the many facets of the truth that gives life may be glimpsed. In addition, he constantly juxtaposes his theme words with their antitheses, the so-called Johannine dualism, and utilizes editorial explanations and discourses by Jesus to make his point clear.

The basic conceptual framework for John's meditative narration can be briefly summarized. The Word of God became man in Jesus. This is fundamental for John. For him, the truth is not theory, it is a living Person, and this explains the wealth of detail in his narratives. The Word came accredited. God Himself bore witness to him, as did John the Baptist, the Scriptures, the disciples, as well as Jesus through his signs and life-giving words. Nevertheless, Jesus was rejected by the World (specifically, by his own, the Jewish authorities) and died as a sacrifice of love in accordance with the Divine plan to bring light, sight, belief, and life into the darkness and blindness of the World. Yet to those who believe, Jesus still offers life, and his resurrection is a witness to his victory and his life-giving power, not as a symbol but as a fact that has been seen and touched. And when we believe the witness that is given we begin to live the life that Jesus has shown us; we begin to know that God is Love.

A. 1:1-18   Prologue: Jesus, the Preexistent Word and Incarnate Son of God. Themes: The Word brings life and truth; conflict between light and darkness; rebirth in God; hostility of this world to the Word; opposition of flesh and Spirit; witness; glory of the Son through the Father.

B. 1:19-51   Witness of the Baptist and the first disciples. Themes: Witness; baptism of water and Spirit; sight.

C. 2:1-12   The "first sign" at Cana. Themes: Jesus replaces water purification of the old covenant with the wine of the new; revelation of his glory.

D. 2:13-25   The first Passover of Jesus' ministry, in Jerusalem; the cleansing of the Temple. Themes: Jesus replaces the Temple with the new temple of his body and replaces animal sacrifice with himself.

E. 3:1-21   The dialogue with Nicodemus. Themes: Opposition of flesh and Spirit and need for rebirth in the Spirit; knowledge and sight; faith in the Son of Man as the source of eternal life; opposition of light and darkness.

F. 3:22-4:3   Renewed witness of the Baptist; Jesus withdraws to Galilee. Themes: Witness; sight; truth; faith and life; Spirit.

G. 4:4-45   Encounter with the Samaritan woman en route to Galilee. Themes: Jesus is the inner well of water for eternal life; Spirit and truth; true worship; witness.

H. 4:46-54   Jesus performs his "second sign," in Galilee. Themes: Jesus is the source of life; belief and sight.

I. 5:1-47   Jesus returns to Jerusalem for a festival, is embroiled in Sabbath controversy and defends his witness. Themes: Jesus claims equality with God; sight; the Son gives life; witness, belief and life.

J. 6:1-71   Return to Galilee; Jesus feeds the crowd at Passover time and walks on the sea; controversy and unbelief. Themes: Jesus is the true food for everlasting life; need to eat and drink Jesus' body and blood; as Jesus and the Father live in each other, so do Jesus and believers; the Spirit, not flesh, gives life; his words are Spirit and life.

K. 7:1-8:59   Jesus at the Feast of Tabernacles. Themes: Knowledge, truth, and witness; Jesus gives life-giving water, the Spirit; Jesus is the light of life; contrast of worlds, above and below; Jesus' glory.

L. 9:1-41   The man born blind. Themes: Sight and blindness, faith and unbelief; witness.

M. 10:1-21   The Good Shepherd. Themes: Jesus lays down his life; he has come to give life; as Jesus and the Father know each other, so Jesus and the believer do, too; mission to the other sheep; one flock and one Shepherd.

N. 10:22-39   Jesus at Hanukkah. Themes: Sheep and Shepherd; Jesus gives eternal life to his sheep; "the Father and I are one."

O. 10:40-11:54   Jesus raises Lazarus and the Jews resolve that he should die for the nation. Themes: Light and darkness; Jesus is the resurrection and life; faith gives life; witness; faith gives sight to see the glory of God in the Son; Jesus will gather the scattered sheep.

P. 11:55-12:50   Jesus returns to Jerusalem for Passover and proclaims the hour of his glorification. Themes: Glorification of the Son; death brings eternal life; Jesus will draw all people to himself; darkness and light, blindness and sight.

Q. 13:1-30   The Last Supper. Themes: Water; humility in exercise of authority; darkness.

R. 13:31-17:26   Jesus' farewell to his disciples.

13:31 - 14:31   "Love, fear not, I'll send the Advocate." Themes: Glorification of Father and Son; faith, sight, life; way, truth, life; the world and blindness; the Spirit will abide; ask.

	15:1-16:15	"I am the true vine, love and bear fruit in face of persecution." Themes: Unity and faithfulness; abide in me and I will in you; abide in love; hostility of the world; witness; Advocate will guide; glorification.
	16:16-33	"I'm going to the Father! The Victory is mine!" Themes: The world has been vanquished.
	17:1-26	Prayer to the Father for the disciples. Themes: Glorification of Father and Son; knowledge and life; unity, "that they may be one"; hostility of the world; the Word is truth.
S.	18:1-19:42	The Passion. Themes: Truth; Jesus is not of this world.
T.	20:1-31	Resurrection and appearances to Mary Magdalen, the disciples, and Thomas. Themes: Faith, sight, and life.
U.	21:1-25	Appearance in Galilee, commission to Peter. Themes: Sheep and shepherd; glorification; truth and witness.

THE GOSPEL ACCORDING TO
J O H N

A. PROLOGUE

1   **1**   In the beginning was the Word,
And the Word was with God,

And the Word was God.
   2   He was in the beginning with God.

   3   All things were made through him,
And without him nothing was made.

What came to be **4** through him was life,
And the life was the light of men,

   5   And the light shines in the darkness,
And the darkness did not overcome it.

6 There was a man sent by God named John. **7** He came as a witness to bear witness concerning the light, so that all might believe through him. **8** He was not the light, but was to bear witness concerning the light. **9** It was the true light that enlightens every man which had come into the world.

  10   He was in the world, and the world was made by him,
Yet the world did not know him.

  11   He came to his own home,
Yet his own people did not receive him.

12 But all who did receive him, to them he gave the power to become sons of God, to those who believe in his name, **13** those who were born, not of blood nor of the will of flesh nor of the will of man, but of God.

14   And the Word became flesh
And dwelt among us,

And we saw his glory,
Glory as of the only begotten of the Father,

Full of grace and truth.

15 John bore witness concerning him and cried out, saying, "This was the one of whom I said, 'The one who's coming after me is above me, because he was before me.'"

16   For we have all received of his fullness,

and grace upon grace,

17   For the Torah was given through Moses,
Grace and truth came through Jesus Christ.

18   No one has ever seen God;
The only begotten Son of God,

who is in the bosom of the Father

he has revealed Him.

B. THE BAPTIST AND THE FIRST DISCIPLES

19 [a] And this was John's witness when the Jews of Jerusalem sent priests and Levites to ask him, "Who are you?" **20** He stated plainly and

---

[a] Mt 3:1-12; Mk 1:2-8; Lk 3:15-17.

1:12-13   "... to those who believe in the name of him who was born, not by blood or the urge of the flesh or the will of man, but of God himself." A variant and possibly original rendering of the text (cf. Justin, Hippolytus, Irenaeus and esp. Tertullian's *De Carne Christi*, 19, 1-2 [CCL 2, 907]), in which the obscure phrase "not by blood" would arguably refer to the virgin birth of Jesus.

1:14   The verb translated "dwelt" literally means, "set his tent," and referred in the Old Testament to Yahweh's presence in the tabernacle. "Glory" refers to God's power as manifested, then in the tabernacle, and now in the person of Jesus.

1:17   "Torah," or "law," referred to the totality of God's revelation which could serve as a guide for one's life. Torah was, therefore, quintessentially, the Decalogue, but it also extended far beyond the confines of the Pentateuch to areas which we would never characterize as "law," as can be seen in several New Testament passages.

1:18   Another manuscript tradition omits "Son of" in this passage.

didn't deny it, and he stated plainly, "I'm not the Messiah." **21** And they asked him, "Then who are you? Are you Elijah?" He said, "I'm not." "Are you the Prophet?" And he answered, "No." **22** So they said to him, "Who are you? Let us give an answer to those who sent us! What do you say about yourself?" **23** He said,

> "I am **the voice of one crying out in the desert,**
> **Make straight the way of the Lord,"**

as Isaiah the prophet said. **24** Those who had been sent were from the Pharisees, **25** and they asked him, "Then why do you baptize if you aren't the Messiah or Elijah or the Prophet?" **26** John answered them and said, "I baptize with water; among you stands one you don't know, **27** the one who comes after me, the strap of whose sandal I'm not worthy to untie." **28** These things took place at Bethany beyond the Jordan, where John was baptizing.

29 The next day he saw Jesus coming toward him and said, "Here is the Lamb of God who takes away the sin of the world! **30** This is the one of whom I said, 'After me comes a man who is above me, because he was before me.' **31** I didn't know him; instead, I came baptizing with water for this reason — so he might be revealed to Israel." **32** And John bore witness and said, "I saw the Spirit descending like a dove from Heaven, and it remained upon him. **33** I didn't know him, but He Who sent me to baptize with water, He said to me, 'Whoever you see the Spirit descending upon and remaining upon, he's the one who baptizes with the Holy Spirit.' **34** And I've seen and have borne witness that this is the Son of God."

35 The next day John was again standing there, as well as two of his disciples, **36** and he looked right at Jesus as he was walking by and said, "Here is the Lamb of God." **37** His two disciples heard him speaking and they followed Jesus. **38** Now when Jesus turned and saw them following him he said to them, "What are you looking for?" So they said to him, "Rabbi" — which, translated, means "Teacher" — "where are you staying?" **39** "Come and see," he said to them. So they came and saw where he was staying, and they stayed with him that day; it was about four in the afternoon. **40** Now Andrew, the brother of

---

1:21, 25   "The Prophet" is the figure referred to in Dt 18:15-19. Cf. Jn 6:14; 7:40.

1:23   Is 40:3 (Septuagint).

1:39   "About four in the afternoon." Lit., "about the fourth hour."

Simon Peter, was one of the two who were listening to John and had followed him. **41** He first found his own brother, Simon, and said to him, "We've found the Messiah!" — which, translated, is "Christ." **42** He led him to Jesus. Jesus looked at him and said, "You are Simon son of John; you shall be called 'Cephas'" — which is translated, "Peter."

43 The next day he decided to go to Galilee, and he found Philip. And Jesus said to him, "Follow me!" **44** Now Philip was from Bethsaida, from Andrew's and Peter's city. **45** Philip found Nathanael and said to him, "We've found the one Moses wrote about in the Torah, as well as the Prophets — Jesus son of Joseph from Nazareth!" **46** And Nathanael said to him, "What good can come from Nazareth?" Philip said to him, "Come and see!" **47** Jesus saw Nathanael coming towards him and said about him, "Here's a true Israelite, in whom there's no guile!" **48** Nathanael said to him, "Where do you know me from?" Jesus answered and said to him, "Before Philip called you, while you were under the fig tree, I saw you." **49** Nathanael answered him, "Rabbi, you're the Son of God, you're the king of Israel!" **50** Jesus answered and said to him, "Do you believe because I told you I saw you beneath the fig tree? You'll see greater things than this!" **51** And he said to him, "Amen, amen, I say to you, you'll see **Heaven opened up and the angels of God ascending and descending** upon the Son of Man!"

C. A SIGN AT CANA

2 **1** On the third day there was a wedding in Cana of Galilee, and Jesus' mother was there. **2** Now Jesus was also invited to the wedding as well as his disciples, **3** and when the wine ran out Jesus' mother said to him, "They have no wine." **4** Jesus replied to her, "What do you want from me, woman? My hour hasn't come yet." **5** His mother said to the servants, "Do whatever he tells you." **6** Now six stone water jars were standing there, in accordance with the Jewish purification rites, each holding twenty or thirty gallons. **7** Jesus said to

---

1:51   Gn 28:12.

2:4   "What do you want from me, woman?" This difficult idiom literally means: "What to you and to me?" The context seems to indicate that the meaning cannot be the brusque dismissal many interpreters have made it sound like, since Jesus, quite to the contrary, is fully cooperative. "Woman" was a respectful form of address.

2:6   "Gallons." Lit., "measures." A measure was about nine or ten gallons.

them, "Fill the water jars with water." And they filled them to the brim. **8** Then he said to them, "Now draw some out and take it to the head steward." So they took it. **9** Now when the head steward tasted the water which had become wine — and he didn't know where it came from, while the servants who had drawn the water did know — the head steward called the bridegroom **10** and said to him, "Every man first puts out the good wine, then when they're drunk [he puts out] the lesser wine; *you've* kept the good wine till *now!*" **11** Jesus did this, the first of his signs, at Cana in Galilee and revealed his glory, and his disciples believed in him.

12 After this he, as well as his mother and brothers and his disciples, went down to Capharnaum and stayed there for a few days.

D. THE CLEANSING OF THE TEMPLE

13 [b] When the Jewish Passover was near Jesus went up to Jerusalem. **14** He found in the Temple those who sold oxen and sheep and doves, and the money-changers were also sitting there. **15** Then he made a whip out of rope and drove them all out of the Temple, along with the sheep and the oxen. He poured out the moneylenders' coins and overturned their tables, **16** and he told those who were selling the doves, "Get them out of here! Don't make my Father's house a market house!" **17** His disciples remembered that it is written, **Zeal for Your house will consume me. 18** So in response the Jews said to him, "What sign can you show us to justify your doing these things?" **19** Jesus answered and said to them, "Destroy this sanctuary, and in three days I'll raise it up." **20** So the Jews said, "This sanctuary has been forty-six years in the building, and you claim you can raise it up in three days?"

---

[b] Mt 21:12-13; Mk 11:15-17; Lk 19:45-46.

2:12 In Semitic usage, close relatives such as cousins could be referred to as brothers or sisters. That these "brothers" were not additional sons of Mary, the mother of Jesus, can be seen from other passages such as Mt 27:60. Cf. Mt 13:55 for a further discussion.

2:14 The presence of the money-changers indicates that this was Passover time, since their purpose was to change money for the Temple tax which was collected once a year, at Passover.

2:16 Zc 14:21.

2:17 Ps 69:10.

21 But he was speaking about the sanctuary of his body. **22** So, when he rose from the dead, his disciples remembered that he'd said this, and they believed the scripture and the word Jesus had spoken.

23 Now when he was in Jerusalem for the Passover, at the festival, many believed in his name when they saw the signs he was doing, **24** but Jesus didn't trust himself to them because he understood everyone **25** and because he had no need for anyone to tell him about human nature —he knew himself what was in men.

E. JESUS AND NICODEMUS

3 **1** Now there was a man of the Pharisees named Nicodemus, a ruler of the Jews. **2** He came to Jesus at night and said to him, "Rabbi, we know that you're a teacher come from God, because no one can do the signs you're doing unless God is with him." **3** Jesus answered and said to him, "Amen, amen, I say to you, unless you're born from above, you cannot see the Kingdom of God." **4** Nicodemus said to him, "How can a man be born when he's old? Surely he can't go into his mother's womb and be born a second time?" **5** Jesus answered, "Amen, amen, I say to you, if you're not born of water and the Spirit you cannot come into the Kingdom of God. **6** What's born of the flesh is flesh and what's born of the Spirit is spirit. **7** Don't wonder that I say to you, 'you must be born from above.' **8** The wind blows where it pleases and you hear its voice, but you don't know where it comes from or where it goes. So it is with everyone who's born of the Spirit." **9** Nicodemus answered and said to him, "How can these things be?" **10** Jesus answered and said to him, "You're a teacher of Israel and don't know these things? **11** Amen, amen, I say to you,

> We speak about what we know,
> and we bear witness to what we've seen,
> yet you don't accept our witness.

3:3 "From above." This Greek adverb also means "again," which is how Nicodemus (v. 4) misunderstands it.

3:8 The Greek word *pneuma* means both "wind" and "spirit," and is used in both senses in this verse. Such word play is very typical of Semitic style.

12   If I told you about earthly things and you
               didn't believe,
      How will you believe if I tell you about
               heavenly things?
13   Yet no one has gone up to Heaven
      Except the one who came down from Heaven,
               the Son of Man.

14   And just as Moses lifted up the serpent
               in the desert,
         so must the Son of Man be lifted up
15   so that everyone who believes in him
               may have eternal life."

16   For God so loved the world
         that He gave His only begotten Son,
      So that everyone who believed in him would not die
         but would have eternal life.
17   For God didn't send His Son into the world
         to judge the world,
      But so the world would be saved through him.

18   Whoever believes in him is not condemned;
         whoever doesn't believe in him
            is already condemned,
         because he hasn't believed in the name
            of the only begotten Son of God.

19 And this is the condemnation —

      The light came into the world,
      Yet men loved the darkness rather than the light,
         for their works were evil.
20   For everyone who does evil hates the light,
      And doesn't come into the light
         lest his works be made known,
21   But whoever does the truth comes to the light
     So his works may be revealed
         as wrought in God.

F. THE WITNESS OF THE BAPTIST

22 After this Jesus and his disciples went to the Judean country-side and he stayed there with them and baptized. **23** Now John was also baptizing at Aenon near Salim because water was plentiful there, and people came and were baptized — **24** John had not yet been thrown into prison. **25** So a dispute arose between some of John's disciples and the Jews regarding purification. **26** And they came to John and said to him, "Rabbi, the one who was with you beyond the Jordan, to whom you bore witness, here he is, baptizing, and everyone is going to him!" **27** John answered and said, "A man can receive nothing unless it's given to him from Heaven. **28** You yourselves bear witness to me that I said, 'I'm not the Messiah,' but that I'm the one sent before him. **29** The one who has the bride is the bridegroom. The one who is the friend of the bridegroom, who stands and listens to him, rejoices with joy at the bridegroom's voice. So this my joy has been fulfilled. **30** He must increase while I must decrease."

31   Whoever comes from above is above everything,
  Whoever is from the earth is of the earth
      and speaks of the earth.

32   What he has seen and heard,
        this he bears witness to,
  Yet no one receives his witness.

33   Whoever receives his witness
        attests that God is true.

34   For the one God sent speaks the words of God,
        for He gives the Spirit without measure.

35   The Father loves the Son
  And has given all things into his hand.

36   Whoever believes in the Son has eternal life;
  Whoever doesn't obey the Son shall not see life,
        but God's wrath remains upon him.

4 **1** So when Jesus learned that the Pharisees had heard that Jesus was making and baptizing more disciples than John — **2** al-

---

3:23   "At Aenon near Salim" may possibly mean "near the springs of Salim."
3:29   "With joy" is a typical Semitism, intensifying the preceding verb: "rejoices."

though Jesus himself wasn't baptizing; his disciples baptized instead —
3 he left Judea and went off to Galilee again.

G. THE SAMARITAN WOMAN

4 Now he had to pass through Samaria, **5** and he came to a Samaritan city named Sychar, near the field Jacob gave to his son Joseph. **6** Now Jacob's well was there. So Jesus, tired out from the journey, simply sat down at the well. It was about noon.

7 A Samaritan woman came to draw water. Jesus said to her, "Give me a drink" — **8** his disciples had gone off to the city to buy food. **9** So the Samaritan woman said, "How is it that you, a Jew, ask me, a Samaritan woman, for a drink?" — Jews don't use vessels in common with Samaritans. **10** Jesus answered and said to her, "If you knew the gift of God and who it is who's saying to you, 'Give me a drink,' you would have asked him and he would have given you living water." **11** The woman said to him, "Lord, you have no bucket and the well is deep, so where do you get the living water from? **12** Surely you're not greater than our father Jacob who gave us the well and drank from it himself, as well as his sons and his herds?" **13** Jesus answered and said to her, "Everyone who drinks this water will thirst again. **14** But whoever drinks the water I'll give him will never thirst; instead, the water I'll give him will become a spring of water welling up in him to eternal life." **15** The woman said to him, "Lord, give me this water so I'll neither be thirsty nor have to come over here to draw water."

16 He said to her, "Go call your husband and come here." **17** The woman answered and said to him, "I don't have a husband." Jesus said to her, "You said well, 'I don't have a husband' — **18** you've had five men and the one you have now isn't your husband. You've spoken the truth." **19** The woman said to him, "Lord, I see that you're a prophet. **20** Our fathers worshipped on this mountain but you say that Jerusalem is the place where we should worship." **21** Jesus said to her, "Believe me, woman, the hour is coming when you'll worship the Father neither

---

4:6   "About noon." Lit., "about the sixth hour."
4:16-18   In Greek the word translated "man" and "husband" is the same, as in many other languages.

on this mountain nor in Jerusalem. **22** You worship what you don't know; we worship what we know, because salvation is from the Jews. **23** But the hour is coming, and is now, when the true worshippers will worship the Father in spirit and truth, for the Father also seeks such people who worship Him. **24** God is spirit, and those who worship Him must worship in spirit and truth." **25** The woman said to him, "I know that the Messiah is coming, who is called the Anointed; when he comes he'll tell us everything." **26** Jesus said to her, "I who am speaking to you am he."

27 At this point his disciples came, and they were amazed that he was speaking to a woman. Nevertheless, no one said, "What do you want?" or, "Why are you speaking with her?" **28** So the woman left her water jar and went off to the city and said to the men, **29** "Come see a man who told me everything I've done! Could this be the Messiah?" **30** They went out of the city and came to him.

31 In the meantime the disciples were urging him, "Rabbi, eat!" **32** But he said to them, "I have food to eat that you don't know about." **33** So the disciples said to each other, "No one brought him anything to eat, did they?" **34** Jesus said to them, "My food is to do the will of the One Who sent me, and to bring His work to completion. **35** Don't you say, 'There are still four months, and then comes the harvest?' Behold, I tell you, lift up your eyes and look at the fields, because they're white for the harvest. Already **36** the reaper receives his pay and gathers fruit for eternal life, so that the sower and reaper rejoice together. **37** For in this the saying is true, 'One is the sower and another the reaper.' **38** I sent you to reap what you didn't labor for. Others have labored and you've come into their labor."

39 Now many of the Samaritans from that city believed in him, based upon the word of the woman who bore witness that "He told me everything I've done!" **40** So when the Samaritans came to him they asked him to stay with them, and he stayed there for two days. **41** And far more believed based upon his word, **42** and they said to the woman, "No longer do we believe because of what you said — we've heard for ourselves and we know that this man is truly the savior of the world."

43 [c] Now after the two days he set out from there for Galilee, **44** because Jesus himself bore witness that a prophet gets no honor in

[c] Mt 8:5-13; Lk 7:1-10.

his own country. **45** So when he came to Galilee the Galileans received him because they'd heard all the things he did in Jerusalem during the festival, since they, too, had gone to the festival.

H. A SECOND SIGN IN GALILEE

46 So he came to Cana of Galilee again, where he made the water into wine. There was a royal official there whose son was ill in Caphar-naum, **47** and when he heard that Jesus had come from Judea into Galilee he went off to him and urged him to come down and cure his son, because he was about to die. **48** So Jesus said to him, "Unless you see signs and wonders you don't believe." **49** The royal official said to him, "Lord, come down before my child dies!" **50** Jesus said to him, "Go your way, your son will live." The man believed the word Jesus spoke to him and went his way. **51** Now while he was going down his servants met him and said that his son was alive. **52** So he asked them the hour at which he got better, and they said to him, "Yesterday at about one in the afternoon the fever left him." **53** The father realized that it was at that hour that Jesus said to him, "Your son will live," and he believed, along with his whole household. **54** Jesus did this second sign as he was coming from Judea into Galilee.

I. CONTROVERSY IN JERUSALEM

5 **1** After these things there was a festival of the Jews, and Jesus went up to Jerusalem. **2** Now in Jerusalem by the Sheep Gate is a pool — called *Bethzatha* in Hebrew — which has five porticoes. **3** In these would lie a crowd of sick people — blind, lame, paralyzed. [**4**] **5** Now a man was there who'd been sick for thirty-eight years. **6** When Jesus saw him lying there and learned that he'd already been there a long time he said to him, "Do you want to be healthy?" **7** The sick man

---

4:52   "About one in the afternoon." Lit., "at the seventh hour."

5:2   Although John states that *Bethzatha* is a "Hebrew" word, it is, in fact, Aramaic. This illustrates the very close relationship between the two languages.

5:4   The best manuscript tradition omits this verse: "They were waiting for the troubling of the water, for from time to time an angel of the Lord went down into the pool and troubled the water, and whoever first entered the pool afterwards was healed of whatever disease he had."

answered him, "Lord, I have no man to put me into the pool when the water's been troubled, so when *I* come, another goes down before me." **8** Jesus said to him, "Get up, pick up your cot and walk!" **9** And at once the man became healthy and picked up his cot and walked.

Now that day was the Sabbath. **10** So the Jews said to the man who had been cured, "It's the Sabbath, and it's not lawful for you to carry your cot." **11** But he answered them, "The one who made me healthy, he told me, 'Pick up your cot and walk!'" **12** They asked him, "Who's the man who said to you, 'Pick it up and walk'?" **13** Now the man who had been cured didn't know who it was — Jesus had left without being noticed, since there was a crowd at the place. **14** After these things Jesus found him in the Temple and said to him, "Here you are, made healthy! Sin no more, lest something worse happen to you!" **15** The man went off and told the Jews, "Jesus is the one who made me healthy." **16** And this is why the Jews persecuted Jesus, because he did these things on the Sabbath. **17** But Jesus answered them, "My Father is still working, so I'm working, too." **18** So this is why the Jews sought all the harder to kill him — not only did he break the Sabbath, but he even said God was his own Father, making himself equal to God.

19 So in response Jesus said to them,

> "Amen, amen, I say to you,
> The Son can do nothing on his own
>> except what he sees the Father doing —
> What He does,
>> likewise the Son, too, does.

20   For the Father loves the Son
>> and shows him everything He does,
> And He'll show him greater works than these,
>> so that you'll be amazed.

21   For just as the Father raises the dead
>>> and gives them life,
>> so too the Son gives life to those he wants to.

22   For the Father judges no one;
>> instead, He's given all judgment to the Son,

23   So all may honor the Son,
>> just as they honor the Father.

Whoever doesn't honor the Son,
    doesn't honor the One Who sent him.

24 Amen, amen, I say to you,
    Whoever listens to my word
        and believes in the One Who sent me
    Has eternal life and doesn't come to judgment,
        but, instead, crosses over from death to life.

25 Amen, amen, I say to you,
    The hour is coming, and is now, when the dead
        will hear the voice of the Son of God,
    and those who listen to it will live.

26 For just as the Father has life in Himself,
        so too has He given the Son life to have
            in himself,

27 And has given him authority to pass judgment,
        because he's Son of Man.

28 Don't be amazed at this,
    Because the hour is coming in which all those
        in the tombs will hear his voice,

29   and they'll come out,
    Those who did good to the resurrection of life,
        but those who wrought evil to the resurrection
            of judgment."

30 "I can do nothing on my own;
        just as I hear, I judge,
    And my judgment is just because I seek,
        not my own will,
        but the will of the One Who sent me.

31 If I bear witness to myself,
        my witness isn't true.

32 There's Another Who bears witness to me,
        and I know that the witness He bears to me
            is true.

33 You sent to John and he bore witness
        to the truth,

5:27   This is the only instance in the Gospels where "Son of Man" is not preceded by an article.

5:28-29   Dn 12:2.

34   but I don't receive witness from a man;
Instead, I say these things
         so you may be saved.

35   He was a lamp burning and shining,
         so you wanted to rejoice in his light
              for a time.

36   But I have witness greater than John's,
              for the works the Father has given me
                   to bring to completion,
The very works I do,
         bear witness to me that the Father sent me,

37   And the Father Who sent me,
         He has born witness to me.
You've never heard His voice,
         nor seen His image,

38   And you don't have His word abiding in you,
         because you don't believe the one He sent.

39   You search the scriptures
         because you think you have eternal life
              in them,
Yet *they* bear witness to *me*,

40   and you don't want to come to me
              to have life."

41   "I don't receive glory from men,
42   but I know you,
         that you don't have the love of God
              within you.

43   I've been sent in the name of my Father,
         yet you don't receive me;
If another should come in his own name,
         him you'll receive.

44   How *can* you believe, who receive glory
              from each other,
         yet don't seek glory from God alone?

45   Don't think that *I'll* accuse you
              before the Father;
         your accuser is *Moses*, in whom you hoped!

46   For if you'd believed Moses, you would have
believed me,
because he wrote about me!
47   So if you don't believe *his* writings,
how can you believe what *I* say?"

J. SIGNS, CONTROVERSY, AND UNBELIEF

6 **1** ^d After this Jesus went off to the other side of the Sea of Galilee of Tiberias. **2** Now a large crowd was following him because they saw the signs he was performing on the sick. **3** So Jesus went up the mountain and sat down there with his disciples. **4** Now the Passover, the festival of the Jews, was near. **5** When Jesus raised his eyes and saw that a large crowd was coming toward him he said to Philip, "Where can we buy loaves for them to eat?" **6** He said this to test him — he knew what he was going to do. **7** Philip answered him, "Two hundred *denarii* worth of bread wouldn't be enough to allow each of them to have a little!" **8** One of his disciples, Andrew, Simon Peter's brother, said to him, **9** "There's a boy here who has five barley loaves and two fish, but what are they for so many?" **10** Jesus said, "Have the people sit down" — now there was a lot of grass at that spot. **11** So Jesus took the loaves and after blessing them he distributed them to those who were reclining, and likewise with the fish, as much as they wanted. **12** When they were full he said to his disciples, "Gather the left-over fragments so nothing will be lost." **13** So they gathered them and filled twelve baskets with fragments of the five barley loaves which were left by those who had eaten. **14** When the people saw the sign he'd done they said, "Truly this is the Prophet who is to come into the world!" **15** But when Jesus realized that they intended to come and take him by force to make him king he withdrew alone to the mountain again.

    16 ^e Now when evening came his disciples went down to the sea, **17** and they got into a boat and began to go across the sea to Capharnaum.

---

^d Mt 14:13-21; Mk 6:30-44; Jn 9:10-17. ^e Mt 14:22-27; Mk 6:45-52.

6:9   "Barley loaves." This bland fare was the staple of the poor, as opposed to the tastier, but more expensive, wheat bread.

6:14 Cf. footnote to Jn 1:21, 25.

6:15 Other manuscript traditions put it more strongly: "he fled" those who would make him king.

9. The Alba House Gospels

Darkness had already come and Jesus had not yet come to them, **18** and the sea became rough, with a strong wind blowing. **19** After they'd rowed about three or four miles they saw Jesus walking on the sea and coming near the boat, and they were frightened. **20** But he said to them, "It's me, don't be afraid!" **21** So they wanted to take him into the boat, and at once the boat came to land where they were going.

22 The next day the crowd which had stayed on the other side saw that there had been no other boat there except the one, and that Jesus had not gone into the boat with his disciples, but instead only his disciples had gone off; **23** in addition boats came from Tiberias to near the place where they'd eaten the bread after it was blessed by the Lord. **24** So when the crowd saw that neither Jesus nor his disciples were there they got into the boats and went to Capharnaum in search of Jesus. **25** And when they found him on the other side of the sea they said, "Rabbi, when did you come here?" **26** Jesus answered them and said, "Amen, amen, I say to you,

> You seek me not because you saw signs,
>> but because you ate of the loaves
>> and were satisfied.

27 Labor not for food that perishes,
>> but for food that remains for life eternal,
> Which the Son of Man will give you,
>> for God the Father has set His seal on him."

28 So they said to him, "What should we do to do the works of God?" **29** Jesus answered and said to them,

> "This is the work of God,
>> to believe in the one He sent."

30 So they said to him, "Then what sign do you do, so we can see and believe in you? What work do you perform? **31** Our fathers ate manna in the desert, as it is written, **He gave them bread from Heaven to eat.**" **32** Jesus said to them, "Amen, amen, I say to you,

> It wasn't Moses who gave you bread from Heaven;
> On the contrary, my Father gives you
>> the true bread from Heaven,

6:19 "Three or four miles." Lit., "twenty-five or thirty *stadious*." A *stadioi* was about 607 feet.

33   For God's bread is he who comes down from Heaven
       And gives his life for the world."

34 So they said to him, "Lord, give us this bread always." **35** Jesus said to them,

> "*I* am the bread of life;
> Whoever comes to me shall not hunger,
> And whoever believes in me shall never thirst.

36   But I said to you that you saw me,
           yet you don't believe.

37   Everything the Father gives to me
           shall come to me,
       And whoever comes to me I will not cast out,

38   Because I've come down from Heaven
           not to do *my* will,
       But to do the will of Him Who sent me.

39   Now this is the will of Him Who sent me,
               that I should lose nothing of what He gave me,
                   but should raise it up on the last day.

40   For this is the will of my Father,
               that everyone who sees the Son and believes
                   in him should have eternal life,
               and I'll raise him up on the last day."

41 So the Jews complained about him because he said, "I am the bread come down from Heaven," **42** and they said, "Isn't this fellow Jesus son of Joseph? Don't we know his father and mother? How can he now say, 'I've come down from Heaven'?" **43** Jesus answered and said to them, "Don't complain to each other.

44   No one can come to me unless the Father
               Who sent me draws him,
           and I'll raise him up on the last day.

45   It is written in the Prophets,
           And they will all be taught by God.
       Everyone who listens to the Father and learns,
           comes to me.

6:35   Is 55:1-3.
6:45   Is 54:13.

46   Not that anyone has seen the Father except
           he who is from the Father;
        he has seen the Father.

47 Amen, amen, I say to you,

        Whoever believes has eternal life.

48   *I* am the bread of life.

49   Your fathers ate manna in the desert
        yet they died.

50   This is the bread that came down from Heaven,
        so that you can eat of it and *not* die.

51   I am the living bread that comes down from Heaven.
        If anyone eats of this bread he'll live forever,
    but the bread that *I'll* give for the life
        of the world
        is my flesh."

52 So the Jews quarrelled among themselves and said, "How can this fellow give us his flesh to eat?" **53** But Jesus said to them, "Amen, amen, I say to you,

    Unless you eat the flesh of the Son of Man
        and drink his blood,
        you will not have life in yourselves.

54   Whoever feeds on my flesh and drinks my blood
        has eternal life,
        and I'll raise him up on the last day,

55   For my flesh is true food,
        and my blood is true drink.

56   Whoever feeds on my flesh
        and drinks my blood
    Remains in me,
        and I in him.

57   Just as the living Father sent me,
        and I live because of the Father,
    Whoever feeds on me
        will live because of me.

58   *This* is the bread come down from Heaven,
        not like your fathers ate and they died.

> Whoever feeds on this bread
> will live forever."

59 He said these things while teaching in a synagogue in Capharnaum.

60 Many of his disciples who were listening said, "This teaching is hard; who can listen to it?" **61** Now Jesus knew in himself that his disciples were complaining about this and he said to them, "Does this offend you? **62** What if you see the Son of Man ascending to where he was before?

> **63** The Spirit is the life-giver,
> The flesh is profitless;
> The words I speak to you are Spirit and are life.
> **64** But there are some of you who don't believe."

For Jesus knew from the beginning who they were who didn't believe, and who was the one who would hand him over. **65** And he said, "This is why I told you that no one can come to me unless it's given to him by the Father."

66 From this time on many of his disciples went back and no longer walked with him. **67** So Jesus said to the Twelve, "Do you, too, wish to turn back?" **68** Simon Peter answered him, "Lord, who would we go to? You have the words of eternal life, **69** and we've believed and come to know that you're the Holy One of God." **70** Jesus answered them, "Didn't I choose you Twelve? Yet one of you is a devil." **71** Now he was speaking about Judas son of Simon Iscariot, because this fellow, one of the Twelve, intended to hand him over.

K. JESUS AT THE FEAST OF TABERNACLES

7 **1** And after these things Jesus moved about in Galilee — he didn't want to go about in Judea because the Jews were trying to kill him. **2** Now it was near the Jewish Festival of Tabernacles. **3** So his brothers said to him, "Leave here and go to Judea so your disciples, too, can see the works you do. **4** After all, no one does something in private if he wants to be before the public. If you do these things, make yourself known to the world." **5** For his brothers didn't believe in him either. **6** So Jesus said to them, "My time hasn't come yet, but your time is always at hand. **7** The world can't hate you, but it hates me because I bear witness against it that its works are evil. **8** *You* go up to the festival; I'm not going up to this festival because my time hasn't been brought to completion yet." **9** Now after he said these things he stayed in Galilee.

10 But after his brothers had gone up to the festival he went up, too — not openly, but in secret. **11** So the Jews were looking for him at the festival and saying, "Where is he?" **12** and there was a great deal of arguing about him among the common people. Some said, "He's a good man!" while others said, "No! On the contrary, he's leading the people astray!" **13** No one spoke openly about him, however, for fear of the Jews.

14 When the festival was already half over Jesus went up to the Temple and began to teach. **15** The Jews were amazed and said, "How could the fellow get this learning, since he hasn't studied?" **16** So Jesus answered them and said, "My teaching isn't mine but is from the One Who sent me. **17** If anyone wishes to do His will, he'll know whether the teaching is from God or if I'm speaking on my own. **18** Whoever speaks on his own is seeking his own glory, while whoever seeks the glory of the one who sent him, he's truthful and there's no falsehood in him. **19** Didn't Moses give you the Torah? Yet none of you keeps the Torah. Why are you trying to kill me?" **20** The crowd answered, "You have a demon! Who's trying to kill you?" **21** Jesus answered and said to them, "I did one work and all of you were amazed **22** by it. Moses gave you circumcision — not that it's from Moses; it's actually from the fathers — yet you'll circumcise a man on the Sabbath. **23** If a man can receive circumcision on the Sabbath so as not to break the Torah of Moses, why be angry with me because I made a whole man healthy on the Sabbath? **24** Don't judge by outward appearances; render *just* judgment, instead."

25 So some of the Jerusalemites were saying, "Isn't this fellow the one they're trying to kill? **26** Yet here he is, speaking openly, and they say nothing to him. Could it be that the rulers really know that he's the Messiah? **27** But we know where he's from, whereas when the Messiah comes no one will know where he's from." **28** So while Jesus was teaching in the Temple he cried out and said, "You both know me and know where I'm from, yet I haven't come on my own; but the One Who

---

7:15 "Since he hasn't studied," i.e., Jesus had not had a formal rabbinical education.

sent me, Whom you don't know, is true. **29** *I* know Him because I'm from Him and He sent me." **30** So they wanted to arrest him, yet no one laid a hand on him because his hour had not yet come. **31** But many of the common people believed in him and said, "When the Messiah comes will he do more signs than this man has done?"

32 The Pharisees heard when the people were whispering these things about him, and the chief priests and the Pharisees sent Temple attendants to arrest him. **33** So Jesus said,

> "A little while yet I'll be with you,
> And then I'm going to the One Who sent me.
> **34** You'll seek me, yet you won't find me,
> And where *I* am, you cannot come."

35 So the Jews said to themselves, "Where is he going to go that we won't find him? He's not going to travel to the Diaspora among the Greeks and teach the Greeks, is he? **36** What does it mean when he said,

> 'You'll seek me, yet you won't find me,
> And where *I* am, you cannot come'?"

37 Now on the last day of the festival, the most important day, Jesus stood up and cried out,

> "If anyone thirsts, let him come to me;
> **38** Whoever believes in me, let him drink!

As scripture said, **From within him shall flow rivers of living water!"** **39** Now he said this about the Spirit which those who believed in him were going to receive — the Spirit hadn't come yet, because Jesus had not yet been glorified.

40 Some of the people who heard these words said, "He's the Prophet!" **41** Others said, "He's the Messiah!" But some said, "The Messiah certainly doesn't come from Galilee, does he? **42** Hasn't

---

7:32 "Attendants." The Jewish authorities had a Temple police force, armed with staves, to keep order.

7:35 "Greeks." Cf. 12:20. While it is possible that this term refers to Gentiles, it is more likely that it refers to Jews of the Diaspora who spoke Greek.

7:37-38 Part of the ritual of the Feast of Tabernacles involved the priests pouring water over the altar. Jesus may have used this rite as the occasion for proclaiming himself the "living water."

7:38 Pr 18:4, Is 58:11, Ex 17:6, Ezk 47:1.

7:40 Cf. footnote to Jn 1:21, 25.

7:42 2 S 7:12; Ps 89:3-4.

scripture said that the Messiah comes from **the seed of David** and **from Bethlehem,** the village David was from?" **43** There was a split among the people over him. **44** Some of them wanted to arrest him, but no one laid hands on him.

45 So the attendants came back to the chief priests and Pharisees, and they said to them, "Why haven't you brought him?" **46** The attendants answered, "Never did a man speak like that!" **47** So the Pharisees answered them, "You haven't been led astray too, have you? **48** None of the rulers or Pharisees have believed in him, have they? **49** But this rabble that doesn't know the Torah is under God's curse." **50** Nicodemus said to them — the one who had come to Jesus previously, he was one of them — **51** "Our Torah doesn't judge a man unless it first hears from him and learns what he's doing, does it?" **52** They answered and said to him, "You're not from Galilee, too, are you? Look it up and you'll see that no prophet comes from Galilee!"

53 And each departed for his own house,

8 **1** but Jesus departed for the Mount of Olives. **2** Now early in the morning he again came to the Temple and all the people came to him, and he sat down and taught them. **3** Then the scribes and the Pharisees brought a woman who had been caught in adultery, and after standing her out in the middle **4** they said to him, "Teacher, this woman was caught in the act of adultery. **5** Now in the Torah Moses commanded us to stone such women. So what do *you* say?" **6** They said this to test him, so they could accuse him of something. But Jesus bent down and began to write on the ground with his finger. **7** When they kept asking him, he straightened up and said to them, "Let whoever is without sin among you be the first to throw a stone at her." **8** And once again he bent down and began to write on the ground. **9** Then those who had been listening began to go away, one by one, beginning with the elders, and he was left alone, with the woman still in the middle. **10** Jesus

---

7:49 "Rabble"; this Greek word, which literally means "crowd," also refers to the common people, here pejoratively, as used by the authorities. Cf. 7:40. The rabbis maintained that the common people were under a curse because of their ignorance of the Torah. Bonsirven notes that this followed from their teaching that a man's primary duty — even before prayer and charitable works — was to study the Torah.

7:53-8:11 While this passage is accepted by the Church as authentic and canonical, its exact position is a matter of some question. The earliest texts omit it entirely from the Gospel of John, while other texts place it elsewhere in John or, sometimes, in the Gospel of Luke, with which it appears to have stylistic affinities. In this latter manuscript tradition, it appears after Lk 21:38.

straightened up and said to her, "Woman, where are they? Has no one condemned you?" **11** "No one, Lord," she said. Then Jesus said, "Neither do I condemn you. Go your way, and from now on sin no more."

12 Jesus spoke to them again and said,

> "I am the light of the world;
> Whoever follows me shall not walk in darkness,
> But shall have the light of life."

13 So the Pharisees said to him, "You're bearing witness to yourself! Your witness isn't true!" **14** Jesus answered and said to them, "Even if I bear witness to myself my witness is true, because I know where I came from and where I'm going, but you don't know where I came from or where I'm going. **15** You judge according to the flesh. I judge no one. **16** But even if I do judge, my judgment is true because I'm not alone; rather, I and the Father Who sent me bear witness, **17** and in your Torah it is written that the witness of two men is true. **18** I bear witness to myself, and the Father Who sent me also bears witness to me." **19** So they said to him, "Where *is* your father?" Jesus answered, "You know neither me nor my Father. If you knew me you'd know my Father, too." **20** He spoke these words while teaching near the Temple treasury in the Temple, and no one arrested him because his hour had not yet come.

21 So he said to them again, "I'm going away and you'll seek me, yet you'll die in your sin; where I'm going you cannot come." **22** So the Jews said, "He won't kill himself, will he?" since he said, "Where I'm going you cannot come." **23** And he said to them,

> "You're from below,
> I'm from above;
> You're *of* this world,
> I'm *not* of this world.

The Jewish authorities thought they were putting Jesus on the horns of a dilemma: either call for the woman's execution, in which case he would run afoul of the Romans who reserved the power of punishment in capital cases, or recommend leniency and caution, in which case Jesus would reveal himself as less than zealous for the Torah and willing to acquiesce in Roman interference in Jewish affairs.

8:12 The Feast of Hanukkah featured a torchlight procession and, as at 7:37, this may have been the occasion for Jesus' proclamation. Unfortunately, there are no other clear indications in the text which would allow us to say definitely that that was when this scene occurred. From a narrative standpoint, this passage belongs to the section on Jesus at the Feast of Tabernacles.

24 That's why I said to you that you'll die in your sins — if you don't believe that I am, you'll die in your sins." 25 So they said to him, "Who are you?" Jesus said to them, "Why do I talk to you in the first place? 26 I have many things to say about you and to condemn, but the One Who sent me is true, and these things I heard from Him I speak to the world." 27 They didn't realize that he was speaking about the Father. 28 So Jesus said, "When you've lifted up the Son of Man, then you'll realize that I am, and I do nothing on my own; I proclaim these things just as the Father taught me to. 29 And the One Who sent me is with me. He hasn't left me alone because I always do what's pleasing to Him." 30 Many believed in him when he said these things.

31 So Jesus said to those Jews who had believed in him,

> "If you abide in my word,
> You're truly disciples of mine,
> 32   And you'll know the truth,
> And the truth will set you free."

33 They answered him, "We're Abraham's offspring and have never been enslaved! How can you say, 'You'll be freed'?" 34 Jesus answered them, "Amen, amen, I say to you,

> Everyone who commits sin
> is a slave of sin.
> 35   Now the slave doesn't stay in the house forever;
> the *son* stays forever.
> 36   So if the son frees you,
> you will, indeed, be free.

37 I know that you're Abraham's offspring, but you're trying to kill me because my word finds no place in you. 38 I speak of what I've seen with my Father, just as you, too, do what you've heard from your father."

39 They answered and said to him, "Our father is Abraham!" Jesus said to them, "If you're Abraham's children, do the *works* of Abraham! 40 But now you're trying to kill me, a man who's told you the truth he heard from God — something Abraham did *not* do. 41 You're doing the works of your father!" They said to him, "We weren't born from fornication! We have one father, God!" 42 Jesus said to them, "If

---

8:25 This difficult idiom has also been translated, "What I have been telling you right from the beginning." Good arguments can be advanced for both readings.

God were your father you would have loved me, because I came forth from God and have come from God — I haven't spoken on my own, but He sent me. **43** Why don't you understand what I say? Because you're unable to hear my word. **44** You're from your father the Devil, and you long to do your father's desires. He was a murderer from the beginning, and doesn't stand with the truth because there's no truth in him. When he lies, he's speaking according to his nature, because he's a liar and the father of lies. **45** But because I speak the truth, you don't believe me. **46** Which of you can convict me of sin? If I speak the truth, why don't you believe me? **47** Whoever is from God hears the words of God, which is why you don't hear, because you're not from God."

48 The Jews answered and said to him, "Aren't we right to say that you're a Samaritan and have a demon?" **49** Jesus answered, "I don't have a demon, but I honor my Father, and you dishonor me. **50** Now I'm not seeking *my* glory. One there is Who seeks it, and He's also the One Who judges! **51** Amen, amen, I say to you, if anyone keeps my word, he'll never see death." **52** The Jews said to him, "Now we *know* you have a demon. Abraham died, as well as the prophets, yet *you* say, 'If anyone keeps my word he'll never taste death'! **53** Are you greater than our father Abraham, who died? The prophets died, too! What are you making yourself out to be?" **54** Jesus answered, "If I glorify myself, my glory is nothing. It's my *Father* Who glorifies me, Who you say is your God. **55** Yet you haven't recognized Him, while I know Him. And if I were to say that I don't know Him, I'd be like you, a liar. But I know Him and I keep His word. **56** Your father Abraham rejoiced to see my day; he saw it and was glad." **57** So the Jews said to him, "You're not fifty years old yet, and you've seen Abraham?" **58** Jesus said to them, "Amen, amen, I say to you, before Abraham came to be, I am." **59** They picked up stones to throw at him, but Jesus hid himself and went out of the Temple.

L. THE MAN BORN BLIND

9 **1** As he passed along he saw a man who was blind from birth. **2** The disciples asked him, "Rabbi, who sinned, this fellow or his parents, that he should be born blind?" **3** Jesus answered, "Neither he nor his parents sinned, but he was born blind so that the works of God might be revealed through him! **4** We must do the works of the One Who sent me while it's day; when night comes, no one is able to work. **5** As long as I'm in the world, I'm the light of the world." **6** Having said these things he spit on the ground and made clay out of the spittle, and he smeared the clay on his eyes **7** and said to him, "Go wash yourself in the pool of Siloam," which is translated, "Sent." So he went off and washed himself and came back seeing. **8** His neighbors and those who used to see him as a beggar said, "Isn't this the man who used to sit and beg?" **9** Some said, "It *is* him!" others said, "No, it's not! but he's similar to him." He said, "I'm the one!" **10** So they said to him, "How were your eyes opened?" **11** He answered, "The man called Jesus made clay and smeared it on my eyes and said to me, 'Go to Siloam and wash yourself'! When I went off and washed myself I could see." **12** And they said to him, "Where is he?" He said, "I don't know."

13 They brought him to the Pharisees — the man who was formerly blind. **14** Now it was the Sabbath on the day Jesus made the clay and opened his eyes. **15** Once again they as well as the Pharisees asked him how it was that he could see. But he said, "He put clay on my eyes, and I washed myself and now I can see." **16** So some of the Pharisees said, "This man isn't from God because he doesn't keep the Sabbath!" Others said, "How can a sinful man do such signs?" And there was a split among them. **17** So they said to the blind man again, "What do you say about him, since it was your eyes he opened?" Then *he* said, "He's a prophet."

18 The Jews didn't believe that the man had been blind and had gained his sight until they called the parents of the man who was now able to see **19** and questioned them and said, "Is this your son, the one you say was born blind? How can he now see?" **20** His parents answered, "We know that this is our son and that he was born blind, **21** but how he can now see we don't know, nor do we know who opened his eyes. Ask *him*; he's of age! He'll speak for himself!" **22** His parents said these things because they were afraid of the Jews, for the Jews had already agreed that if anyone declared him to be the Messiah he'd be banished from the synagogue. **23** Therefore, his parents said, "He's of age, ask *him*!"

24 So for a second time they called the man who had been blind and said to him, "Give glory to God! We know this man's a sinner." **25** He answered, "Whether he's a sinner, I don't know. One thing I *do* know — I was blind, but now I can see." **26** So they said to him, "What did he do to you? How did he open your eyes?" **27** He answered them, "I've already told you but you didn't listen. Why do you want to hear again? Surely you don't want to become his disciples, too, do you?" **28** Then they began to insult him and said, "You're his disciple, but we're Moses' disciples! **29** We know that God spoke to Moses, but we don't know where this fellow's from!" **30** The man answered, "The wonder is certainly in this, that you don't know where he's from, yet he opened my eyes. **31** We know God doesn't listen to sinners, but if anyone is God-fearing and does His will He listens to him. **32** It hasn't been heard of from all eternity that someone opened the eyes of a man blind from birth. **33** If this man weren't from God, he wouldn't have been able to do anything." **34** They answered, "You were completely born in sin, and *you're* teaching *us*?" And they threw him out.

35 Jesus heard that they'd thrown him out, and when he found him he said, "Do you believe in the Son of Man?" **36** He answered, "And who is he, Lord, so I can believe in him?" **37** Jesus said to him, "You have seen him, and the one who is speaking with you is he." **38** Then he said, "I believe, Lord," and worshipped him. **39** And Jesus said, "For judgment I came into this world, so that

> Those who do not see may see,
> And those who see may become blind."

40 Those of the Pharisees who were with him heard, and they said to him, "We're not blind, too, are we?" **41** Jesus said to them, "If you were blind you'd have no sin, but since you say, 'We see!' your sin remains."

M. THE GOOD SHEPHERD

10

1 "Amen, amen, I say to you,
> Whoever doesn't go in by the gate
> into the sheepfold

9:34 "Threw him out." This probably means he was banished from the synagogue, although he may also have been physically ejected.

but enters by another way,
he's a thief and robber.

2   But whoever comes in by the gate,
he's the shepherd of the sheep.

3   The gate keeper opens to him,
and the sheep hear his voice,
and he calls his own sheep by name,
and leads them out.

4   When he drives out all his own sheep
he goes before them,
and the sheep follow him
because they know his voice.

5   But they don't follow a stranger,
instead, they flee from him,
because they don't know
the voice of strangers."

6 Jesus told them this figure of speech, but they didn't realize what it was
he was telling them.

7 So once again Jesus said, "Amen, amen, I say to you,

I am the gate for the sheep!

8   All those who came before me
are thieves and robbers,
But the sheep didn't listen to them.

9   I am the gate!
Whoever comes in through me will be saved
And will enter and leave and find pasture.

10   The thief comes only to steal and slaughter
and slay;
I've come that you might have life
and have it abundantly.

11   I am the *good* shepherd;
The good shepherd lays down his life
for his sheep.

10:1ff. The following poem is based upon Burney's retroversion of a rhyming Aramaic original and
the format must be considered somewhat speculative. The translation, however, does not
rely in any way on the retroversion. The image of Yahweh as a shepherd is common in the
Old Testament.

12 But since the hired man is not a shepherd —
     the sheep are not his own —
   When he sees the wolf coming he leaves the sheep
     and flees,
   And the wolf carries them off
     and scatters them,
13 Because he's a hired man and doesn't care
     about the sheep.
14 I am the *good* shepherd,
   And I know mine and mine know me,
15 Just as the Father knows me and I know the Father,
   And I lay down my life for my sheep.
16 I have other sheep who are not
     of this fold,
   And I must lead them,
   And they'll listen to my voice,
   And become one flock, one shepherd.
17 This is why the Father loves me,
   Because I lay down my life in order to take
     it up again.
18 No one takes it from me;
   On the contrary, I lay it down on my own.
   I have power to lay it down and I have power
     to take it up again.
   This is the command I've received from my Father."

19 Once again a split arose among the Jews because of these words. **20** Now many of them said, "He has a demon and is out of his mind! Who can listen to him?" **21** Others said, "These are not the words of a demon-possessed man! Can a demon open the eyes of the blind?"

N. JESUS AT HANUKKAH

22 At that time Hanukkah was taking place in Jerusalem. It was winter **23** and Jesus was walking in the Temple in the Portico of

10:22   Hanukkah, or the Feast of Dedication, celebrates the rededication of the Temple by the Maccabees in 164 B.C., after it had been profaned by Antiochus IV Epiphanes, the Seleucid ruler.

10:23   The Portico of Solomon provided a shelter from the cold winter winds.

Solomon. **24** So the Jews surrounded him and said, "How long will you keep us in suspense? If you're the Messiah, tell us openly!" **25** Jesus answered them,

> "I told you and you don't believe.
> The works I do in the name of my Father —
>> these bear witness to me,
> **26** But you don't believe because you're not
>> from among my sheep.
> **27** My sheep listen to my voice,
> And I know them, and they follow me,
> **28** And I give them eternal life and they'll
>> never die,
> And no one will snatch them from my hand.
> **29** My Father, Who has given them to me,
>> is greater than all,
> And no one can snatch them
>> from the hand of the Father.
> **30** The Father and I are one."

31 Once again the Jews picked up stones in order to stone him. **32** Jesus answered them, "I've shown you many good works from the Father. For which of those works are you going to stone me?" **33** The Jews answered him, "We're not stoning you for a good work but for blasphemy, and because you, a man, are making yourself God!" **34** Jesus answered them, "Isn't it written in your Torah, **I said, you shall be gods?** **35** If he called them gods, to whom the word of God came, and scripture cannot be set aside, **36** are you saying to the one the Father consecrated and sent into the world, 'You're blaspheming!' because I said, 'I'm the Son of God'? **37** If I'm not doing my Father's works, don't believe me! **38** But if I am, and you don't believe *me*, believe the *works*, so you may know and understand that the Father is in me and I am in the Father." **39** Once again they tried to arrest him, yet he came out from their hands.

O. THE RAISING OF LAZARUS

40 He went off again to the other side of the Jordan where John first baptized and stayed there. **41** Many people came to him because they said, "John did no sign, but all the things John said about this man were true." **42** And many believed in him there.

11 **1** Now a certain man was sick, Lazarus of Bethany, from the village of Mary and her sister Martha. **2** Mary was the one who had anointed the Lord with oil and wiped his feet dry with her hair — it was her brother Lazarus who was sick. **3** So the sisters sent to him and said, "Lord, behold, the one you love is sick." **4** When Jesus heard this he said, "This sickness will not bring death — it's for the glory of God so the Son of Man may be glorified through it." **5** Now Jesus loved Martha and her sister and Lazarus, **6** but when he heard that Lazarus was sick he stayed where he was for two more days. **7** Then after this he said to the disciples, "Let's go into Judea again." **8** The disciples said to him, "Rabbi, the Jews were just trying to stone you, and now you're going back there again?" **9** Jesus answered, "Aren't there twelve hours in a day?

> If someone walks in the day he doesn't stumble,
>> because he sees the light of this world,
> **10** But if someone walks in the night he stumbles,
>> because the light isn't with him."

11 He said these things, and then he said to them, "Our friend, Lazarus, has fallen asleep, but I'm going now to wake him up." **12** So the disciples said to him, "Lord, if he's fallen asleep he'll recover." **13** But Jesus had spoken about his death, while they thought he was speaking about natural sleep. **14** So then Jesus said to them openly, "Lazarus has died, **15** and I rejoice for your sake that I wasn't there, so you may believe." **16** So Thomas, who was called the Twin, said to his fellow disciples, "Let's go, too, so we can die with him!"

17 When Jesus came he found that Lazarus had already been in the tomb for four days. **18** Now Bethany was near Jerusalem, about two miles away, **19** and many of the Jews had come to Martha and Mary to

---

11:2   Jn 12:3.
11:18   "Two miles." Lit., "fifteen *stadious*." A *stadioi* was about 607 feet.

console them over their brother. **20** So Martha, when she heard that Jesus was coming, met him, but Mary sat in the house. **21** Martha said to Jesus, "Lord, if you'd been here my brother wouldn't have died! **22** but even now I know that whatever you ask God for, God will give you." **23** Jesus said to her, "Your brother will rise!" **24** Martha said to him, "I know that he'll rise at the resurrection on the last day." **25** Jesus said to her,

> *"I* am the resurrection and the life!
> Whoever believes in me, even if he should die,
>   will live,
> **26**   And everyone who lives and believes in me
>   shall never die!

Do you believe this?" **27** She said to him, "Yes, Lord, I've come to believe that you're the Messiah, the Son of God who has come into the world!"

28 After she said these things she went off and called her sister Mary, saying quietly, "The Teacher is here and he's asking for you." **29** When she heard that, she got up quickly and went to him. **30** Now Jesus had not yet come to the village, but was still at the place where Martha had met him. **31** So the Jews who were with her in the house, consoling her, when they saw that Mary had quickly gotten up and gone out they followed her, thinking, "She's going to the tomb to weep there." **32** When Mary came to where Jesus was and saw him she fell at his feet and said to him, "Lord, if you'd been here my brother wouldn't have died!" **33** So when Jesus saw her weeping, and the Jews who had come with her weeping, he groaned in spirit and was troubled **34** and he said, "Where have you laid him?" They said to him, "Lord, come and see!" **35** Jesus began to weep. **36** So the Jews said, "See how he loved him!" **37** But some of them said, "Couldn't the one who opened the eyes of the blind man have caused this man not to die?"

38 So Jesus, again groaning within himself, came to the tomb. Now it was a cave, and a stone lay on it. **39** Jesus said, "Take the stone away!" Martha, the sister of the dead man, said to him, "Lord, by now he'll smell — it's been four days!" **40** Jesus said to her, "Didn't I tell you that if you believe you'll see the glory of God?" **41** So they took the stone away. Then Jesus lifted up his eyes and said, "Father, I give you thanks, because You heard me. **42** Now I knew that You always hear me, but I said this for the sake of the crowd standing around me, so they may believe that You sent me." **43** And after saying this he called out with a loud voice, "Lazarus, come out!" **44** The dead man came out with his hands and feet bound with thongs and his face wrapped with a cloth. Jesus said to them, "Untie him and let him go!"

45 [f] Many of the Jews who had come to Mary, and had seen what he did, believed in him, **46** but some of them went off to the Pharisees and told them what Jesus had done. **47** So the chief priests and Pharisees gathered the Sanhedrin and said, "What should we do? — this man is doing many signs! **48** If we leave him like this everyone will believe in him, and the Romans will come and destroy both our place and our nation!" **49** One of them, Caiaphas, who was the high priest that year, said to them, "You don't know anything! **50** Don't you realize that it's better for one man to die than to have the whole people be destroyed?" **51** Now he didn't say this on his own, but since he was high priest that year he prophesied that Jesus would die for the nation, **52** and not only for the nation but also so that the scattered children of God might gather into one. **53** So from that day they resolved to put him to death.

54 So Jesus no longer went about openly among the Jews, but instead he went away from there to the country near the desert, to a city called Ephraim, and there he remained with the disciples.

P. JESUS' GLORIFICATION IN JERUSALEM

55 The Passover of the Jews was near, and many of them went up to Jerusalem from the country before the Passover to purify themselves. **56** So they were looking for Jesus and would say to each other as they stood in the Temple, "What do you think? He won't come to the festival, will he?" **57** Now the chief priests and Pharisees had given an order that if anyone knew where he was he should report it, so they could arrest him.

12 **1** [g] Six days before the Passover Jesus came to Bethany, where Lazarus was, whom Jesus had raised from the dead. **2** They

---

[f] Mt 26:1-5; Mk 14:1-2; Lk 22:1-2. [g] Mt 26:6-13; Mk 14:3-9.

11:48   "Place," i.e., the Temple.
11:51   The high priest was believed to have the gift of prophecy.

had a banquet for him there and Martha served, while Lazarus was one of those who were reclining at table with him. **3** So Mary took a pound of very expensive pure oil of nard and anointed Jesus' feet and wiped his feet dry with her hair, and the house was filled with the fragrance of the oil. **4** Then Judas Iscariot, one of his disciples, the one who was going to hand him over, said, **5** "Why wasn't this oil sold for three hundred *denarii* and given to the poor?" **6** Now he said this not because he was concerned about the poor but because he was a thief, and since he kept the money bag he used to take what was put in it. **7** So Jesus said, "Let her be; let her keep it for the day of my burial, for

8   The poor you always have with you,
        But me you do not always have."

9 So a large crowd of the Jews found out that he was there and they came, not just because of Jesus, but also to see Lazarus, whom he'd raised from the dead. **10** Now the chief priests were plotting to kill Lazarus, too, **11** because many of the Jews were leaving on account of him and were coming to believe in Jesus.

12 ^h The next day, when the large crowd that had come to the festival heard that Jesus was coming to Jerusalem, **13** they took the branches of palm trees and went out to meet him, and they cried out,

> **"Hosanna!**
> **Blessed is he who comes in the name of the Lord,**
> and the king of Israel!"

14 But Jesus found a young donkey and sat on it, as it is written,

15   **Fear not, daughter Zion!**
         Behold, your king is coming,
          sitting on a donkey's colt.

16 His disciples didn't understand these things at first, but when Jesus was glorified, then they remembered that these things had been written about him and had been done for him. **17** So the crowd that had been with him when he called Lazarus out of the tomb and raised him from

---

h Mt 21:1-11; Mk 11:1-11; Lk 19:28-40.

12:5   A *denarius* was a silver coin worth about a day's wage.

12:13   Ps 118:26.

12:15   Jesus took the mount of the King of Peace for all nations (Zc 9:9), as a sign that he was not a nationalistic Messiah come to wreak vengeance on the Gentiles.

the dead was bearing witness. **18** This is why the crowd met him —
because they'd heard that he'd done this sign. **19** So the Pharisees said
to themselves, "You see there's no use! Look, the whole world has gone
off after him!"

20 Now there were some Greeks among those who had come up
to worship at the festival, **21** so they came up to Philip, who was from
Bethsaida in Galilee, and asked him, "Sir, we want to see Jesus."
22 Philip came and spoke to Andrew; Andrew and Philip came and
spoke to Jesus. **23** Jesus answered them by saying, "The hour has come
for the Son of Man to be glorified! **24** Amen, amen, I say to you,

> If the grain of wheat that falls to the ground
>> does not die,
>> it remains alone,
> But if it dies,
>> it bears much fruit.

25 Whoever loves his life,
>> loses it,
> And whoever hates his life in this world
>> will save it for eternal life.

26 If anyone would serve me,
>> let him follow me,
> And where *I* am,
>> there will my servant be.
> If anyone would serve me,
>> the Father will honor him."

27 "Now my soul is troubled! And what shall I say? 'Father, save
me from this hour'? But it was for *this* that I came to this hour. **28** Father,
glorify your name!" A voice came from Heaven, "I have glorified it and
I will glorify it again!" **29** So when the crowd standing there also heard
it they said that it had thundered. Others said, "An angel spoke to him!"
30 Jesus answered and said, "This voice came, not for my sake, but for
your sake.

31 Now is the judgment of this world,
> Now the ruler of this world will be driven out!

12:20   "Greeks" probably refers to Jews of the Diaspora whose first language was Greek.

32   And when I'm lifted up from the earth
            I'll draw all men to myself."

33 He said this to indicate the kind of death he was going to die. **34** So the crowd answered him, "We've heard from the Torah that the Messiah is to stay forever, so how can *you* say that the Son of Man must be lifted up? Who *is* this Son of Man?" **35** So Jesus said to them, "The light will be with you for a little while, yet. Walk about while you have the light, so the darkness doesn't overtake you, and whoever walks in the dark doesn't know where he's going. **36** While you have the light, believe in the light, so you may become sons of light."

Jesus said these things and went off and hid from them. **37** Though he'd done so many signs in front of them, they didn't believe in him **38** so that the word Isaiah the prophet spoke might be fulfilled,

**Lord, who has believed our report?
And to whom has the arm of the Lord been revealed?**

39 This is why they were unable to believe, because Isaiah said once again,

40   **He has made their eyes blind
            and made their hearts stubborn,
Lest they see with their eyes
            and understand with their hearts
and return,
            and I will heal them.**

41 Isaiah said these things because he saw His glory and spoke about Him. **42** Nevertheless, even many of the rulers believed in him, but because of the Pharisees they didn't admit it, lest they be banished from the synagogue, **43** for they loved the glory of men more than the glory of God.

44 Then Jesus cried out, "Whoever believes in me doesn't believe in me but in the One Who sent me, **45** and whoever sees me sees the One Who sent me. **46** I've brought light to the world so that no one who believes in me will remain in darkness. **47** And if anyone hears my words and doesn't keep them, *I* don't judge him—I didn't come to *judge* the world, but to *save* the world. **48** Whoever rejects me and doesn't

---

12:38   Is 53:1 (Septuagint).
12:40   Is 6:10 (Septuagint).

accept my words has something to judge him; the word I spoke — *that* will judge him on the last day, **49** because I haven't spoken on my own; it's the Father Himself Who sent me who has commanded me what to say and what to speak. **50** And I know that His command is eternal life. So the things I say — as the Father has spoken to me, so do I speak."

Q. THE LAST SUPPER

13 **1** Now before the festival of the Passover Jesus, knowing that his hour had come to leave this world for the Father, having loved his own in the world, he loved them to the end. **2** During the banquet, when the Devil had already put it into the heart of Judas son of Simon Iscariot to hand Jesus over, **3** knowing that the Father had given all things into his hands and that he had come from God and was now returning to God, **4** he got up from the banquet and laid aside his clothing, and he took a towel and wrapped it around himself. **5** Then he poured water into the washbasin and began to wash the disciples' feet and wipe them dry with the towel he'd wrapped around himself. **6** When he came to Simon Peter, Peter said to him, "Lord, are *you* going to wash *my* feet?" **7** Jesus answered and said to him, "What I'm doing you don't understand just now, but later you'll understand." **8** Peter said to him, "You'll *never* wash my feet!" Jesus answered him, "Unless I wash you, you'll have no share in me." **9** Simon Peter said to him, "Lord, wash not only my feet, but my hands and head as well!" **10** Jesus said to him, "Whoever has bathed has no need to wash his feet; on the contrary, he's completely purified; and you *are* pure, but not all of you." **11** For he knew who was to hand him over; that's why he said, "Not all of you are pure."

12 After he'd washed their feet and had put his clothing on he sat down again and said to them, "Do you understand what I've done for you? **13** You call me 'The Teacher' and 'The Lord,' and rightly so, because I am. **14** So if I, the Lord and Teacher, have washed your feet, you, too, ought to wash each others' feet, **15** because I've given you an example so that, just as I've done for you, you, too, may do. **16** Amen, amen, I say to you,

> A servant isn't greater than his lord,
> Nor is a messenger greater than the one who sent him.

17   If you *know* these things,
       Blessed are you if you *do* them.

18 I'm not speaking about all of you. I know whom I've chosen, but let the scripture be fulfilled, **The one who ate my bread has raised his heel up against me.** **19** I tell you this now before it happens so you may believe, when it does happen, that I am he. **20** Amen, amen, I say to you,

       Whoever receives anyone I send receives me,
       While whoever receives me receives the One
         Who sent me."

21 [i] After saying these things Jesus was troubled in spirit, and he bore witness and said, "Amen, amen, I say to you, one of you will hand me over!" **22** The disciples looked at one another, uncertain whom he was speaking about. **23** One of the disciples, the one Jesus loved, was reclining at his bosom, **24** so Simon Peter nodded to him to ask whom he could be speaking about. **25** So, simply leaning onto Jesus' chest, he said to him, "Lord, who is it?" **26** Jesus answered, "It's the one I'll dip the piece of bread for, and give to him." When he'd dipped the piece of bread he gave it to Judas son of Simon Iscariot. **27** And then, after the piece of bread, Satan went into him. So Jesus said to him, "Do what you're doing quickly." **28** Now none of those reclining at table knew why he said this to him — **29** some thought, since Judas kept the money bag, that Jesus was telling him, "Buy what we need for the festival," or to give something to the poor. **30** So after taking the piece of bread he went out at once; now it was night.

R. JESUS' FAREWELL TO HIS DISCIPLES
THE WAY, THE TRUTH, AND THE LIFE

31 After Judas went out Jesus said,

       "Now is the Son of Man glorified,
       and God is glorified in him!

---

[i] Mt 26:21-25; Mk 14:17-21; Lk 22:21-23.

Jn 13:23-25   The disciple Jesus loved is normally understood as being the disciple John. Cf. Jn 18:15-16, 19:26-27, 21:7, 20-24.

32   If God is glorified in him,
       God will also glorify him in Him.

33   Little children, I'll be with you
       yet a little while;
   you'll seek me,
   And just as I told the Jews,
       'Where I'm going you cannot come,'
   I now tell you also.

34   I give you a new commandment —
   love one another;
   As I have loved you,
       you, too, love one another.

35   All will know by this that you're
       my disciples,
   if you have love for one another."

36 [j] Simon Peter said to him, "Lord, where are you going?" Jesus answered, "Where I'm going you cannot follow me now, but you'll follow later." **37** Peter said to him, "Lord, why can't I follow you now? I'll lay down my life for you!" **38** Jesus answered, "You'll lay down your life for me? Amen, amen, I say to you, the cock will not crow until you deny me three times!"

14 **1**   "Let not your hearts be troubled!
   Believe in God and believe in me.

2   In my Father's house are many rooms;
   Were it not so, would I have told you that I'm
       going to prepare a place for you?

3   And if I go and prepare a place for you,
   I'll come again and take you to myself,
   So that where I am, you, too, may be.

4   Yet where I'm going, you know the way."

5 Thomas said to him, "Lord, we don't know where you're going! How can we know the way?" **6** Jesus said to him,

      "I am the way and the truth and the life;

---

[j] Mt 26:31-35; Mk 14:27-31; Lk 22:31-34.

13:18   Ps 41:10.

13:34   As at the Sermon on the Mount, Jesus here proclaims himself capable of establishing laws or commandments — considered by the Jews to be a divine prerogative — and thus, implicitly, proclaims his equality with the Father.

No one comes to the Father except through me.

7 If you'd recognized me you would have recognized
  the Father, too,
And from now on you'll know Him and will see Him."

8 Philip said to him, "Lord, show us the Father and we'll be satisfied."
9 Jesus said to him,

"Have I been with you so long and yet you
  don't recognize me, Philip?
Whoever has seen me has seen the Father!
How can you say, 'Show us the Father'?

10 Don't you believe that I am in the Father
  and the Father is in me?
The words I speak to you I don't speak on my own,
But the Father Who abides in me does His works.

11 Believe *me* when I say that I am in the Father
  and the Father is in me,
But if you don't, believe because of the works
  themselves.

12 Amen, amen, I say to you,

Whoever believes in me,
  the works I do he, too, will do,
And he'll do greater works than these,
  because I'm going to the Father!

13 And whatever you ask for in my name, I'll do it,
  so the Father may be glorified in the Son;

14 If you ask me for anything in my name,
  I'll do it."

15 "If you love me, you'll keep my commandments,

16 And I'll ask the Father and He'll give you
  another Intercessor to be with you forever,

17 The Spirit of truth, whom the world cannot accept
  because it doesn't see or know Him.
You'll know Him, because He'll remain with you
  and be in you.

18 I won't leave you orphaned — I'll come to you.

19 Yet a little while and the world will no longer
         see me, but *you'll* see me;
Because *I* will live, you, too, will live.

20 On that day you'll realize that I am in my Father,
         and you in me and I in you.

21 Whoever keeps my commandments and obeys them —
         he it is who loves me,
While whoever loves me is loved by my Father,
         and I'll love him and reveal myself to him."

22 Judas, not the Iscariot, said to him, "Lord, why is it that you're going to reveal yourself to us but not to the world?" **23** Jesus answered,

         "If anyone loves me he'll keep my word,
           and my Father will love him,
And We'll come to him and make our abode
         with him.

24 Whoever doesn't love me doesn't keep my words,
And the word you hear is not mine,
         but the Father's Who sent me."

25 "I've told you these things while I'm still with you, **26** but the Intercessor, the Holy Spirit the Father will send in my name, He'll teach you everything and will remind you of all the things I told you.

27 Peace I leave with you,
         my peace I give to you;
Not as the world gives
         do I give to you.
Let not your hearts be troubled
         nor afraid.

28 You've heard that I told you,
         'I'm going away and I'm coming to you.'
If you loved me you'd rejoice
         that I'm going to the Father,
        because the Father is greater than I.

29 And now I've told you before it happens,
         so that when it happens you'll believe.

14:26   "Intercessor." The Spirit intercedes for us, or serves as our Advocate, with God in Heaven.

30 I'll speak of many things with you no longer, for the ruler of the world is coming. And he has no claim over me, **31** but so the world may know that I love the Father, and because the Father has commanded me, I'll do it this way. Get up, arise!"

THE TRUE VINE

15 **1** "I am the true vine,
And my Father is the vinedresser.

2 Every branch in me not bearing fruit He'll remove,
And every one bearing fruit He'll prune
so it will bear more fruit.

3 You're already pure because of the word I've spoken
to you;

4 Abide in me, and I'll abide in you.
Just as the branch cannot bear fruit on its own
unless it remains on the vine,
Likewise *you* cannot unless you abide in me.

5 I am the vine, you are the branches.
Whoever abides in me, and I in him,
He it is who bears much fruit,
For apart from me you can do nothing.

6 Unless someone abides in me he's thrown out
like a branch and withers,
And they gather them and throw them into the fire
and they're burned.

7 If you abide in me, and my words abide in you,
Ask whatever you wish and it will happen for you.

8 In this is my Father glorified,
That you bear much fruit and become my disciples.

9 Just as the Father has loved me, I, too, have
loved you;
Abide in my love.

10 If you keep my commandments you'll abide in my love,
Just as I've kept my Father's commandments
and I abide in Him."

11 "I've told you these things so that my joy
    may be in you
    and your joy may be complete.
12 This is my commandment,
    that you love one another as I have loved you.
13 Greater love than this no man has —
    to lay down his life for his friends.
14 You're my friends
    if you do what I command you.
15 I no longer call you servants,
    because the servant doesn't know
        what his lord does.
I've called you friends
    because everything I've heard from the Father
        I've made known to you.
16 You haven't chosen me;
    on the contrary, I've chosen you,
And I've designated you to go and bear fruit
    and that your fruit should abide,
So that whatever you ask the Father for in my name
    He'll give to you.
17 This I command you,
    that you love one another."

18 "If the world hates you,
    remember that it hated me before you.
19 If you had been of the world
    the world would have loved its own,
But because you're not of the world, but instead
    I chose you from the world,
    therefore, the world hates you.
20 Remember the word I spoke to you,
    'A servant isn't greater than his lord.'
If they've persecuted me,
    they'll also persecute you,
If they've kept my word,
    they'll keep yours as well.

21 But they'll do all these things to you
   because of my name,
    because they don't know the One Who sent me.

22 If I hadn't come and spoken to them they'd
   have no sin,
    but now they have no excuse for their sin.

23 Whoever hates me
   also hates my Father.

24 If I hadn't done among them works that no one
   else has done,
    they'd have no sin,
  But now they've both seen and hated
   both me and my Father.

25 But let the word written in their Torah
   be fulfilled,
   They hated me without cause."

26 "When the Intercessor comes, whom I'll send to you
   from the Father

   — the Spirit of truth that comes forth
   from the Father —

   He'll bear witness to me,

27 But you, too, will bear witness,
   because you've been with me from the beginning."

16 1 "I've told you these things so you won't lose faith. 2 They'll have you banished from the synagogue, but the hour is coming when everyone who kills you will think he's performing a service to God. 3 And they'll do these things because they knew neither my Father nor me. 4 But I've told you these things so that when their hour comes you'll remember that I told you."

  "I didn't tell you these things from the beginning
   because I was with you.

5 But now I'm returning to the One Who sent me,
   yet none of you asks me, 'Where are you going?'

6 But because I've told you these things,
   grief has filled your hearts.

15:25 Ps 69:5.

7   Still I tell you the truth,
  it's for your good that I should go away,
 Because if I don't go
  the Intercessor won't come to you,
 But if I depart,
  I'll send Him to you.
8   And when He comes
  He'll expose sin and righteousness and judgment
   to the world for what it is;
9   sin,
  because they don't believe in me,
10   then righteousness,
  because I'm returning to the Father
   and you'll no longer see me,
11   then judgment,
  because the ruler of this world has been judged."

12   "I still have many things to tell you,
 But for now you can't bear it,
13   But when He comes — the Spirit of truth —
 He'll lead you to the whole truth,
 For He won't speak on His own,
 But instead He'll say what He hears,
 And He'll proclaim to you the things to come.
14   He'll glorify me because He'll receive what's mine
  and proclaim it to you.
15   Everything the Father has is mine;
 That's why I said that He receives what's mine
  and proclaims it to you."

THE VICTORY IS MINE

16   "A little while and you'll no longer see me,
  yet again a little while and you *will* see me."

17 So some of his disciples said to one another, "What is this he's telling us, 'A little while and you won't see me, yet again a little while you *will* see me' and, 'Because I'm returning to the Father'?" 18 So they said,

"What is this 'little while'? We don't know what he's saying." **19** Jesus knew what they wanted to ask him, and he said to them, "Are you asking each other about this because I said, 'A little while and you won't see me, yet again a little while and you *will* see me'? **20** Amen, amen, I say to you,

> You'll wail and mourn,
> > but the world will rejoice;
> You'll grieve,
> > but your grief will turn to joy.

21   When a woman is giving birth
> she grieves
> > because her hour has come,

> But when she bears a child
> > she no longer remembers her suffering
> > > out of joy that a man has come into the world.

22   So you, too, are in grief now,
> but I'll see you again
And your hearts will rejoice,
> and no one will take your joy from you.

23 And on that day you'll ask nothing of me. Amen, amen, I say to you, whatever you ask the Father for in my name He'll give you. **24** Up till now you've asked for nothing in my name; ask and you'll receive, so your joy may be complete."

25 "I've told you these things in figures of speech; the hour is coming when I'll no longer speak to you in figures of speech but will openly tell you about the Father. **26** On that day you'll ask in my name and I won't tell you that I'll ask the Father for you, **27** for the Father Himself loves you because you've loved me and have believed that I've come from God. **28** I came from the Father and came into the world, and now I 'm leaving the world and going to the Father." **29** His disciples said, "Look, now you're speaking openly and aren't speaking in a figure of speech! **30** Now we know that you know everything and have no need for someone to question you! Because of this we believe that you came forth from God." **31** Jesus answered them, "Do you believe for now? **32** Behold, the hour is coming, and has come, when each will be scattered to his home and you'll leave me alone; yet I'm not alone, because the Father is with me. **33** I've told you these things so you'll have peace in me; you'll have suffering in the world, but take courage! I've conquered the world!"

JESUS' PRAYER TO THE FATHER

17 **1** Jesus said these things, and then he lifted his eyes up to Heaven and said,

"Father, the hour has come!
Glorify Your Son so Your Son may glorify You,
2   Just as You gave him authority over all flesh
So You may give eternal life to all those
     You've given to him.
3   Now this is eternal life, to know You —
     the One, True, God —
And the one You sent, Jesus Christ.
4   I glorified You on earth by completing the work
     You gave me to do,
5   And now You glorify me in Your presence, Father,
     with the glory I had with You before the world
     was."

6   "I've made Your name known
     to those men You gave me from the world.
They were Yours and You gave them to me,
     and they've kept Your word.
7   Now they know that everything You've given me
     is from You,
8   because I've given them the words You gave me,
And they received them and they truly know
     that I came from You,
     and they believe that You sent me.
9   I'm praying for *them;* I'm praying, not for the world,
     but for those You've given me,
Because they're Yours **10** and everything of mine
     is Yours and Yours is mine,
     and I am glorified in them.

11   Yet I'm no longer in the world and they *are*
           in the world,
        and I'm coming to You.
  Holy Father, keep in Your name those You've given me,
      that they may be one as We are one.

12   When I was with them I kept those You gave me
          in Your name
        and guarded them,
  And none of them is lost except the son of perdition,
      so that scripture may be fulfilled.

13   But now I'm coming to You, and I'm speaking these
          things in the world
      that they may have my joy fulfilled in them.

14   I've given them Your word
      and the world has hated them
  Because they're not of the world,
      just as I'm not of the world.

15   I don't pray for You to take them out of the world,
      but for You to preserve them from the Evil One.

16   They're not of the world,
      just as I'm not of the world.

17   Make them holy in the truth;
      Your *word* is truth.

18   Just as You sent me into the world,
      I, too, have sent them into the world.

19   And I consecrate myself for their sake
      that they may be made holy in truth."

20   "But I'm praying not only for them
      but also for those who believe in me
        through their word,

21   So that all may be one,
      just as You, Father, are in me and I in You,
  So they, too, may be in Us,
      so the world may believe that You sent me.

22   And I've given them the glory You gave me,
      so they may be one as We are one,

23   I in them and You in me,
      so they may be perfectly one,

So the world may know that You sent me
    and You loved them just as You loved me.
24 Father, I desire that they, too, may be with me
    where I am —
those You gave me —
So they may see my glory which You gave me,
    because You loved me
    before the beginning of the world.
25 Righteous Father, the world also doesn't know You,
    but I know You and these know that You sent me,
26 And I made Your name known to them
    and I'll make it known,
That the love with which You have loved me
    may be in them,
    and I in them."

S. THE PASSION

18 **1** [k] After Jesus said these things he went out with his disciples to the other side of the Kedron Valley where there was a garden, which he and his disciples went into. **2** Now Judas, who handed him over, also knew the spot because Jesus had often met there with his disciples. **3** So Judas took the cohort, as well as Temple attendants from the Pharisees and the chief priests, and came there with torches and lanterns and weapons. **4** Jesus, knowing all that was to befall him, came out and said to them, "Who are you looking for?" **5** They answered him, "Jesus of Nazareth!" He said to them, "I am he!" Now Judas, who handed him over, was also standing with them. **6** When Jesus said to them, "I am he!" they drew back and fell to the ground. **7** So he asked them again, "Who are you looking for?" Then they said, "Jesus of Nazareth!" **8** Jesus answered, "I told you that I am he, so if you're looking for *me,* let these others go," **9** so what he said might be fulfilled: "I lost none of those who were given to me." **10** Simon Peter, who had

---

[k] Mt 26:47-56; Mk 14:43-50; Lk 22:47-53.

18:3 A "cohort" was, technically, the tenth part of a Roman legion, or about 600 men. It may here mean simply a group of soldiers.

18:9 Cf. Jn 6:39, 10:28, 17:12.

a sword, drew it and struck the servant of the high priest and cut off his right ear. Now the servant's name was Malchus. **11** Jesus said to Peter, "Put the sword in its scabbard. Am I not to drink the cup my Father has given me?"

12 [i] So the cohort and their tribune and the attendants of the Jews seized Jesus and bound him **13** and led him first to Annas — he was the father-in-law of Caiaphas, who was high priest that year — **14** for it was Caiaphas who had advised the Jews that it was better for one man to die for the people.

15 [m] Simon Peter and another disciple followed Jesus. Now that disciple was known to the high priest and so he went in with Jesus to the high priest's courtyard **16** while Peter stood outside near the gate. The other disciple, who was known to the high priest, went out and spoke to the maidservant at the gate and led Peter in. **17** So the gatekeeper, the maidservant, said to Peter, "Aren't you one of this man's disciples, too?" He said, "I'm not." **18** Now the servants and the Temple attendants had made a charcoal fire and were standing warming themselves, because it was cold; Peter was with them, too, standing and warming himself.

19 [n] So the high priest questioned Jesus about his disciples and about his teaching. **20** Jesus answered him, "I've spoken openly to the world; I've always taught in a synagogue or in the Temple" — where all the Jews gather — "and I've said nothing in secret. **21** Why are you questioning me? Ask those who heard what I said to them. After all, they know what I said." **22** Now when he said these things one of the attendants who was standing by gave Jesus a slap and said, "Is that how you answer the high priest?" **23** Jesus answered him, "If I've spoken wrongly, bear witness against the wrong, but if I've spoken rightly, why do you hit me?" **24** So Annas sent him bound to Caiaphas, the high priest.

25 [o] Now Simon Peter was standing and warming himself. So they said to him, "Aren't you one of his disciples, too?" He denied it and said, "I'm not." **26** One of the servants of the high priest, a kinsman of

---

[i] Mt 26:57-58; Mk 14:53-54; Lk 22:54. [m] Mt 26:69-70; Mk 14:66-68; Lk 22:55-57. [n] Mt 26:59-66; Mk 14:55-64; Lk 22:66-71. [o] Mt 26:71-75; Mk 14:69-72; Lk 22:58-62.

18:15   The disciple known to the high priest is normally identified with the disciple John. Cf. footnote to Jn 13:23.

the one whose ear Peter had cut off, said, "Didn't I see you with him in
the garden?" **27** Again Peter denied it, and at once a cock crowed.

28 [p] So they led Jesus from Caiaphas to the praetorium. Now it
was early morning, and they didn't go into the praetorium so they
wouldn't be defiled and could eat the Passover. **29** Pilate came out to
them and said, "What charge are you bringing against this man?" **30**
They answered, "If the fellow weren't a wrongdoer we wouldn't have
handed him over to you." **31** So Pilate said to them, "*You* take him and
judge him according to your law." The Jews said to him, "It's not lawful
for us to put anyone to death," **32** so that Jesus' word might be fulfilled,
which he said to indicate the kind of death he was going to die. **33** So
Pilate went into the praetorium again and called for Jesus and said to
him, "Are you the King of the Jews?" **34** Jesus answered, "Are you
saying this on your own or have others told you about me?" **35** Pilate
answered, "Am I a Jew? It was your nation and the chief priests who
handed you over to me; what have you done?" **36** Jesus answered, "My
Kingdom is not of this world; if my Kingdom *were* of this world my
attendants would fight so that I wouldn't be handed over to the Jews,
but as it is my Kingdom is not from here." **37** So Pilate said to him, "So
you *are* a king?" Jesus answered, "*You* say that I'm a king. For this I was
born and for this I came into the world — to bear witness to the truth.
Everyone who is of the truth hears my voice." **38** [q] Pilate said to him,
"What's truth?"

After saying this he went out again to the Jews and said to them,
"I find no case against him. **39** But it's your custom to have me release
one man to you on the Passover. So do you want me to release the King
of the Jews to you?" **40** But they cried out again, "Not this one, but
Barabbas, instead!" Now Barabbas was a robber.

19
1 So then Pilate took Jesus and had him scourged. **2** And the
soldiers wove a crown of thorns and placed it on his head, and
they put a purple robe on him, **3** and they'd come up to him and say,

---

[p] Mt 27:1-2, 11-14; Mk 15:1-5; Lk 23:1-5. [q] Mt 27:15-31; Mk 15:6-20; Lk 23:13-25.

18:30 The Romans normally allowed subject populations to rule themselves according to their own law. It is understood here that the offense is a breach of Roman law, i.e., rebellion, rather than solely of Jewish law, otherwise Jesus would not have been brought to Pilate.

18:32 Cf. Jn 12:32-33.

18:40 "Robber." This term was often applied to rebels against Roman rule.

"Hail, King of the Jews!" and slap him. **4** Pilate went outside again and said to them, "Look, I'm bringing him out to you so you'll know that I find no case against him." **5** So Jesus came outside, wearing the crown of thorns and the purple robe. And Pilate said to them, "Look at the man!" **6** When they saw him the chief priests and their attendants cried out and said, "Crucify him, crucify him!" Pilate said to them, "*You* take him and crucify him—I find no case against him!" **7** The Jews answered him, "We have the Torah, and according to the Torah he deserves to die, because he made himself the Son of God!"

8 Now when Pilate heard *this* being said he became more afraid than ever, **9** and he went into the praetorium and said to Jesus, "Where are you from?" But Jesus gave him no answer. **10** So Pilate said to him, "You won't speak to me? Don't you know that I have power to release you and I have power to crucify you?" **11** Jesus answered him, "You'd have no power over me unless it had been given to you from above; that's why the one who handed me over to you has the greater sin." **12** From then on Pilate tried to release him, but the Jews kept shouting, saying, "If you release this man you're no 'Friend of Caesar'; everyone who makes himself a king is rebelling against Caesar!"

13 So when Pilate heard these words he led Jesus outside and sat on the judgment seat at a place called "the Pavement," but in Hebrew, *Gabbatha*. **14** Now it was the Day of Preparation for the Passover; it was about noon. And he said to the Jews, "Here is your king!" **15** They shouted, "Away with him, away with him! Crucify him!" Pilate said to them, "Shall I crucify your king?" The chief priests answered, "We have no king but Caesar!" **16** ʳ Then he handed him over to them to be crucified.

So they took Jesus in charge. **17** And carrying the cross himself he went out to what was called "the Place of the Skull," in Hebrew, *Golgotha*, **18** where they crucified him and with him two others, on either side, while Jesus was in the middle. **19** Now Pilate wrote a notice and

---

ʳ Mt 27:32-44; Mk 15:21-32; Lk 23:26-43.

19:12 "Friend of Caesar" was a title given high-ranking Roman officials. As used by the Jews here it takes on a threatening tone: if Pilate refuses to condemn Jesus he may be accused of declining to defend the supremacy of the Roman Emperor against pretenders to the royal dignity.

19:14 "About noon." Literally, "at about the sixth hour."

19:17 *Golgotha* is in reality an Aramaic rather than a Hebrew word. Cf. 5:2.

placed it on the cross, but it was written, "Jesus of Nazareth, the King of the Jews." **20** Many of the Jews read this notice, because the place where Jesus was crucified was near the city, and it was written in Hebrew, Latin, and Greek. **21** So the chief priests of the Jews said to Pilate, "Don't write, 'The King of the Jews' but, 'He said, I am the King of the Jews.'" **22** Pilate answered, "What I have written I have written!"

23 When the soldiers had crucified Jesus they took his clothes and made four parts, one for each soldier, plus the tunic. Now the tunic was seamless, woven from the top in one piece. **24** So they said to each other, "Let's not tear it; let's draw lots for it instead," so the scripture would be fulfilled which said,

> They divided my garments among them,
> and for my clothing they cast lots.

So the soldiers did these things. **25** Now standing by Jesus' cross were his mother and his mother's sister, Mary the wife of Clopas, and Mary Magdalen. **26** When Jesus saw his mother and the disciple he loved standing by he said to his mother, "Woman, here is your son." **27** Then he said to the disciple, "Here is your mother." And from that hour the disciple took her into his home.

28 [s] After this Jesus, knowing that everything had already been accomplished, in order to fulfill the scripture, said, **"I'm thirsty."** **29** There was a container there full of sour wine; so after putting a sponge full of sour wine on some hyssop they held it up to his mouth. **30** When he took the sour wine Jesus said, "All has been fulfilled!" and bowing his head he gave up the spirit.

31 The Jews, since it was the Day of Preparation and so the bodies wouldn't remain on the crosses — for that Sabbath was a great day — asked Pilate to let them break their legs and take them away. **32** So the soldiers came and they broke the legs of the first one and the other who

---

[s] Mt 27:45-46; Mk 15:33-41; Lk 23:44-49.

19:24   Ps 22:19.
19:26-27   Cf. footnote to Jn 13:23-25.
19:28   Ps 22:16.
19:29   Ps 69:22.
19:30   "Gave up." Most literally this means "to hand over," and is also used in the sense of "to betray." While the sense of "to entrust" is also possible, a more neutral translation has been chosen here.

had been crucified with him, **33** but when they came to Jesus and saw he'd already died they didn't break his legs, **34** but, instead, one of the soldiers stabbed him in the side with a spear, and at once blood and water came out. **35** And the one who saw it has borne witness and his witness is true, and he knows that he's speaking the truth so you, too, may believe. **36** For these things happened so the scripture might be fulfilled, **Not a bone of his shall be broken.** **37** And again another scripture says, **They shall look on him whom they have pierced.**

38 ᵗ Now after these things Joseph of Arimathea asked Pilate — since he was a disciple of Jesus, but a secret one for fear of the Jews — to let him take Jesus' body, and Pilate let him. So he came and took his body. **39** Then Nicodemus came, too — the one who had first come to him at night — bringing a mixture of myrrh and aloes, about a hundred pounds. **40** So they took Jesus' body and bound it in linen cloths with the spices, as is the custom among the Jews in preparing for burial. **41** Now at the place where he had been crucified there was a garden, and in the garden a new tomb in which no one had been laid yet, **42** so because of the Jewish Day of Preparation, because the tomb was near, they laid Jesus there.

T. RESURRECTION AND APPEARANCES OF JESUS

20 **1** ᵘ On the first day of the week Mary Magdalen came to the tomb in the early morning while it was still dark, and she saw the stone, which had been taken away from the tomb. **2** So she ran and came to Simon Peter and to the other disciple whom Jesus loved, and she said to them, "They've taken the Lord out of the tomb and we don't know where they've put him!" **3** So Peter and the other disciple went out and they went to the tomb. **4** The two of them were running together, but the other disciple ran faster than Peter and came to the tomb first, **5** and when he bent down he saw the linen cloths lying there, but he didn't go in. **6** Simon Peter came, too, following him, and he went

---

ᵗ Mt 27:57-61; Mk 15:42-47; Lk 23:50-56. ᵘ Mt 28:1-10; Mk 16:1-8; Lk 24:1-12. .

19:36   Nb 9:12, Ps 34:21.
19:37   Zc 12:10.
20:2-10   The beloved disciple; cf. footnote to Jn 13:23-25.

into the tomb and saw the linen cloths lying there, **7** and the face covering, which had been on his head, wasn't lying with the linen cloths but was wrapped up separately in its own place. **8** So then the other disciple, who had come first, went in, too, and he saw and believed, **9** for they didn't yet understand the scripture that he had to rise from the dead. **10** So the disciples went off home again.

11 ᵛ Now Mary stood near the tomb, weeping outside. As she wept she looked into the tomb **12** and saw two angels in white sitting where Jesus' body had been, one at the head and one at the feet. **13** And they said to her, "Woman, why are you weeping?" She said to them, "They've taken my Lord and I don't know where they've put him!" **14** After she said this she turned around and saw Jesus standing there, yet she didn't realize that it was Jesus. **15** Jesus said to her, "Woman, why are you weeping? Who are you looking for?" Thinking that it was the gardener she said to him, "Lord, if you removed him tell me where you put him, and I'll take him away." **16** Jesus said to her, "Mary!" She turned and said to him, in Hebrew, *"Rabboni!"* which means, "Teacher!" **17** Jesus said to her, "Don't touch me — I haven't yet ascended to the Father. But go to my brothers and tell them,

> 'I am ascending to my Father and your Father,
> And to my God and your God.'"

18 Mary Magdalen came and told the disciples, "I've seen the Lord!" and that he told her these things.

19 ʷ When it was evening on that first day of the week, and the doors had been locked where the disciples were for fear of the Jews, Jesus came and stood in their midst and said to them, "Peace be with you!" **20** And after saying this he showed them his hands and side. So the disciples rejoiced to see the Lord. **21** He said to them again, "Peace be with you! As the Father has sent me, I, too, send you." **22** And after saying this he breathed on them and said, "Receive the Holy Spirit!

> **23** Whoever's sins you forgive,
> they've already been forgiven;

ᵛ Mk 16:9-11 ʷ Mt 28:16-20; Mk 16:14-18; Lk 24:36-49.

20:23   i.e., the disciples will be guided by the Holy Spirit to perform what God has already decided from all eternity.

Whoever's you retain,
    they've already been retained."

24 Now Thomas, one of the Twelve, called the Twin, wasn't with them when Jesus came. **25** So the other disciples told him, "We've seen the Lord!" But he told them, "Unless I see the mark of the nails in his hands and put my finger into the mark of the nail and put my hand into his side, I won't believe!" **26** And a week later his disciples were once again inside, and Thomas was with them. Although the doors had been locked, Jesus came and stood in their midst and said, "Peace be with you!" **27** Then he said to Thomas,

"Bring your finger here
    and look at my hands,
And bring your hand
    and put it in my side,
And be not unbelieving,
    but believing!"

28 Thomas answered and said to him, "My Lord and my God!" **29** Jesus said to him,

"You've believed because you've seen me;
Blessed are they who haven't seen
    yet have believed!"

30 Jesus also did many other signs in the presence of the disciples which are not written in this book, **31** but these things have been written so you may believe that Jesus is the Messiah, the Son of God, and so that by believing you may have life in his name.

U. JESUS AND PETER IN GALILEE

21 **1** After these things Jesus again showed himself to the disciples at the Sea of Tiberias; now he appeared in this way. **2** Simon Peter and Thomas, who was called the Twin, and Nathanael, who was from Cana in Galilee, and the sons of Zebedee and two other of his disciples were together. **3** Simon Peter said to them, "I'm going fishing." They said to him, "We're going with you, too." They went out and got in the boat and that night they caught nothing. **4** Now as day was breaking Jesus stood there on the shore, but the disciples didn't know that it was Jesus. **5** So Jesus said to them, "Children, do you have any fish?" They answered him, "No." **6** Then he said to them, "Cast the net to the right side of the boat and you'll find some." So they cast it, and now they were unable to draw it in because of the number of fish. **7** So the disciple Jesus loved said to Peter, "It's the Lord!" Simon Peter, when he heard that it was the Lord, put on his outer garment — he was stripped — and threw himself into the sea. **8** Then the other disciples came with the boat — they weren't far from land, about a hundred yards away — dragging the net of fish. **9** So as they were coming up onto land they saw a charcoal fire started and a fish laid on it and bread. **10** Jesus said to them, "Bring some of the fish you caught just now." **11** So Simon Peter went aboard and dragged the net to land, full of large fish — a hundred and fifty-three — yet, even though there were so many, the net wasn't split. **12** Jesus said to them, "Come eat breakfast." Now none of the disciples dared to ask him, "Who are you?" because they knew it was the Lord. **13** Jesus came and took the bread and gave it to them, and likewise the fish. **14** This was already the third time Jesus had appeared to the disciples after rising from the dead.

15 After they'd eaten breakfast Jesus said to Simon Peter, "Simon son of John, do you love me more than they do?" He said to him, "Yes, Lord, you know that I love you!" He said to him, "Feed my lambs!" **16** Again he said to him a second time, "Simon son of John, do you love me?" He said to him, "Yes, Lord, you know that I love you!" He said to him, "Tend my sheep!" **17** He said to him a third time, "Simon son of John, do you love me?" Peter was distressed because he said to him a third time, "Do you love me?" and he said to him, "Lord, you know everything; you know that I love you!" He said to him, "Feed my sheep! **18** Amen, amen, I say to you, when you were young you fastened your belt and went where you wanted, but when you're old you'll stretch out your hands and another will fasten you and bring you where you don't

---

21:7   Cf. footnote to Jn 13:23-25.

21:8   "A hundred yards." Lit., "two hundred cubits." A cubit was about 18 inches.

21:15   This passage could also be translated, "Do you love me more than these?"

21:15-19   This passage strongly stresses the primacy of Peter. Just as Jesus is the Good Shepherd who has a unique relationship to the Father, he now designates Peter to be that good shepherd in his stead, to tend and lead the flock Jesus loves and for which he has suffered and died.

wish to go." **19** Now he said this to indicate by what type of death he'd glorify God. And after saying this he said to him, "Follow me!"

20 When Peter turned he saw the disciple Jesus loved following — the one who had leaned at his bosom onto his chest and said, "Lord, who is it who will hand you over?" — **21** so when Peter saw him he said to Jesus, "Lord, what about him?" **22** Jesus said to him, "If I want him to stay till I come, what's it to you? Follow me!" **23** So this report went out to the brothers, that that disciple wouldn't die. But Jesus didn't say to him that he wouldn't die, but, instead, "If I want him to stay till I come, what's it to you?"

24 This is the disciple who bears witness to these things and has written them, and we know that his witness is true.

25 Now there are also many other things that Jesus did; if every one of them were written down, I don't suppose the world itself would have room for the books that would be written.

21:20, 24 "The disciple Jesus loved." It is generally agreed that this refers to the disciple John, son of Zebedee. In verse 24 an unknown writer attests that the Gospel is the witness or testimony of John.

THE ALBA HOUSE GOSPELS
"So You May Believe"

Distributed in collaboration with

Daughters of St Paul
50 St Paul's Avenue
Boston, MA 02130

Australia

St Paul Publications
60-70 Broughton Road
Homebush, NSW 2140

Canada

St Paul Books & Media
3022 Dufferin Street
Toronto, Ont. M6B 3T5

England

St Paul Multi Media
199 Kensington High Street
London WA 6BA

Italy

San Paolo Multimedia
Via del Mascherino, 94
Rome 00193

Ireland

St Paul Publications
Moyglare Road
Maynooth, Co. Kildare

India

St Paul Publications
23rd Road, T.P.S. III
Bandra, Bombay 400 050

Philippines

St Paul Publications
7708 St Paul Road
Makati, Metro Manila

Scotland

St Paul Multi Media
5-7 Royal Exchange Square
Glasgow G43 1DB